The Millenarian World of Early Mormonism

The Millenarian World
of Early Mormonism

GRANT UNDERWOOD

UNIVERSITY OF ILLINOIS
Urbana and Chicago

This book is printed on acid-free paper.

Library of Congress Cataloging-in-Publication Data

Underwood, Grant, 1954–
    The millenarian world of early Mormonism / Grant Underwood.
        p.   cm.
    Includes bibliographical references and index.
    ISBN 0-252-02037-5 (alk. paper)
    1. Millennialism—History of doctrines—19th century. 2. Mormon
Church—History—19th century. I. Title.
BX8643.M54U63   1993
236'.9'088283—dc20   93-374
                                                             CIP

Contents

Acknowledgments

The publication of this book culminates the scholarly activity of more than a decade. Not surprisingly, a number of debts were incurred along the way. Thanks are due all the scholars of Mormon history and members of the Mormon History Association with whom portions of this work have been discussed at various conferences and symposia over the years. Among those who have been most influential are Tom Alexander, James Allen, Richard Bushman, Milton Backman, Michael Quinn, Jan Shipps, and Dean May. Special thanks are due Leonard J. Arrington, the dean of Mormon history, who repeatedly took time to notice and encourage this young scholar. A number of historians of religion in America have also been helpful, especially Edwin S. Gaustad, Martin Marty, and Richard Hughes. As this work passed through a dissertation stage, it was enriched by the keen mind and kind manner of a true gentleman and scholar, Daniel Walker Howe.

Earlier versions of some of the material in this book have appeared in *Journal of Mormon History, BYU Studies, Dialogue,* and *John Whitmer Historical Association Journal; Mormons in Victorian Britain,* edited by Richard Jensen and Malcolm Thorp (Salt Lake City: University of Utah Press, 1989); and *The Old Testament and the Latter-day Saints* (Orem, Utah: Randall Book Co., 1986).

Finally, I express deep love and appreciation to Sheree, my wife and friend. The happy association with her and our seven wonderful children—Jared, Sarah, Rebecca, Diana, Renee, Rachel, and Amy—has always provided me with an oasis of peace and pleasure which makes life worth living and efforts such as this worth undertaking.

Introduction

This book is an effort to link two fascinating realms in the world of knowledge—the study of Mormonism and the study of millennialism. In 1990, the Mormon History Association celebrated its twenty-fifth anniversary. While nonpolemical, scholarly works had been written before the founding of the MHA, the organization's birth provides a convenient milestone in Mormon historiography.[1] Greater access to church archives, professional organization and activism, new documentary discoveries, a rapidly proliferating body of practitioners, and the rise of a number of new publication outlets have all combined to make the past three decades a period in which the writing of Mormon history has flourished.[2] Many aspects of the Latter-day Saint experience needing reassessment were lifted beyond the distorting confines of polemical or propagandistic history by an impressive array of scholarly articles and monographs. That a reliable retelling of the entire span of LDS history is now available will be disputed by few.[3]

The 1960s and 1970s also produced what one historian has called "a veritable blizzard of scholarly and popular writings in the often stormy field of millennialism."[4] Nor has interest in this topic dissipated with the passage of time. By the mid-1980s, that same historian wrote, "the word millennialism has become almost synonymous in recent years with American religious history."[5] Another added, "even this statement errs on the side of timidity." Enthusiasm aside, one can hardly argue with the latter's assessment that "in recent years, millennialism has proven to be one of the most fertile areas of investigation in American religious history" and that "scholars have found millennialism almost everywhere."[6]

It is all the more surprising, then, that its presence in early Mormonism has received little more than passing mention. Mormon studies and millennial studies have never really converged in a systematic manner, and cross-pollination has been occasional at best. Previous studies of Mormonism have correctly identified the first Latter-day Saints as Christian primitivists—seekers after the "primitive" or New Testament church, or have viewed them from within the context of frontier communitarianism, or have even depicted Mormonism as a "new religion."[7] But if important parts of the building have been recognized before, the foundation supporting it needs to be fully revealed. That undergirding essence was the Mormons' millennial worldview.

Millennialism, it must be stressed, is far more than simply believing that the millennium is near. It is a comprehensive way of looking at human history and an integrated system of salvation. It is a type of eschatology, a term derived from Greek for "doctrine of the last things" or "end times," and used to refer broadly to people's ideas about the final events in individual human lives as well as the collective end of human history.[8] This study of Mormon eschatology, therefore, deals with more than just what Latter-day Saints thought about the Second Coming of Christ or how they envisioned the millennium. It probes many related aspects of their mental universe and, in the process, demonstrates how one of the most satisfactory models for understanding Mormonism during its earliest phase (1830–46) is from the standpoint of millenarianism.

When the story of the past is told with full attention to ideas as the principal determinants of human behavior, it is called intellectual history. While not dismissing the influence of social or economic factors, intellectual history harbors a profound respect for the power of ideas—the product of the human intellect—to shape history. This book is such a work in intellectual history. It takes Latter-day Saint thought seriously and argues for its causative priority in Mormon history. Along the way, it challenges the old scholarly chestnut that millenarianism is best accounted for as a result of socioeconomic deprivation. On the one hand, demographic study of Kirtland Mormons demonstrates that, overall, the Saints had almost the same wealth distribution pattern as their neighbors.[9] More broadly, within the past generation, it has been shown that rather than a compensatory ideology for those on the fringe of social and economic progress, "millennialism is a natural, rational and sometimes normative force that can exert formative influence over all strata of society."[10]

This is not to suggest, however, that the Saints did not feel alienated, for in their eyes the gospel always alienated Christ's disciples from the worldly. But their concern was for the kingdom of God rather than the kingdoms of this world. It was the "riches of eternity" they were seeking and the right to rule with Christ during the millennium, not material profit or political power in "Babylon." As is made clear in subsequent chapters, if the Saints wished to see the contemporary world replaced by the millennial world, it was because it had deprived them of spiritual, not economic, opportunity. Thus, only by attending to the intellectual and spiritual dimensions of Mormonism can the movement adequately be accounted for.

A hurdle to be overcome at the outset is the matter of definitions. As is often the case in fields enjoying interdisciplinary interest like millennial studies, there is an unfortunate lack of consensus on nomenclature. Writers oriented toward theological studies tend to use terms like *premillennialism* or *postmillennialism*. At the same time, social scientists talk of "millenarian movements," and historians of antiquity discuss "apocalypticism." Yet while utilizing a different name, these scholars are often describing the same thing. Thus, it is possible at several points to bridge the terminology gap between disciplines.

Chapter 1 illustrates how millennialist notions evolved out of apocalypticism by adding the expectation of a future "golden age" on earth *before* the final, apocalyptic transformation at the end of time. Some versions of the millennial dream retained the vivid and dramatic spirit of their eschatological progenitor, lashing out against contemporary society and promising imminent vindication for the beleaguered faithful. Others drifted toward a more irenic view of the world around them and interpreted the prophecies figuratively. By the time the Mormons appeared on the scene there were basically two rival millennial visions of the future. What is today labeled postmillennialism constituted one approach. What most accurately should be called millenarian apocalypticism, but more commonly is simply designated millenarianism or premillennialism, represented the other.[11]

Simplistic differentiations about whether Christ will come before (pre-) or after (post-) the millennium are hardly sufficient to distinguish these two schools of thought. The historian Robert Clouse warns that "the distinctions involve a great deal more than the time of Christ's return. The kingdom expected by the premillennialist is quite different from the kingdom anticipated by the postmillennialist, not only with respect to the time and manner in which it will be established but also in regard to its nature and the way Christ will exercise control over it."[12] Historically, both groups have maintained that Christ personally would return to the earth, and both associated with that return a resurrection and a day of judgment. As the prefix implies, however, the postmillennialists felt that these events would conclude the millennium, that is, that there would be only one general resurrection of all humankind and one Day of Judgment, and that both would coincide with Christ's return to earth at the end of the thousand years.

On the other hand, premillennialists believed that there would be *two* comings, two physical resurrections, and two judgments. The first resurrection would occur at the time of Christ's premillennial advent and would involve only the faithful dead. The rest of humanity would come forth after the millennium as the second resurrection. Like their postmillennialist counterparts, millenarians believed that Christ would come after the millennium to execute final judgment, but they also felt that there would be a kind of preliminary judgment (primarily the destruction of the wicked) that would accompany his appearance to inaugurate the millennium.

Shifting from the events surrounding it to the nature of the millennium itself and how Christ will exercise control over it, other important differences are noticeable. Perhaps the most helpful distinction to make pertains to the way each group approached the interpretation of Scripture. In the early nineteenth century, postmillennialism "was often designated 'Spiritualist' because its advocates believed that the promised Kingdom of Christ would be manifested in the reign of the Holy Spirit over the hearts of his people" rather than in some material way.[13] On the other hand, literal interpretation of prophetic passages, in the words of historian Ernest Sandeen, "was the foundation stone of millenarian theology."[14] "As a general rule," summarizes another scholar, premillennialists were "literalists [who] stressed the discontinuities between the mundane world and the future," while postmillennialists were "allegorists" who emphasized "the continuities, with respect to both the means of change and the result of change."[15]

This distinction was plainly manifest in their differing perceptions of the millennial age. For the millenarian, the lamb really would lie down with the lion, immortal beings really would mingle freely with mortals, and Christ indeed would reign personally over the earth from some terrestrial capital. To all of these prophetic promises the postmillennialists gave a spiritualized interpretation. The scene of the lamb and the lion was just a pastoral metaphor to describe an age of peace and cooperation; the resurrection was the process of burying the old sinful self and "rising" to a new spiritual life in Christ; and it was Christ's spirit, not his body (if indeed they felt he still had one) that would reign during the millennium. As one scholar has observed, "The pre-millennialists are clearly closer to the meaning of the texts both accepted. . . . Pre-millennialism is the basic stance; postmillennialism a compromise in the form of a metaphor."[16]

Not surprisingly, the two schools of thought also maintained differing expectations for the salvation of humanity. For the postmillennialists, the thousand years represented the culmination of the gradual Christianization of the entire world and would be achieved largely through successful evangelists. The premillennialists, on the other hand, could be just as active in missionary work but merely hoped to convert a relative handful before Christ came personally to purge the earth and usher in the millennium. Other differences between the two groups could be added, but most reflect their contrasting scriptural hermeneutics (principles of interpretation).

With these distinctions carefully delineated by historians of religion, the groundwork is laid to bridge the terminology gap between disciplines by examining the standard typology of millenarian movements worked out by social scientists at a famous 1960 University of Chicago conference. According to that definition, a religious movement is said to be millenarian when it views salvation as (a) *collective,* to be enjoyed by the faithful as a group; (b) *terrestrial,* to be realized here on earth; (c) *total,* to completely transform life on earth; (d) *imminent,* to come soon and swiftly rather than gradually; and (e) *miraculous,* to be accomplished by, or with the help of, supernatural agencies.[17] In comparing this definition to the pre/post differences discussed above, it is clear that only premillennialism matches each point. Aspects (c) and (e) can hardly be said to describe the postmillennial ethos, and while some postmillennialists expected an imminent millennium, contrary to (d), they saw it coming gradually rather than swiftly. Thus, while acknowledging that no translation from one language or scholarly discipline to another is ever exact, it is possible to see the terms *premillennialism* and *millenarianism* as basically synonymous. Throughout this book, therefore, these terms will be used interchangeably.

As detailed in chapter 2, Mormon eschatology consistently exhibits its closest conceptual correspondence with premillennialism. Despite the propriety of seeing Latter-day Saints as premillennialists, this has not been the standard evaluation. In the 1960s, one scholar summarized millennial scholarship in part by describing the Mormons as an "eccentric embodiment" of the "postmillennial idea."[18] Another thought that they "fit awkwardly" into the postmillennial movement but argued that they could not "be completely excluded either."[19] The weakness of such studies is that they are based on a very superficial examination of early Mormon sources.[20] On the other hand, those more familiar with Mormonism have tended to lack an adequate understanding of Judeo-Christian eschatologies in general. Relying on either a simple dictionary definition or even an outright misunderstanding of eschatological categories, they have argued that Latter-day Saint eschatology vacillated between pre- and postmillennialism during the 1800s and that by the turn of the century it had moved away from premillennialism for good.[21]

The problem is basically one of dated stereotypes. It used to be assumed that because premillennialists were pessimistic about society's future, they were therefore largely uninvolved in evangelism or social reform, expecting Christ to set up his kingdom supernaturally and singlehandedly. Postmillennialists, on the other hand, were supposed to be optimistic about human possibilities, actively involved in missionary work and social reform, and convinced that Christ could work only through them or other natural means to establish the millennium. Thus, when commentators on Mormonism noticed the Saints' kingdom-building rhetoric, they felt compelled to label it postmillennial. They also interpreted the Saints' energetic evangelism in the same light. Additionally, because a sense of the imminent end was assumed to be the essence of what was premillennial about the Mormons, when such rhetoric subsided around the turn of the century it looked as if Mormonism was turning postmillennial.[22]

The latest scholarship, however, has made it clear that such characterizations and conclusions are unwarranted on several counts.[23] First, American historians "have been pre-occupied with studying nineteenth-century postmillennialism" and have therefore "made uninformed generalizations (some of a formulaic if not predictive character) about premillennialism and its association with quietism, pessimism, and catastrophism as opposed to the optimism, activism, and progressivism inherent in the 'post' outlook."[24] It has now been demonstrated that naturalism and supernaturalism, progress and cataclysm, optimism and pessimism indeed can be found side by side in any millennial scenario. "The millennial hope is a paradoxical one," explains Moorhead, "and one can extrapolate a dismal or optimistic view of history, encompassing temporal disaster or progress, or both. . . . Efforts to seize the Kingdom by violence, passive withdrawal from corruption to await the Second Coming, or melioristic reform efforts—all these and other responses have been adduced from eschatological symbols."[25]

Those who have studied premillennialism in depth find, for instance, that millenarians could be just as dedicated to missionary work as any postmillennialists.[26] In exploring the renaissance of American premillennialism in the final quarter of the nineteenth century, one scholar found that it actually brought a heightened interest in missionism: "Just as D. L. Moody [said he] 'felt like working three times as hard' after becoming a premillennialist, others experienced a new desire to bring the gospel to a dying world."[27] George Duffield, a contemporary of Joseph Smith, defended his premillennialism against the charge that it dampened missionary efforts in these words: "The groans of a world perishing in its corruption calls for quickened, multiplied effort, and for zeal irrepressible and inextinguishable. The Gospel of the Kingdom must be preached in all the world, for a witness unto all nations; and then shall the end come."[28] Early Mormon motivation for missionary work, or "raising the warning voice" as they often called it, was similarly rooted in an eschatological evaluation of the world's imminent fate. Orson Hyde, one of the original LDS apostles, expressed it in verse:

> Shall I behold the nations doomed
> To sword and famine blood and fire?
> And not the least exertion make
> But from the scene in peace retire?
> No. While kind heaven shall lend me breath
> I'll sound repentance far abroad
> And tell the nations to prepare
> For Jesus Christ, their coming Lord.[29]

If premillennialists' zeal was equal or superior to that of postmillennialists, their expectations for numerical success were not. Millenarians were "conservative" in their views of "the possibility of salvation."[30] Their idea was that "God had absolutely no intention of saving the world before the second coming of Christ. His chief purpose in this dispensation was to 'visit the Gentiles, to take out of them a people for his name,' not to convert the world."[31] Likewise, the Mormons did not expect to convert the world, only to warn it. To modify a phrase from Leonard Sweet, the Saints have always believed that they were called to bring to pass the gathering of the elect, not the broad electorate, of humankind.

As for millenarians being distinguished by an acute sense of the imminence of the Second Coming, the example of Charles G. Finney, one of the most famous of all postmillennialists, is instructive. On 28 November 1830, he told an audience in Rochester, New York, that if Christians would unite and dedicate themselves to the task at hand, they could "convert the world and bring on the millennium in three months."[32] Such pronouncements (and he issued other similar ones) make the speculations of premillennialist Millerites and Mormons seem tame in comparison. Postmillennialists have been just as ebullient in their hopes and just as anxious for an imminent millennium as have any millenarians. In fact, after having studied both schools of thought in the nineteenth century, one scholar concluded that actually "the [post]millennialists were more given to date-setting than their millenarian contemporaries."[33]

The point is that even though the Saints urged human efforts to build the kingdom, or were mission-minded, or occasionally waned in their enthusiasm for the imminence of paradisiacal glory, these attitudes do not warrant changing the classification of Mormons as premillennialists. Mormon eschatology will be shown to exhibit a much closer kinship to millenarian apocalypticism than it does to allegorist postmillennialism. It would be as misleading to label Mormons postmillennialists simply because of a few shared views and rhetorical emphases as it would be to consider them Baptists because they believed in baptism by immersion or eschewed worldliness as vigorously as Baptist preachers.

A key component in most apocalyptic and millenarian eschatologies is their dualism. Millenarian apocalypticists divide the world into opposing factions, with the status quo and its supporters as the enemy and themselves as the last remnant of righteousness. Added to this sociological dualism is a satisfying soteriological (salvation-related) dualism which ultimately damns the opposition and consigns them to perdition, while the elect live on triumphantly in a transformed world. That early Mormonism provides an excellent example of such apocalyptic dualism, however, has often been overlooked. In part, this is due to the eventual popularity of Joseph Smith's "Vision of the Three Degrees of [post-mortal] Glory" which has seemed to church member and outsider alike to dismiss the dualism of heaven and hell. Yet both social and soteriological dualism were fundamental aspects of the early LDS thought world. This intellectual phenomenon is explored at length in chapter 3.

For Christians, eschatology is integrally related to the interpretation of scripture. Consequently, to probe the depth and breadth of Mormon millenarianism, a careful examination must be made of exactly how Latter-day Saints invoked the word of God to explicate their doctrine. In chapters 4 and 5, as the effort continues to recreate the mental world of early Mormonism, LDS use of both the Bible and the Book of Mormon is examined in detail. Millenarianism exerted a profound influence on what the Saints noticed in scripture, as well as on how they interpreted what they read. Premillennially construable passages effectively constituted a "canon within the canon" for them. As a result, a pronounced emphasis is discernible on topics such as the fate of the proud but apostate Christian world around them and the glorious restoration of Israel, with which they associated themselves. On an even broader basis, their millenarian worldview provided the conceptual context for a number of interpretive emphases heretofore seen as unrelated but which also are discussed in these two chapters.

The latter portion of the book provides a comparative dimension. Careful consideration in chapter 6 of what Mormons both criticized and supported in early nineteenth-century society allows a more accurate identification of their place on the cultural map of antebellum America. LDS perceptions of the institutions and values prevalent in pre–Civil War America show them to be "moderate" millenarians and a good example of how some millenarian groups can level a withering critique at the world around them and yet still be very much a part of the dominant culture. Cultural deviance and millenarianism do not always go hand in hand. Herein lies a crucial distinction, often missed in earlier studies which characterized Mormons as radically countercultural, even revolutionary. Latter-day Saints, it will be seen, actually deviated little from the morals and mores of nineteenth-century evangelicalism, at that time the prevailing religious ethos in America. Upon close examination, the attitudes and behavior of early Mormons seem more mainstream and the alleged radicalism of their marital, economic, and political relations more superficial than has often been assumed.

Narrowing the focus to premillennialism per se, chapter 7 analyzes similarities and differences between the two major American millenarian groups of the day—the Mormons and the Millerites. In this way, the distinctiveness of Mormon premillennialism is made clear, as well as the thorough immersion of many Latter-day Saints in the contemporary "community of discourse" dealing with Biblical prophecies. The Mormon interaction with Millerism in the early 1840s also provided the basis for the later abatement among Latter-day Saints of the sense that the Second Coming was imminent. By concentrating on the numbers of days mentioned within various biblical prophecies and by assigning them an equivalency in years, William Miller calculated that the Second Coming would occur "about the year 1843." During the final eighteen months of his life Joseph Smith responded to Millerism by clearly and repeatedly denouncing any notion that the advent of Christ was near.

The last chapter tests the essentiality of millenarianism to Mormonism by examining the rise of Mormonism in England to see if millenarianism was merely a manifestation of *American* Mormonism. As it turns out, millenarianism seems to have been as integral a part of English Mormonism as it was of American Mormonism. Mormonism tapped the prominent strain of charismatic millenarianism found within the religious world of early Victorian England. By the end of the book, from any vantage point, the fundamental importance of millenarianism to early Mormonism stands out in bold relief. Because of this, some comment is in order as to what has become of this relationship beyond the period covered in this study. An epilogue, therefore, carries the story into the twentieth century.

1

The Eschatological Background
of Early Mormonism

Along the wide spectrum of thought created by a nearly universal fascination with the "end times" lies a particular kind of eschatological thinking called apocalypticism. Despite its common usage in the late twentieth century, *apocalypse* is actually a technical term employed by scholars to refer to a particular type of Jewish or Christian literature that flourished between the years 200 B.C. and A.D. 150. The word is borrowed from Greek and means "to disclose" or "to reveal." As with most categorizations, characteristics of the apocalypses differ somewhat from scholar to scholar, but most include the following: (1) Apocalypses disclose the future by predicting a coming cosmic transformation in which the suffering righteous will be vindicated and their evil opposers vanquished. (2) This revelation of future triumph is delivered through a vision or dream by an angel or other heavenly messenger. (3) Famous ancient figures such as Daniel, Abraham, and Ezra appear as the recipients of such visions. It should be pointed out that since most scholars do not believe in predictive prophecy, at least not with the specificity found in the apocalypses, and because they discern evidence for late dating, they often title this characteristic pseudonymity, or false authorship attribution. (4) Apocalypses are usually highly esoteric, filled with bizarre symbols, images, colors, and numbers that conceal the message from the persecuting majority and reserve it only for the enlightened elect.[1]

Because of their importance to later Christian eschatology, portions of Daniel in the Old Testament and Revelation in the New Testament are probably the most famous apocalypses, but other lesser-known writings such as the Enoch literature, 4 Ezra, and the Testament of the Twelve Patriarchs more closely approximate the foregoing model in all aspects. It is also important to clarify that the Book of Mormon would *not* be viewed as a modern-day apocalypse. While some of the characteristics are similar, it lacks the esoteric and overwhelmingly eschatological nature of the apocalypses. Just as in the Bible, where books and portions of books are singled out as apocalypses, some chapters and groups of chapters in the Book of Mormon may be so classified, but they will be important in this study only as they reflect and reinforce the broader apocalyptic worldview apparent in early Mormonism.

Strictly speaking, *apocalypticism* refers to the particular outlook on life and human history found in apocalyptic literature. However, even in scholarly circles, it is a term that has outgrown its original definition and has become a useful shorthand for such ideas wherever encountered in history, even if unaccompanied by a written apocalypse.[2] Apocalypticism is the dream of "the great reversal." Growing out of a profound discontent with the status quo and seeing society and its power brokers as evil and antagonistic, it promises that the first will be last and the last first. Because the forces of sin are felt to be in control, apocalypticists see little hope in working through "the system." Power structures fully controlled by the adversary can hardly be expected to yield to the efforts of the godly. Only God can make the situation right, and such divine intervention is expected to come dramatically, even cataclysmically, as superhuman forces square off in the final showdown of good and evil. This is where apocalypticism presents a different means to the end of world transformation, which it shares with many reformers and revolutionaries.

Such a faith engenders hope. It is consoling to know that no matter how bleak the contemporary scene may appear, God and good will ultimately prevail.[3] What is more, apocalypticism inevitably portrays the transformation as imminent. Apocalypticists live not in the latter days but in the last days.[4] Though the present is viewed with profound pessimism, a period of tribulation or "messianic woes," as it has been variously called in Judeo-Christian tradition, is felt to be a necessary prerequisite to the end. Thus, if the present generation is viewed as ripe in iniquity, and especially if the righteous are being persecuted, the faithful are thereby provided with additional assurance that all is proceeding according to plan, that everything is in place for the great reversal soon to be effected by the divine deliverer.

From a sociological perspective apocalypticists would be considered sectarians since their ideals stand in sharp contrast not only to unbelievers but to whatever entrenched religious establishment is being opposed. As such, they react strongly against the comfortable accommodation to the world evidenced by the dominant faith. They call for a purification and a return to old-time religion. They are fighting against attempts to make God present only in clerically mediated worship and in ordinary events of history. They want to free God to do the remarkable things he has done in the past. Their apocalypticism promises that he will do them again. From sectarian Jews in the second century B.C. to Mormons in the nineteenth century A.D., a variety of groups over the course of the last two millennia have met the vicissitudes of life with attitudes such as these. It is their story, so vital to a proper appreciation of early Mormonism, that constitutes the remainder this chapter.

For a relative handful of Palestinian Jews, the messianic deliverer came in the form of Jesus of Nazareth early in the first century A.D. What role apocalypticism played in the rise of Christianity and how it has continued to inform its character has been a matter of lively debate for over a century. In his influential book *The Quest for the Historical Jesus,* Albert Schweitzer reviewed the writings of hundreds of scholars who since the eighteenth century had attempted nondevotional biographies of Christ in an effort to separate the Jesus of history from the Jesus of faith and dogma. Schweitzer believed his study actually demonstrated how thoroughly unscientific were the methods and how unhistorical were the conclusions of this self-proclaimed scientific quest for the "Life of Jesus." Tired of explicit or implicit confessional overlays, Schweitzer proposed his own allegedly objective reading of the documents to produce what has been called the apocalyptic Jesus.[5]

Schweitzer argued that Jesus (and later Paul) believed in an imminent and radical transformation of the world which would occur in his own lifetime. Schweitzer focused on several key Biblical passages to make his case. Matthew 24:34 (and parallels in Mark 13:30 and Luke 21:32) records that Jesus, after detailing events surrounding the "end of the world," declared, "Verily, I say unto you, This generation shall not pass, till all these things be fulfilled." In Matthew 10:23, Jesus sends off his disciples with these words: "Verily, I say unto you, Ye shall not have gone over the cities of Israel, till the Son of man be come." And in Mark 9:1, Jesus declares, "Verily I say unto you, That there be some of them that stand here, which shall not taste of death, till they have seen the kingdom of God come with power." Whatever the best interpretation of these passages actually may be, it is at least clear how a literal reading could give one the ideas that Schweitzer (and others) set forth.

Most scholars concede that at least among Jesus' followers, particularly his early Jewish converts, apocalypticism was common.[6] Apocalyptic literature was responsible for bequeathing to the Jews of Palestine a sense of the decisive culmination of history, the restoration of Israel, the resurrection of Jewish dead, an imminent messianic age of peace variously ranging from several hundred to one thousand years, a final judgment, and a glorious age to come.[7] Such ideas had become so pervasive in Palestine by the first century A.D. that they constituted the "common currency in the Judaism of Jesus' day."[8] Some Biblical scholars have elaborated an entire model of the development of early Christianity based on the assumption of the centrality of apocalypticism and have traced its transmutations throughout the first century.[9]

A theme common in the study of early Christianity is the notion of the "delay of the 'Parousia' (Coming)."[10] This theory holds that the earliest Christians expected the end in their lifetimes and argues that when it did not take place, the Catholic Church was born. In other words, by the second century, the delay in the Lord's return was obvious, and Christians settled in for the long haul. Institutionalization occurred as a church hierarchy was established, creeds were formalized, and a canon was fixed. By applying cognitive dissonance theory to early Christianity, it has been argued that the delay intensified a sense of mission, as Christians subconsciously sought to convince themselves, through successfully converting others, that the movement was right after all. Thus, disconfirmation (of prophecy regarding a "this generation" conclusion to history) did not necessarily result in discreditation.[11]

As Catholicism evolved, apocalypticism diminished. Late in the second century, however, in reaction to a diverse movement known as Gnosticism, which stressed secret knowledge (gnosis) as the key to salvation from this evil, material world, Christian millenarianism, as a particular subset of apocalypticism, emerged. Also known as chiliasm, from the Greek root for "thousand," it expounded the idea of an interim golden age of a thousand years' duration inaugurated by Christ's return and followed by the final, cosmic transformation envisioned in the apocalypses. Chiliasm drew on Jewish thought influenced by Persian Zoroastrianism and Babylonian astrology to divide the span of history into seven millennia under the seven planets. Christians saw in this "Cosmic Week" schema a recapitulation of the creation account in Genesis. After six thousand years of earthly existence, a final, millennial "day" of rest, or Sabbath of Creation, as it would later be called, could be expected.[12]

In combating the figurative, anti-materialist views of the Gnostics, early Christian apologists tended to describe the millennium in literal, physical terms as an actual paradise on earth. In ways similar to the contemporary Jewish Apocalypse of Baruch and 4 Ezra, which envisioned a millennium of such material abundance that a thousand grapes would grow on every vine, Irenaeus, in his famous polemic *Against Heresies,* countered Gnostic spiritualism with the idea that the millennial Kingdom of God would be both earthly and Edenic.[13] Such ideas were also present in the Asia Minor writings of Papias, as well as in the Latin discourses of Justin Martyr. With the passing of the Gnostic controversy, however, the doctrine of an earthly millennium became unpopular, particularly in the East where the tendency was to take it as a metaphor for heaven.[14]

Despite its Jewish roots, millenarianism was more directly an outgrowth and modification of early Christian apocalypticism. By linking the commencement of the millennium to the return of Christ in glory, the early fathers provided a peculiarly Christian twist to the doctrine of a final period of peace and prosperity on earth. This was facilitated by eschatological reflection on a single passage in the Apocalypse of John—the one place in the New Testament where the "thousand years" are specifically mentioned:

> And I saw thrones, and they sat upon them, and judgment was given unto them: and I saw the souls of them that were beheaded for the witness of Jesus, and for the word of God, and which had not worshipped the beast, neither his image, neither had received his mark upon their foreheads, or in their hands; and they lived and reigned with Christ a thousand years. But the rest of the dead lived not again until the thousand years were finished. This is the first resurrection. Blessed and holy is he that hath part in the first resurrection: on such the second death hath no power, but they shall be priests of God and of Christ, and shall reign with him a thousand years. (Revelation 20:4–6)[15]

Before leaving the second century, mention must be made of the Montanist movement. Montanism originated in Asia Minor in the latter half of the second century. It was led by a former priest, Montanus, and two prophets, Priscilla and Maximilla. They inveighed against the loss of the apostolic gifts of the spirit and claimed that through them the Holy Ghost was speaking afresh. Not only were the Montanists charismatics (believers in the present availability of spiritual gifts), they were also chiliasts. They believed that the end was near and that the New Jerusalem would soon descend in their neighborhood where they would reign with Christ during the millennium. Though declared a heresy and excoriated by Catholic ecclesiastics, Montanism represented that apocalyptic blend of charisma (in the original Greek sense of "spiritual giftedness" rather than the modern notion of a dashing personality) and chiliasm which had existed in the first century and which thereafter would reappear at various times and in various places throughout the course of Christian history.[16] As the original term implied, apocalypticism presumes a belief in additional revelation, by which, among other things, the apocalypticist is convinced that the end truly is nigh. Early apocalypticists such as the Montanists would have had little trouble understanding young Joseph Smith, who claimed angelic ministrations and heavenly visions disclosing the future.

Though the nascent Catholic church, especially after the coronation of Constantine, glorified the present, seeing in the contemporary prosperity of Christianity the millennium already underway, millenarian apocalypticism was never fully extinguished in subsequent centuries. For one thing, persecution is the incubator for apocalypticism. Millenarian apocalypticism almost never attracts those satisfied with the world around them. By definition, it portrays the status quo as intolerably corrupt and evil and proclaims its imminent overthrow. Once Catholicism became the state religion in the fourth century, it needed to protect itself against such ideas. Augustine became the great architect of the antimillenarian or amillennial perspective which would prevail in Western Christianity until the time of the Reformation. He taught that with the rise of Christianity the promised Kingdom of God had already come, and that the millennial reign mentioned in Revelation 20 was merely a metaphor for the prosperous career of the church thenceforth to the end of time. Ironically, Augustinian eschatology amounted to an ecclesiastical version of the Gnostic notions his predecessor presbyters had combated two hundred years earlier. Of course, one could hardly expect belief in a earthly, political millennium from the man who wrote an entire book to distinguish the "City of God" from the "City of Man."

In 431, the Council of Ephesus ruled that belief in a temporal and paradisiacal millennium was superstition, and millenarian apocalypticism went underground. Nonetheless, it had a thriving existence in the Middle Ages.[17] An innovation from the eleventh century on was that certain poor and oppressed people appropriated apocalyptic ideology in quasipolitical ways, as a revolutionary response to their plight.[18] The Bohemian followers of Jan Huss, for instance, determined that mankind was ripe for destruction and took the cleansing of society into their own hands.[19] As might be expected, apocalypticism also continued to serve as a vehicle for prophetic excoriation of corruption in the church. The Avignon captivity in the 1300s and the Great Schism which followed, in which there were simultaneously two, and for a while three popes, could hardly have failed to engender apocalyptic speculations that the Antichrist was reigning supreme and that the end surely was near.[20]

During the 1500s, in the wake of the Reformation, apocalypticism emerged widely into the light of day. This was so particularly in Germany, where throughout the sixteenth century there existed "a level of apocalyptic expectation that finds few parallels in Western history."[21] Scholars have long recognized the apocalyptic aspects of Radical Reformation movements like Anabaptism, but more recent studies have also documented such mentalities among literate lay burghers, classically trained professors, and educated Lutheran pastors.[22] A mood of eschatological expectancy was also apparent in England.[23] Here the more specifically millenarian type of apocalyptic eschatology came to prevail. Unlike second-century notions of a paradisiacal millennium, however, these commentators spiritualized the thousand years and equated them with the "latter day glory" of the church. The prosperity of English Protestantism in the late sixteenth century made more plausible the medieval musings of Joachim of Fiore and the Spiritual Franciscans about a prolonged and glorious age of the Spirit before the End.[24] Later, as Puritan congregationalism gained strength in seventeenth-century England and America, numerous individuals thought they saw in these gathered churches of the elect "a glimpse of Syon's glory."[25]

Thomas Brightman was initially responsible for mediating these ideas to his fellow Englishmen and he did so through his emphasis on the threefold coming of Christ.[26] Between Jesus' incarnation and his Second Coming at the end of time, there would be a "Middle Advent." This was not to be a personal appearance but an unparalleled outpouring of the Spirit which would revolutionize human history by inaugurating an extended golden age of genuine Christianity. In important ways, Brightman's ideas foreshadowed the later rise of postmillennialism. While the Biblical idea of a brief (generally calculated to last 45 years) "time of refreshing" just before Judgment day had been a popular medieval notion, Brightman expanded the concept both quantitatively and qualitatively.[27] No mere coda to the somber music of mortality, Brightman envisioned this to be an entire symphony of saintliness lasting approximately six hundred years. So resplendent would be the glory of that era that Brightman felt compelled to break with the traditional interpretation of the "New Jerusalem" mentioned in Revelation 21 and 22 as a metaphor for heaven and claimed that those chapters actually described what would yet take place on earth.

While not all his supporters were willing to go as far as Brightman, the idea of a Spirit-revitalized, final flourishing of Christianity before the end caught on. Important Puritan figures such as Henry Finch, Thomas Goodwin, John Cotton, and John Owen all interpreted the "first resurrection" mentioned in Revelation 20 as a future revival of the primitive faith. For a minority of Puritans, however, their millennialism retained the somber tone of medieval apocalypticism and the idea of a paradisiacal millennium reminiscent of patristic chiliasm. In this they were influenced by Johann Alsted's *Beloved City, or the Saints Reign on Earth a Thousand Years* and Joseph Mede's commentary on Revelation. Alsted espoused a literal, thousand-year millennium, cataclysmically inaugurated and peacefully presided over by the resurrected righteous.[28] Mede argued that the Day of Judgment would actually last a thousand years and would be bracketed chronologically by *two* bodily resurrections, one of the righteous dead at the beginning and another of the rest of humanity at the end. The contours of what would come to be called premillennialism first appear here.

What distinguished such a view from the more widespread allegorical millennialism seemed to be scriptural hermeneutics. Referring to

John Henry Archer's *Personall Reigne of Christ,* an opponent wrote in 1650:

> That which is the generall fault not of this Author onely, but of all others that look towards the Millenary way, and indeed the main grounde of all their heterodoxie in this point, is that they put a meerly-literall construction upon the prophesies and promises of Scripture which the Holy Ghost intended onely to be spiritually understood; hence it is that those frequent predictions which we meet in every page of the Prophets concerning the Kingdome of Christ, the re-edifying of the Jewish cities, the pompe and magnificence of restored Israel, their large priviledges and marvailous achievements, are altogether drawn to a grosse, corporall, and syllabicall sense, which the judgment of the whole Christian Church, seconded by the event, hath upon good grounds ever construed not of the letter but the Spirit.[29]

Literal exegesis of the prophecies led to an emphasis on the social and political aspects of the millennium, as in the case of the Fifth Monarchists, who expected the imminent arrival of Christ's millennial kingdom as the fifth and final world monarchy mentioned in scripture.[30] Traditional resistance to the "sensuality" of patristic chiliasm also gradually gave way. Creature comforts were anticipated enthusiastically. John Bunyan invoked the same Isaianic passage (25:6) as Joseph Smith would two hundred years later in his description of the New Jerusalem when he promised that the Lord "would make unto his people a feast of fat things, a feast of wine on the lees, of fat things full of marrow." In *Zion's Joy in her King,* John Fenwick envisioned the Saints idyllically experiencing "sweet and refreshing walks in fair and pleasant vallies and green pastures, by the still and limpid waters." And Mary Cary projected a millennial arcadia in which ravenous carnivores such as the lion would literally eat straw with the ox.[31]

In short, millenarian apocalypticism provided the same antidote to anxiety in times of great upheaval that apocalypticism in general always had. Bernard Capp's summary of its appeal in mid-seventeenth century England is equally applicable to other times and places, including antebellum America into which Mormonism was born:

> At a popular level, the millennium seems to have meant a future world freed from the insecurity of the seventeenth century. Wars

would cease. Crops would be gathered without the age-old fear of harvest failure and famine. The worker alone, liberated from taxes, tithes, and rent, would benefit from his labour. Family life would be transformed by the assurance of perfect health and long life. Fears that a large family meant inevitable poverty disappeared with the guarantee of plenty in a land of milk and honey. In a period of recession, fighting, and confusion, such promises had an obvious appeal. . . . It was more comprehensible than the traditional picture of heaven itself and far more attractive.[32]

Millennialism, whether apocalyptic or allegorical, did not die out with the Restoration in 1660. Among the educated classes of subsequent decades, "millennial speculation never ebb[ed] seriously at any time."[33] Above all, however, there was continuity of apocalyptic millenarianism at the popular level. As the historian Hillel Schwartz put it, scholars have been accustomed to regarding "the Restoration as a tollbooth in English history beyond which earlier millenarian attitudes could not pass." In actuality, "an entire millenarian way of life flourished in England between 1660 and 1740."[34] A similar flourishing has been demonstrated for Colonial America.[35] In either place, its association with charismatic spirituality, or "enthusiasm" as it was pejoratively labeled, was clear. In the classical sense of the term, enthusiasm meant simply the in-dwelling of God, but by the 1700s, it had become the term of choice for discrediting those whose religiosity seemed to be a little too vibrant.[36] As one historian has noted, "enthusiastic religion [was] intimately associated, in the early eighteenth century, with millenarianism."[37]

Actually, it had been so throughout Christian history. For those in quest of certainty, few sources could be more authoritative than direct revelation from God. Yet inspiration, whether it came to the Camisard prophets in London or to millenarian mystics in Pennsylvania, was no more warmly received by the established religion of the day than the charismatic prophets within Judaism or the Montanists of early Christianity had been in their time. In his *Tale of a Tub,* Jonathan Swift saw millenarianism and enthusiasm as inseparably connected, and this satire, along with the activities of actual millenarians, helped push the Anglican church in the early decades of the eighteenth century to increasingly identify apocalyptic millenarianism with madness and step away from its own, albeit more academic, eschatological interests.[38]

Yet "as the notion of the apocalypse diminishe[d] in immediacy for the established church, it gr[ew] in importance for minority religions and in popular literature."[39] For the next several centuries, there was a noticeable persistence along the religious periphery of both millenarian impulse and charismatic performance. One study of spirit possession and popular religion has noted that "the eighteenth century witnessed possibly the greatest extent and diversity of episodes of spirit possession since the early Church." Not surprisingly, it "persuaded some that God was inaugurating the promised time."[40] This blend of charismatic and millenarian religion reached high tide in the half-century following the American and French Revolutions and flourished on both sides of the Atlantic.[41]

Two specific examples of how enthusiasm and eschatology combined in the early American republic are Joseph Meacham and the New Lights of New Lebanon, New York, and Nathaniel Wood and the New Israelites of Middletown, Vermont. Meacham had Baptist origins but found himself dissatisfied with the infighting among his brethren. In time, he migrated to New Lebanon and was caught up in the revival of 1779. Under his leadership, New Lighters held protracted meetings in which tongues, visions, and prophesying were prominent and pointed to an imminent millennium. As one participant remembered it, the charismatics "testified that the latter day of glory was near at hand, and that Christ would shortly set up his kingdom on earth and make an end of sin."[42] When the Second Coming did not immediately occur, disappointment set in. Soon, however, Meacham found among the Shaker community of Niskayuna what he had been seeking. Convinced by their spiritual giftedness that they were truly the "people of God" on earth and that the millennial kingdom had already been ushered in, he was converted and dubbed Mother Ann's "first-born in America." After her death, he played a major role in institutionalizing the fledgling faith.[43]

Nathaniel Wood and family, of Separate Congregationalist background, migrated to Middletown, Vermont, and became prominent citizens. In the 1780s, however, Wood broke away to found his own conventicle. He claimed that his group constituted the "modern Israelites or Jews, who were under the special guardianship of the Almighty while the Gentiles—all who were opposed to them—would suffer from their hostility."[44] They enjoyed the gifts of the spirit, including prophecy, and predicted dire judgments upon the wicked. By the late 1790s, the group embraced an individual whose gift was the use of a divining rod to discover both treasure and truth. This combination of folk magic, popular prophetism, and millenarian apocalypticism resulted in a divining-rod prophecy that on a certain date the unbelievers would be slain and the Woodites would inherit the region as the millennium commenced. When the promised Parousia did not occur, the group was "warned out" of town and eventually settled in New York.[45]

In the 1800s, however, postmillennialism reigned supreme. The historian James Moorhead has shown that for the first three-quarters of the century, postmillennialism "dominated the popular denominational magazines as well as the weighty theological quarterlies," and that "it commanded allegiance in leading seminaries and pulpits alike."[46] It was the eschatology of the nineteenth-century revivals collectively designated the Second Great Awakening and of the various religious reform organizations known as the Benevolent Empire.[47] Indeed, it has even been argued that it was the essence of an evangelical "civil" or "public" religion in antebellum America, a "root symbol in American life," and that American history itself is "best understood" as a millennial movement. In short, it identified the history of redemption with the history of the Republic.[48]

Still, not everyone shared this vision of a rapidly Christianizing America. It has been commonplace to emphasize the nineteenth century's ebullient optimism and sense of constant, inevitable progress. Despite the grandiloquent rhetoric of Fourth of July orations or of key community leaders, though, a broad cross-section of Americans, in the privacy of their personal jottings, shared a more negative outlook. "Time and time again, when the mood of their age is under discussion," writes the historian Lewis Saum, "Hawthorne and Melville—those 'Nay-sayers' . . . — appear as idiosyncratic counterpoints to the dominant confidence and assertiveness. However out of step they may have been with some optimism in higher circles, their dark brooding about fate and providence bore a powerful resemblance to the outlook of the common American."[49] It has also been noted that "a deep current of pessimism ran through Jacksonian culture, belying the optimistic egalitarianism usually portrayed."[50]

During the formative years of the new American nation, popular premillennialism capitalized on this sentiment and blended comfortably with the democratic critique of traditional society then underway. As the historian Nathan Hatch has pointed out, when ordinary people married the democratic ideals of civil and religious liberty to their eschatology, a popular millenarianism resulted which "resisted traditional norms, particularly the hegemony of elites, insisted that freedom of thought be extended to those outside of power structures, and identified aspirations of common folk with the will of God."[51] For those seeking to condemn the establishment, millenarianism had always provided an effective tool.

The democratization of American Christianity created a critically important precondition for the birth of Mormonism. In the words of the historian Gordon Wood,

> The disintegration of older structures of authority released torrents of popular religiosity into public life. Visions, dreams, prophesyings, and new emotion-soaked religious seekings acquired a validity they had not earlier possessed. The evangelical pietism of ordinary people, sanctioned by the democratic revolution of these years, had come to affect the character of American culture in ways it had not at the time of the Revolution. It now became increasingly difficult for enlightened gentlemen to publicly dismiss religious enthusiasm as simply the superstitious fanaticism of the illiterate and lowborn.[52]

The sociologist Michael Barkun explains that at such times, alternate belief systems "confront a markedly more sympathetic audience. . . . Once ignored, scorned, or suppressed, they now may be perceived in a new and favorable light." The reason is that they "appear to possess a greater ability to address the crisis of meaning. They assert moral order where none may appear to exist, typically by claiming access to previously untapped sources of power, identified with some body of hidden knowledge, and often promulgated by a charismatic figure."[53] Just such a figure was Joseph Smith and just such an ideology was Mormonism. Retiring to a grove of trees near his Palmyra, New York, farm house, Joseph Smith petitioned the Almighty for guidance. The resulting theophany inaugurated a decade of divine dispensations that culminated in 1830 with the publication of the Book of Mormon and the establishment of the "Church of Christ."[54] Plenary inspiration and divine authority were once again on the earth, offering definitive resolution to the religious wranglings of the age.[55] As will be shown throughout the rest of this book, the content of that inspiration was profoundly millenarian in character.

2

Mormons as Millenarians

In Joseph Smith's earliest description of his first encounter with Deity, he recorded the words of the Lord thus: "behold the world lieth in sin at this time and none doeth good no not one they have turned asside from the gospel and keep not my commandments they draw near to me with their lips while their hearts are far from me and mine anger is kindling against the inhabitants of the earth to visit them acording to thir ungodliness and to bring to pass that which hath been spoken by the mouth of the prophets and Apostles behold and lo I come quickly as it [is] written of me in the cloud clothed in the glory of my Father."[1]

Such a stinging indictment of the present religious world, along with the warning of an imminent visitation in judgment, is standard millenarian fare. As Ernest Sandeen has pointed out, a basic premise of nineteenth-century millenarianism "was the assumption that an irreversible deterioration in religion and culture had now reached crisis proportions and that the final act in this era of world history had already begun."[2] From the LDS perspective, what inaugurated that act was foretold in John's Apocalypse: "And I saw another angel fly in the midst of heaven, having the everlasting gospel to preach unto them that dwell on the earth . . . saying with a loud voice, fear God and give glory to him; for the hour of his judgment is come" (Revelation 14:6–7). As Latter-day Saints understood it, this was not symbolic. The angel seen in this vision actually visited Joseph Smith and delivered to him the Book of Mormon which, by its presence, signaled that the end was nigh, and, by its contents, stood in judgment against the contemporary religious world.

During the 1830s, Sidney Rigdon was one of the leading exponents of Mormon millenarianism.[3] A former "Reformed Baptist" colleague of Alexander Campbell, the convert Rigdon provided a much-needed Aaron to the Mormon Moses, Joseph Smith. An early revelation announced that "my servant Sidney should be a spokesman unto this people . . . even to be a spokesman unto my servant Joseph."[4] By writing numerous articles in church periodicals and frequent Sunday sermons, as well as by being a member of the First Presidency, the three-man ruling council of the Church, Rigdon performed his appointed task well.

In the mid 1830s, he wrote an important article entitled "The Latter Day Glory," which conveys well some of the major themes in Mormon millenarianism. In the article, Rigdon acknowledged the impressive impetus to evangelical activity that postmillennialism provided his contemporaries. He called it "the spur to all the efforts of the religious communities of the present day." "The great exertions," he elaborated, "which are made to excite revivals" grow out of the "view of the near approach of the latter day glory, and the coming of the Son of man. All the missionary schemes of the age are founded on the belief of it. . . . The cry Millenium is heard all over the land, and men are required to use all their exertions to usher in the glory of the last days, by converting the world."[5]

Ridgon would have been very familiar with such views through his association with postmillennialist Alexander Campbell, but he vigorously disagreed with him on these eschatological matters.[6] It seems that Rigdon and his fellow seeker after the primitive church Walter Scott had been influenced by the premillennialist writings of Elias Smith and James Begg.[7] In part, this is why after nearly a decade's union, Rigdon broke ranks with Campbell just months before the Mormon missionaries arrived. Campbell's memoirs contain the comment that Ridgon "had been for some time diligently engaged in endeavoring, by obscure hints and glowing millennial theories, to excite the imaginations of his hearers, and in seeking by fanciful interpretations of Scripture to prepare the minds of the churches of Northern Ohio for something extraordinary in the near future."[8] For Rigdon and dozens of his followers, that "something extraordinary" turned out to be Mormonism. According to the most important early source of Disciple (Campbellite) history, "the restoration of the ancient gospel was looked upon as the initiatory movement" leading to the millennium.[9] With such a restoration being proclaimed by Mormon preachers, Campbell remembered that they "gained many proselytes" among his followers, "some even persons of intelligence," who had been "filled with vague expectations of a speedy millennium."[10]

As a millenarian, Rigdon firmly believed that all postmillennially motivated efforts at Christianizing the world would come to naught. He rejected Campbell's conviction that, on their own, "human beings were fully capable of reading Scripture aright, implementing its divine patterns, and restoring in full the grandeur and beauty of the apostolic age." Rigdon felt that the only way to achieve a genuine restoration of the "ancient order of things" in anticipation of the millennial day was for the Lord himself to "prepare the way of his coming by raising up and inspiring apostles, prophets, evangelists, pastors and teachers, and under their ministry restore again to his Saints all the gifts of the church as in days of old." Once this was accomplished, Christ could return again to introduce the millennium and "cut off and consign to the perdition of ungodly men" all those who resisted the restored gospel.[11]

Proclamation of coming judgments, however, was balanced by the uniquely Mormon twist on premillennialism, which held that "before the coming of Christ and the general destruction of the wicked, God will gather his Saints together from every nation, tongue, language and kindred, under the whole heaven unto places before appointed." These gathering spots included Jerusalem in the Old World as well as a New-World "Zion" where Mormon converts could gather "for a defense and for a refuge from the storm, and from wrath when it shall be poured out without mixture upon the whole earth." The eleventh-hour choice was simple: gather with the Saints or be destroyed, for truly "all the rest of the world will without exception be cut off."[12]

These ideas were echoed by another articulate apologist for early Mormonism, Orson Hyde. Before his conversion, he, too, had been impressed with the Campbellite commitment to primitivism, but soon became one of the first elders of Mormonism. When the Quorum of the Twelve Apostles was organized in 1835, he was called to serve and in time became president of that body. His apostolic ministry took him to England with the first Mormon mission in 1837 and alone to the Holy Land in the 1840s to dedicate it for the return of the Jews. Through it all, Hyde was an active publicist for the Church and wrote one of the earliest and most influential LDS tracts—*A Prophetic Warning*.[13] A review of this tract provides an excellent glimpse into the millenarian rationale of early Mormonism.

Hyde begins by claiming that just as the Mosaic laws were given to Israel to prepare that people for the initial appearance of Christ, so the Apostolic teachings were given to Christendom "for the express purpose of preparing them for the Second Coming."[14] Unfortunately, according to Hyde, in like manner to the Jews, "the Gentiles [the standard Mormon term for both Catholics and Protestants] have made void the gospel through the tradition of their Elders." After citing Biblical predictions of apostasy, he continues, "I will now present the Gentile churches before the glass of the holy scriptures, and see if they possess the same form and beauty now, that they did Eighteen Hundred years ago."

The outcome is obviously unfavorable. Priestcraft and liturgical formalism abound. The sick are not healed, and the gift of the Holy Ghost is not conveyed by the laying on of hands. Gone are the charismata, the "signs" which "follow them that believe." "How," asks Hyde, "can the clergy of this day be of God; and yet deny the miraculous powers?" The conclusion is inescapable: "every person who is not biassed by most unhallowed prejudice can see that the churches of this day bear but a faint resemblance to those which existed in the days of the Apostles." Pursuing his analogy with the Jews, Hyde invokes the olive tree allegory of Romans 11 to explain that, having failed to "continue" in the "goodness" of God, Gentile Christendom was destined to be "cut off" in the last days, just as the Jews had earlier, though ultimately the Jews would be "grafted" back in.

For Hyde, all of this stood in frightening contrast to the perceptions of postmillennialist evangelicals. "Many are flattering themselves with the expectation that all the world is going to be converted and brought into the ark of safety. Thus the great millennium, in their opinion, is to be established. Vain, delusive expectation! The Savior said to his disciples that 'as it was in the days of Noah, so shall it be also in the days of the coming of the Son of Man.' Query. Were all the people converted in the days of Noah, or mostly destroyed?" The answer was clear, and events "will soon show to this generation that the hour of God's judgment hath come."

Of course, history could be averted if the Gentiles would "speedily turn to the Lord." After all, the predicted wars, pestilences, and natural disasters were clearly linked to the behavior of the people. "The prime cause of all these calamities coming on the earth," wrote Hyde, "is the apostasy of the church. If the church was all righteous, they could save the nations from destruction. But the salt has lost its savor."

Therefore, temporal judgments would continue until finally the Lord himself returned to finish the work of cleansing and inaugurate the millennium. "When Jesus appears in the clouds of heaven," concluded Hyde in good premillennial fashion, "the Saints who have slept will arise from their graves; and those who are living will be changed speedily, and all be caught up to meet the Lord in the air. Then shall all the wicked, who have escaped the former judgments, be consumed, root and branch. Then shall the earth be cleansed from pollution; and the Lord descend upon it, and all the Saints with him to reign a thousand years while Satan is bound. Then will the Saints inherit this promise: 'Blessed are the meek, for they shall inherit the earth.'"

The themes introduced in Hyde's broadside and Rigdon's article were elaborated in greater detail in the two major treatises on Mormon eschatology produced in the 1830s. The first was Sidney Ridgon's "Millenium," a series of fourteen articles appearing nearly monthly in the Church's periodical from December 1833 to May 1835. The second was the work of prominent Mormon apologist and apostle Parley P. Pratt. Entitled *A Voice of Warning and Instruction to All People, Containing an Introduction to the Faith and Doctrine of the Church of the Latter-Day Saints, Commonly Called Mormons,* it was perhaps the most widely reprinted piece of LDS literature in history, aside from the Book of Mormon.[15]

In his series, Rigdon acknowledged the widespread contemporary interest in the millennium and admitted that "the things spoken of by the ancient prophets, have never been fulfilled, nor never can, unless the Millenium is brought about in the economy of God." But, he argued, "in what manner it is to be introduced, and by what means," the Christian world has "been unable to see, or understand."[16] In particular, the postmillennial vision was fatally flawed. "The ignorance of the religious teachers of the day," declared Rigdon, "never appeared more glaring in any thing, than in an attempt to create a Millennium by converting this generation."[17] Even standard premillennialism also fell short. Responding to a series of articles written by premillennialist Samuel McCorkle for Alexander Campbell's *Millennial Harbinger,* Ridgon remarked, "what a difference between a man of God, and a self authorized and self constituted messenger! The man of God will no sooner cry, Destruction, desolation, and judgment than he will tell them of an ark, a Zoar, a Palla, a Mount Zion, a Jerusalem, or some other place which God has provided for them who will hear his voice. But Mr. M'Corkle, like every other messenger that God has never sent, can cry, Destruction, desolation, fire, and judgment, and write very ingeniously about it, but there it ends."[18] It served little purpose in Rigdon's mind to proclaim a message of doom and gloom as premillennialism typically did and then offer "no way for escape! no hiding place! no city of refuge!"[19]

Here was what was distinctive about Mormon millenarianism. Similar to how the doctrine of the rapture would come to function for Darbyite dispensationalists in later decades, the Mormon doctrine of the "gathering" served to provide a means of escape from much of the anticipated tribulation of the last days.[20] At the same time, it produced a concentration of Saints who could be properly prepared for the coming of the millennium. The gathering, therefore, was the pivotal premillennial event in Mormon eschatology. "The only thing," declared Rigdon, "which God promised to the world, after the great apostacy, which was to corrupt all nations, and defile all the kings of the earth; and terminate in the overthrow of the Gentiles . . . was to return the scattered remnants of Jacob, and gather the house of Joseph; bringing them as he did at the first, and building them as he did at the beginning."[21] So emphatic on this point was Rigdon that he concluded his second article by declaring that "unless the scattered remnants of Jacob should be gathered from all countries whither they had been driven, that no such thing as a Millenium could ever exist; or that God never promised such an era to mankind on any other ground than that of the gathering the house of Jacob to the land of their fathers and that predicated on the fact of the Gentiles having forfeited all claim to the divine favor by reason of their great apostasy."[22]

His logic was simple. Gentile Christendom had had its chance. The end times were to be Israel's great day, and what triggered it in the divine economy was the fullness of Gentile apostasy. Once the glorious gathering and restoration of Israel was completed, the Savior could return, destroy the remaining reprobates, transform the earth, and usher in a thousand years of rest. In order to be restored, though, Israel would first have to be identified, and that, it was thought, would require revelation. With revelation again available through Joseph Smith, it was learned that the Israelite race included not only the Jews and the lost Ten Tribes but the American Indians as well. Even European or American Gentiles like Smith, Ridgon, and the bulk of antebellum Mormons could be "adopted" into the House of Israel through conversion to God's latter-day work and thus became equal participants in the promises of the "new covenant."

As Latter-day Saints used it, the term *gentile* had multiple meanings. It could refer to race, religion, or both. Most often, it meant nonbeliever. Just as ancient Israel used the term to refer to all non-Jews, modern, Mormon "Israel" used it to identify all non-Mormons. Sometimes, though, in Mormon scripture and literature the term denoted people of European stock. In this sense, all white Americans were considered gentiles, and American Mormons could with perfect propriety describe themselves as gentiles. Thus, the dedicatory prayer for the House of the Lord in Kirtland included the Saints' self-description as "us who are identified with the Gentiles."[23] Most commonly, however, the term referred to that group which fit both categories, namely European and American members of other churches. To the Saints it seemed doubly appropriate to label them as gentiles since in addition to being Caucasians they were also perceived as not preaching or practicing the true gospel.

With the passage of time, American and European Saints placed increasing emphasis on literally having the "blood of Israel" in their veins and rarely referred to themselves as gentiles needing to be adopted into Israel. The remark by subsequent Mormon prophet Brigham Young that Joseph Smith was a "pure Ephraimite" is typical.[24] Prominent church leaders often traced their genealogies to the Holy Land, and some to the Holy One himself.[25] There was also some discussion that through the conversion process, even those who formerly were literal gentiles acquired more than a figurative kinship with Israel.[26]

With Israel properly identified, the Saints' literalist hermeneutics helped them to discern in scripture two basic places of gathering. Isaiah 24:23 speaks of a day "when the Lord of hosts shall reign in mount Zion, and in Jerusalem, and before his ancients gloriously." Edward Partridge, the first Bishop of the Church, was typical of Latter-day Saints in his exegesis of this passage when he commented, "Thus we see that the Lord is not only to reign in Jerusalem, but in mount Zion, also, which shows that Jerusalem and Zion are two places."[27] In ways to be detailed later, the Saints believed that "Zion" was the designated gathering spot for Gentile converts and their Indian neighbors, while Jerusalem was for the Jews. As one early revelation expressed it, "let them, therefore, who are among the Gentiles flee unto Zion. And let them who be of Judah flee unto Jerusalem, unto the mountains of the Lord's house."[28] Understandably, most LDS interest focused on the American gathering place, Zion. Since an American Israel had been identified for gathering, advent-anxious Saints did not have to wait, as did other Christian millenarians, for dramatic happenings within world Jewry in order to witness the restoration of Israel. Rather, they were able to see in the U.S. government's Indian-removal policies of the 1830s Gentile "nursing fathers" at work gathering the Lord's covenant people. Even more immediate was their own need, as part of Israel also, to gather to Zion.

Since much of the early history of the Church can be understood only in reference to the doctrine of the gathering, it is essential that its history be reviewed. The Book of Mormon, first available in March 1830 just weeks before the church was officially organized, affirmed that there would be a New Jerusalem in the New World, but had not specified its location.[29] Six months later, a revelation declared that "no man knoweth where the city [Zion] shall be built" but indicated that it would be somewhere near the western "borders" of the United States.[30] Despite the uncertainty over location, the Mormon mission was clear: "ye are called to bring to pass the gathering of mine elect, for mine elect hear my voice and harden not their hearts. Wherefore the decree hath gone forth from the Father, that they shall be gathered in unto one place, upon the face of this land, to prepare their hearts, and be prepared in all things, against the day when tribulation and desolation are sent forth upon the wicked."[31]

Consistent with the spirit of gathering, by the Church's first anniversary, the small band of Mormon converts were in the process of relocating from various New York sites to Kirtland, Ohio.[32] Several revelations in the interim had reassured them that the location of Zion was soon to be revealed. Meanwhile, the Lord instructed the brethren to labor "in my vineyard for the last time, for the last time call ye upon the inhabitants of the earth; for in mine own due time will I come upon the earth in judgment, and my people shall be redeemed, and shall reign with me on earth, for the great Millenium of which I have spoken by the mouth of my servants shall come."[33]

During the summer of 1831, Joseph Smith and other leading elders were called to go to Missouri where "the land of [their] inheritance" was to be made known. Shortly after arriving, a revelation declared that "this land, which is the land of Missouri, is the land which I have

appointed and consecrated for the gathering of the Saints. Wherefore, this is the land of promise, and the place for the city Zion. . . . Behold the place which is now called Independence is the center place;
and a spot for the temple is lying westward, upon a lot which is not far
from the courthouse. Wherefore, it is wisdom that the land should be
purchased by the Saints . . . that they may obtain it for an everlasting
inheritance."[34]

When the elders returned to Kirtland with the news, enthusiasm
was understandably high. Given the Saints' eschatology, it took some
persuasion and several revelations to convince them not to gather "in
haste, lest there should be confusion," and to stress that "the land of
Zion shall not be obtained but by purchase."[35] Nor was it the Lord's
will that Kirtland be abandoned in the near future. Several key mer-
chant and landowning converts were specifically told to stay. Frederick G. Williams, for instance, soon to become one of the First Presidency, was counseled not to sell his farm and emigrate, "for I, the
Lord, will to retain a strong hold in the land of Kirtland for the space
of five years in the which I will not overthrow the wicked, that thereby
I may save some." Of course, it was added, that "after that day, I the
Lord, will not hold any guilty that shall go with an open heart up to
the land of Zion, for . . . now it is called today until the coming of the
son of Man . . . but after today cometh the burning . . . and I will not
spare any that remain in Babylon."[36]

Thus, for the next half-dozen years, there were two American gathering spots—Jackson County, Missouri, known simply as Zion, and
Kirtland, Ohio. Zion, however, with all the biblical prophecies and
promises attached to it, always held pride of place emotionally. This is
poignantly portrayed in Joseph Smith's diary entry about a dinner
party in October 1835:

> After being seated around the table Bishop Whitney observed to
> Bishop Partridge that the thought had just occurred to his mind
> that perhaps in about one year from this time [the conclusion of the
> five-year period mentioned above] they might be seated together
> around a table on the land of Zion. My wife observed that she
> hoped it might be the case that not only they but the rest of the
> company present might be seated around her table in the land of
> promise; the same sentiment was reciprocated from the company
> round the table and my heart responded amen God grant it.[37]

Such sentiments were held despite participation in the growing prosperity of Kirtland and the near completion of its much anticipated temple. In the fall of 1837, the Bishop at Kirtland issued a circular "to the Saints scattered abroad" in which he announced, "Our hopes, our expectations, our glory and our reward, all depend on our building up Zion according to the testimony of the prophets. For unless Zion is built, our hopes perish, our expectations fail, our prospects are blasted, our salvation withers, and God will come and smite the whole earth with a curse." As if any of his readers might have wondered why this was the case, he explained that "this great work of building the Zion of our God" was necessary so that "there may be a place of refuge for you, and for your children in the day of God's vengeance, when he shall come down on Idumea, or the world, in his fury, and stamp them down in his wrath, and none shall escape, but the inhabitants of Zion."[38]

Zion, however, was far from becoming the New Jerusalem. The story of the Saints' trials and persecutions in Jackson County has been told thoroughly elsewhere.[39] It need only be noted here that within two years of the original settlement near Independence, Missouri, the Mormons had run afoul of their neighbors and were driven at gunpoint out of the county. They settled across the Missouri river in Clay County and managed to eke out a meager but peaceful existence for the next few years. By 1836, the Saints were once again being asked to leave. This time they moved north and east within the state to a sparsely settled area and petitioned the legislature for incorporation as a county. When the request was granted, Saints poured into the new Caldwell County and most settled in a town they called Far West. Some went even further north and layed out a settlement designated "Adam-ondi-Ahman, because, said [the Lord], it is the place where Adam shall come to visit his people, or the Ancient of Days shall sit, as spoken of by Daniel the prophet."[40] Joseph and Emma Smith, and most of the other Kirtland Saints, got their wish to settle in the "land of promise" within the next two years. However, problems inside the Church as well as with their Kirtland neighbors forced the faithful to flee town rather than abandon it triumphantly. By the spring of 1838, under somewhat different circumstances and on a somewhat different timetable from what was originally anticipated, the bulk of the Saints—around 5,000—had finally been "gathered in unto one place upon the face of the land"—northwestern Missouri.[41]

Rejoicing was brief, however, for the arrival of summer marked the beginning of the end. Sidney Rigdon's "salt sermon," the election-day fracas at Gallatin, Sampson Avard and the Danites, Haun's Mill Massacre, and ultimately the infamous "extermination order" of Missouri Governor Lilburn Boggs evidenced escalating animosities which resulted in the jailing of Joseph Smith and the wintertime banishment from the state of thousands of Mormons.[42] Never again in the nineteenth century would the Saints return en masse to their Missouri Zion, the site originally and ironically designated for their "defense and refuge."

Shortly after their exile, the Saints purchased land near a sleepy little Mississippi river village known as Commerce, Illinois, and started once again to rebuild their lives. They optimistically called their new gathering place "Nauvoo," a Hebrew term which they understood as "the beautiful place." One of the first public revelations received in Nauvoo announced,

> Verily, verily, I say unto you, that when I give a commandment to any of the sons of men to do a work unto my name, and those sons of men go with all their might and with all they have to perform that work, and cease not their diligence, and their enemies come upon them and hinder them from performing that work, behold, it behooveth me to require that work no more at the hands of those sons of men, but to accept of their offerings. . . . Therefore, for this cause have I accepted the offerings of those whom I commanded to build up a city and a house unto my name, in Jackson county, Missouri, and were hindered by their enemies, saith the Lord your God.[43]

This opened the door for a broader interpretation of Zion. As Joseph Smith later explained, "I have now a great proclamation for the Elders to teach the Church hereafter which is in relation to Zion. The whole of North and South America is Zion."[44] This represented such a dramatic change from the past that in a letter to his brother Orson, Parley Pratt reported the announcement using seven exclamation points.[45] Though Joseph Smith now said that "any place where the Saints gather is Zion," in practice, Mormons responding to the divine command were still counseled to gather to the centers of church population.[46] This meant that for the next few years they would emigrate to Nauvoo and, for the rest of the century, they would gather to Utah.

The obvious benefits in terms of faith and fellowship, as well as the allure of the fresh start and the chance to demonstrate physically one's devotion to God, helped make the gathering remarkably successful. During the nineteenth century, tens of thousands of Latter-day Saints would gather to an American Zion. In the twentieth century, however, Smith's statements would provide the basis for a new, figurative understanding of the gathering in which Zion would be wherever pure Saints congregated to live and worship, even in foreign lands. Abandoning Babylon and gathering to Zion now became more of a spiritual than a geographical move; it involved changing one's heart, not one's home. Ultimately, lifestyle rather than location came to be the distinguishing characteristic of Zion.[47]

Still, the hope for building Zion as a sacred city in Missouri persisted. Within the broader definition of Zion, it came to be referred to as the "center stake" or "center place." As late as 1900, Church President Lorenzo Snow exclaimed that "there are many here now under the sound of my voice, probably a majority who will have to go back to Jackson County and assist in building the temple."[48] During the 1970s, the Church adjusted one of its Articles of Faith in a way that seems to reflect both its continued belief in the future establishment of an actual Holy City in western Missouri, as well as its acknowledgment of an amplified understanding of the term Zion. Rather than "we believe ... that Zion will be built upon this the American continent," the tenth article now reads, "we believe ... that Zion *(the New Jerusalem)* will be built upon the American continent."[49] The addition of the parenthetical explanation, unnecessary in the earliest years when there was basically only one, literal sense for the term Zion, clarifies for modern readers acquainted with its multiple significations which meaning is actually intended in this instance.

While LDS attention historically has focused on the gathering of an American Israel and the building an American Zion, it should be clearly understood that their vision was of a *dual* enactment and that they used many of the traditional passages in the usual way to refer to the restoration of the Jews alone. Parley Pratt's *Voice of Warning* is particularly illustrative of this fact. He cites Isaiah, Jeremiah, Ezekiel, Zechariah, and even John the Revelator to prove that God will "set his hand the second time to recover the remnant of his people" by establishing a "new covenant with them" and miraculously leading them back to Palestine with "outstretched hand." At the end of a long chapter, he presents a scenario which was common among literalist students of Biblical prophecy throughout Christendom:

> Suffice it to say, the Jews gather home, and rebuild Jerusalem. Gog gathers against them in battle. Their armies encompass the city, and have more or less power over it for three years and a half. A couple of Jewish prophets, by their mighty miracles, keep them from utterly overwhelming the Jews; until at length they are slain, and the city is left in a great measure to the mercy of their enemies for three days and a half. The prophets then rise from the dead and ascend up into heaven. The Messiah comes, convulses the earth, overthrows the army of Gog, delivers the Jews, cleanses Jerusalem, cuts off all wickedness from the earth, raises the Saints from the dead, brings them with him, and commences his reign of a thousand years.[50]

Another aspect of Mormon millenarianism is captured in the Church's full name, The Church of Jesus Christ of *Latter-day* Saints. Whether discussing the restoration of the Jews or the gathering of the Gentile elect, there was a pronounced sense of urgency among the Saints. The end was felt to be imminent; they thought they were living in the last days. Numerous early revelations indicated that the Lord would "come quickly" and that his return was "nigh" or "at hand."[51] On one of their first missions to the Eastern states, the newly constituted Quorum of Twelve Apostles reported, "some of our number visited the city of Boston, and held forth to that people this important truth, that the Son of Man will appear in this generation."[52] Edward Partridge wrote to his friends in Ohio that "the signs that have been seen show that this is the very generation spoken of" in Matthew 24.[53]

Nor was the idea restricted to the "leading brethren." On a mission to the South in 1838, Amos Fuller, typical of the numerous individuals who left no legacy in the Church other than a brief proselyting diary which has survived, preached a millenarian discourse to a large congregation, after which "one gentleman asked how that there was men standing in this generation that would not pass away until the saviour came. I told him that I knew by the revelation of Jesus Christ."[54] Many Saints were told in blessings pronounced upon their heads by fellow Saints that they would live to see the Savior come or that they would return to Zion in Jackson County to build the New

Jerusalem or that they would live to participate in other end-time activities.[55] Unlike the Millerites and others, the Saints were not given to prophetic numerology or exact calculations as to the date of Christ's advent. They did, however, very much feel they were living on the eve of the Second Coming.

Their views about the nature of the millennium itself also need to be considered. Contrary to popular postmillennialist notions of Christ's reigning in the hearts of the regenerate, early Latter-day Saints looked forward to the day when the "King of Kings" would physically reign as supreme terrestrial monarch. "Not," remarked Rigdon, "as some have said, a spiritual (which might be more properly called imaginary) reign; but literal, and personal, as much so as David's reign over Israel, or the reign of any king on earth. All the inspired men have said that Christ shall reign over the earth literally; for literally the kingdoms of this world will become the kingdoms of our God and His Christ, and he shall reign on the earth." Lest anyone misunderstand, Rigdon made clear, through allusions to Daniel 2:44, how Jesus would reign politically:

He will as literally break in pieces and destroy all the kingdoms of the world, as ever one king destroyed and broke down the kingdom of another. Never did Cyrus the Great, more literally break down and destroy the kingdom of ancient Babylon, than will Christ, the Great King break in pieces and destroy all the kingdoms of the world; and so completely will he do it, that there will not from one end of the earth to another, be an individual found whose word, or edict will be obeyed but his own: so that he will completely break in pieces and destroy all kingdoms."[56]

But the Lord of Hosts was also the Lamb of God, and the Saints anxiously contemplated the privilege of enjoying a thousand years in his visible presence. An early revelation affirmed that the Lord would "dwell in righteousness with men on earth a thousand years."[57] He would be there personally to bless them with his love and "wipe away all their tears." Numerous early Mormon hymns and poems testify to the emotion with which this millennium-long mutual association was anticipated.[58]

Especially gratifying was to be the Saints' millennial co-regency with Christ. Early Mormons basked in John's promise of being made "kings and priests" to rule and reign with Christ a thousand years.[59] Toward the end of his life, Joseph Smith began stressing the eternal implications of this concept, but before that, the Saints projected all their enthusiasm and expectations for the afterlife on the millennium, rather than on the far-off future state. It was the millennium, not "heaven," to which the editor of the *Messenger and Advocate* was referring when he wrote, "The sure promise of such ravishing bliss enabled the Saints anciently to endure such great tribulations . . . with more than manly fortitude."[60] Whereas modern Mormons anxiously await the day in which they will be crowned with an inheritance in the "Celestial Kingdom," early Saints longed for their millennial inheritance. For them, that was the anticipated day of triumph and glory.

And what a day the millennium would be! Mormons waxed eloquent in their descriptions of an earth renewed to its Edenic state, for such a transformation was the ultimate objective of the "restoration of all things which God [had] spoken by the mouth of all his holy prophets since the world began" (Acts 3:21). Parley Pratt put it, "if we can discover the true state in which [the earth] then existed . . . we shall be able to understand what is to be restored."[61] The primitivist character of the Mormon millennium stands out in bold relief here. Pratt's review of Genesis led him to announce, "from this we learn that there were neither deserts, barren places, stagnant swamps, rough, broken, rugged hills, nor vast mountains covered with eternal snow; and no part of it was located in the frigid zone, so as to render its climate dreary and unproductive." In short, "the whole earth was probably one vast plain, or interspersed with gently rising hills, and sloping vales, well calculated for cultivation, while its climate was delightfully varied." This would have resulted in the "good of man, animal, fowl, or creeping thing; while from the flowery plain or spicy grove, sweet odors were wafted on every breeze and all the vast creation of animated beings breathed naught but health, and peace, and joy."[62] All of this was to be present again in the millennium when the earth would be "renewed and receive its paradisiacal glory."[63] In addition, there would be no death, disease, or even sorrow.[64]

If such a pastoral paradise seems quaint from a modern vantage point, it has been noted that "since the seventeenth century, at least one silent assumption, and working hypothesis, has been that the earthly paradise is concocted out of the elements, and bound to the fortunes, of a mundane earth and its aspiring inhabitants." As such, "even Milton's recreation of Eden is heavily indebted to his generation's daydreams about the good life, rural retirement, estate planning, and gardening."[65] Musings about the millennial paradise always tend to be idealizations of what one yearns for in the here and now.

Marrying millennium to primordium by way of a literalist hermeneutic also led to the striking belief that eventually the continental landmasses would be unified into a sort of prophetic Pangaea. Referring to the Genesis 1:9 declaration that the waters be gathered "unto one place," Pratt expounded, "From this we learn a marvelous fact, which very few have ever realized or believed in this benighted age; we learn that the waters which are now divided into oceans, seas and lakes, were then all gathered together into one vast ocean; and consequently that the land which is now torn asunder, and divided, into continents and islands, almost innumerable; was then one vast continent or body, not separated as it now is."[66]

Such a view of the primordial earth required an explanation for why the globe was so different in modern times. Pratt ventured,

> how far the flood may have contributed to produce the various changes, as to the division of the earth into broken fragments, islands, and continents, mountains and valleys, we have not been informed; but the change must have been considerable. But after the flood, in the days of Peleg, the earth was divided. See Gen. x. 25—A short history to be sure, of so great an event. But still it will account for the mighty revolution, which rolled the sea from its own place in the north, and brought it to interpose between different portions of the earth, which were parted asunder, and moved into their present form: this, together with the earthquakes, revolutions, and commotions, which have since taken place, have all contributed to reduce the face of the earth to its present state.[67]

What was lost, however, would one day be restored. "From the whole and various scriptures we learn," remarked Pratt, "that the continents and islands, shall be united in one as they were in the morn of creation, and the sea shall retire and assemble in its own place where it was before; and all this mighty scene shall take place during the mighty convulsion of nature, about the time of the coming of the Lord."[68] Despite his exclusive use of the Bible to make the point, his understanding was clearly influenced by an 1831 revelation which declared that when the Lord comes again he would "break down the mountains, and the valleys shall not be found. He shall command the great deep, and it shall be driven back into the north countries, and the islands shall become one land. And the land of Jerusalem and the land of Zion shall be turned back into their own place, and the earth shall be like as it was in the days before it was divided."[69]

A final aspect of the Saints' millennial vision and one in which literalism again played an important role was their paradisiacal ecology. Referring to the relevant and famous passages in Isaiah (11:6–9; 65:25), Rigdon explained that the millennium would also "materially affect the brutal creation. The lion and the ox are to eat straw together; the bear and the cow to graze the plain in company, and their young ones to lay down in peace." There was nothing figurative here. "When that day comes," continued Rigdon, "the Spirit of the Lord . . . will make a great revolution on the irrational creation; changing their nature both as to food and habits." As a result, "the lion will be carnivorous no longer; and all the beasts will cease to prey on flesh and blood." Anything less would nullify the word of God. If carnivores are not herbivorized, "they will both hurt and destroy, and the testimony of the prophet fail; and if no such day comes, there will be no Millenium."[70] Publicist Pratt put it more succinctly when he declared that both "man and beast" will become "perfectly harmless, as they were in the beginning, and feed on vegetable food only."[71]

At the conclusion of the millennium, the generation of the new heaven and new earth would turn terra firma into the eternal abode of the blessed. Thus, wrote Parley Pratt, "man is destined forever to inherit this self-same planet, upon which he was first created, which shall be redeemed, sanctified, renewed, purified, and prepared as an eternal inheritance for immortality and eternal life!"[72] The early Mormon editor and hymnwriter W. W. Phelps envisioned heaven as an extension of millennial bliss:

> When we've been there a thousand years,
> Bright shining as the Sun,
> We've no less days to sing God's praise,
> Than when we first begun.[73]

In light of what has been presented thus far, any careful attempt to locate Mormonism within the standard eschatological taxonomy should, while admitting that it represents a unique species, most certainly place it within the genus premillennialism. By way of summary, it is recalled that a religious movement is said to be millenarian when it views salvation as (a) *collective*, to be enjoyed by the faithful as a group; (b) *terrestrial,* to be realized here on earth; (c) *total,* to completely transform earth life; (d) *imminent,* to come soon and swiftly rather than gradually; and (e) *miraculous,* to be accomplished by, or with the help of, supernatural agencies.[74]

Mormons fit this description quite closely. In the formative years, the Saints expected to realize their salvation as a gathered group of the elect, as part of latter-day Israel. In that period, they did not emphasize that the infinite variations in individual righteousness in this life would result in correspondingly varied placement in a multi-leveled heaven in the next, a matter to be discussed in greater detail in the next chapter. As to the second point, Latter-day Saints clearly delighted in the prospects of literally inheriting the earth. Even eternity was to be enjoyed on earth, since spatially, the "Celestial Kingdom" turned out to be a *terrestrial* kingdom after all. What made all this worth seeking, of course, was the totality of the future transformation of life on earth, the third facet of millenarianism. Far from its present fallenness, the earth would be "renewed and receive its paradisiacal glory," including the herbivorization of carnivores, the commingling of mortals and immortals, and a topography that would have tantalized any pre–transportation revolution traveler. Regarding their sense of imminence, the very name of the church discloses the dominant expectation that the Saints were living in the generation that would witness the Second Coming of Christ and the supernatural inauguration of the millennium. In short, early Mormon beliefs correspond closely to each category in this and other millenarian models. Their eschatology is thoroughly premillennial.

3

Apocalyptic Dualism in Early Mormonism

Joseph Smith and Sidney Rigdon once responded to a series of questions which they said were "daily and hourly asked by all classes of people." To the query "will everybody be damned but Mormons?" they replied, "Yes, and a great portion of them, unless they repent and work righteousness."[1] Judging Mormonism by its more inclusive, twentieth-century posture regarding postmortal salvation, many have felt that Smith's response was rather tongue-in-cheek. Actually, he was very much in earnest and, as will be shown, was simply reflecting a dualistic sentiment widely held among the early Saints.

Benjamin Winchester articulated the common assumption that since Mormonism was the restoration of New Testament Christianity, "all who reject [it] will be damned, if the scriptures are true."[2] Such categorical statements were indeed connected to the scriptures, particularly passages like Mark 16:16: "He that believeth and is baptized shall be saved; but he that believeth not shall be damned."[3] One finds this verse frequently and unequivocally invoked in the early literature.[4] In an article for the *Star,* Sidney Rigdon wrote,

> Unless God had sent the apostles, or others authorized as they were, the world must have perished; every creature in it must have been damned: for they were to go into all the world, and preach the gospel to every creature, and he (that is, every creature) that believed and was baptized, should be saved; but he (that is, every creature) that believed not, should be damned. Had there been one creature in all the world who was in a state of salvation, or could have attained that state without the apostles, this commission would not

have been correct, that is, that every creature in all the world who did not believe them and be baptized by their direction should be damned.[5]

But what of the honest and honorable of other churches? A *Times and Seasons* editorial answered bluntly that it did not matter "how often a man prayed, how much alms he gave, how often he fasted, or how punctual he was in paying his tithes, if he believed not, he would be damned."[6] Such either/or thinking was not mere polemical posturing; it permeated the membership from the Prophet on down. In a Nauvoo address, Joseph Smith referred to "the various professors of religion who do not believe in revelation & the oracles of God" and said, "I tell you in the name of Jesus Christ they will be damned & when you get into the eternal world you will find it to be so they cannot escape the damnation of hell."[7] A week later, he mentioned a particular denomination as an example and declared, "If they reject our voice they shall be damned."[8]

That the Saints did not balk at pointing out the consequences of rejecting the message of the restored gospel is also evident from the frequency with which anti-Mormons and other observers commented on this very point, an emphasis they found suffocatingly exclusive. La Roy Sunderland, a Methodist minister who wrote one of the more widely circulated anti-Mormon pamphlets of the 1830s, decried the "monstrous cruelty of Mormonism" in "pretending to consign all to hell who do not believe it."[9] Parley Pratt responded in *Truth Vindicated:* "Every dispensation that God ever sent, is equally cruel in this respect; for God sends all to hell who reject any thing that he sends to save those that believe. And I add, if Methodism be true, God will send every man to hell who rejects it. And a man must be very inconsistent, to come with a message from God, and then tell the people that they can be saved just as well without, as with it."[10]

Such soteriological dualism led inevitably to sociological dualism. Humanity was differentiated not by race or rank but by its response to the gospel message. "Mine elect," declared the Lord, "hear my voice and harden not their hearts."[11] By divine definition, only those who accepted the restored gospel were considered God's elect. A *Times and Seasons* article explained that "when a man is adopted into the church and kingdom of God, as one of his Saints; his name is then enrolled in the book of the names of the righteous."[12] The same criterion was extended to the definition of "goodness": "And there are none that doeth good except those who are ready to receive the fullness of my gospel, which I have sent forth unto this generation."[13]

Conversely, the Lord defined the "wicked" just as succinctly. They were simply those "that will not hear my voice but harden their hearts."[14] Even the casual observer will note that this is phrased as the exact negation of what constituted election. As if it were not already clear enough, a year later the Saints were taught how to distinguish the two types of people: "Whoso cometh not unto me is under the bondage of sin. . . . And by this you may know the righteous from the wicked."[15] Parley Pratt defined "the wicked" as "that portion of the people who were not of the Kingdom of God."[16] Theologically, then, the Saints used the word "wicked" as a sort of generic term for *all* unbelievers, regardless of their personal ethics.

Such social reductionism may seem strange to twentieth-century pluralists, but it was at the heart of the millenarian worldview. What one scholar has called the "rhetoric of polarization" inheres in all millenarian movements.[17] Not surprisingly, for millenarian Mormons, the lines between good and evil, between saintly and satanic, were clearly drawn and had important consequences for how they pictured the world around them.

Dualism colored their perception of groups as well as individuals. Neighboring churches were identified in various revelations as "the congregations of the wicked."[18] Entire cities were also classified collectively. After their initial failure in London, early missionaries wrote home that though it was "the boast of the Gentiles," London contained "one million five hundred thousand souls who are ripening in iniquity and preparing for the wrath of God; and like the ox going to the slaughter, know not the day of their visitation."[19] On an even broader scale, Mormon apostle and later Church president John Taylor wrote that "Babylon, literally understood, is . . . the Roman Catholics, Protestants, and all that have not had the keys of the kingdom."[20] In short, as the Book of Mormon expressed it, "there are save two churches only; the one is the church of the Lamb of God, and the other is the church of the devil; wherefore, whoso belongeth not to the church of the Lamb of God belongeth to that great church, which is the mother of abominations; and she is the whore of all the earth" (1 Nephi 14:10).[21]

That life was perceived in such black-and-white terms is typical of

millenarians. In looking at early Christianity as a millenarian movement, one scholar found that the otherwise complicated moral judgments often required in life were "resolved into a series of binary op-
positions: poor-rich, good-evil, pious-hypocrite, elect-damned. And a
final reckoning was proclaimed for the near future."[22] Similarly, the
anthropologist Kenelm Burridge's studies led him to conclude that
millenarian movements take the disquieting and "unmanageable
manyness" of society and re-order it into "sharply contrasted contrar-
ies."[23] Herein lay one of Mormonism's greatest strengths. In words
first used by E. R. Dodds to describe early Christianity, it can be seen
that Mormonism's

> very exclusiveness, its refusal to concede any value to alternative
> forms of worship, which nowadays is often felt to be a weakness, was
> in the circumstances of the time a source of strength. The religious
> tolerance which was the normal [American] practice had resulted
> by accumulation in a bewildering mass of alternatives. There were
> too many cults, too many mysteries, too many philosophies of life
> to choose from: you could pile one religious insurance on another,
> yet not feel safe. [Mormonism] made a clean sweep. It lifted the
> burden of freedom from the shoulders of the individual: one
> choice, one irrevocable choice, and the road to salvation was clear.[24]

Not only was the gospel path clear; so were the consequences of
rejection. As Parley Pratt explained, "The people of England may repent, and never be destroyed; but if they do not repent, they will perish, in common with all nations who are unprepared for the second
advent of the Messiah: For lo! the time is near—very near, when every
one who does not give heed to Jesus Christ 'will be destroyed from
among the people.' This applies equally to England, and all other
places."[25] Boston, Albany, and Cincinnati were singled out by name for
"desolation and utter abolishment" if they rejected the gospel.[26] Even
close friends were not exempt. Edward Partridge once penned this
earnest entreaty to all his former acquaintances: "O take the advice of
one that wishes you well. . . . humble yourselves before God and embrace the everlasting gospel before the judgments of God sweep you
from the face of the earth."[27]

Dualist mentalities also conditioned the Saints to expect opposition
and in so doing created a sort of siege mentality. When history is seen
as one continual struggle of the forces of God against Satan, "it is nat-

ural for the adherents of the Kingdom to perceive a coherent, sinister intelligence animating the various problems they encounter."[28] Years ago, David B. Davis documented the fear of conspiracy characteristic of antebellum America which manifested itself, in part, as a paranoia that Mormonism was un-American. What seems equally apparent is that Mormon millenarianism disposed the Saints to a similarly conspiratorial view which, clothed in scriptural imagery, leagued the whole sectarian world with Lucifer.[29]

When Gentile neighbors learned that the Saints had fitted them into a larger-than-life battle either as emissaries of Satan or, at least, as the unwitting dupes he manipulated to block the progress of the Kingdom, it is little wonder that their dander was raised. It probably bothered Missourians to read in the *Star* that all those who did not obey the restored gospel would be consumed at Christ's coming and that only Mormons would be worthy to inhabit Jackson County during the millennium. On one occasion, Edward Partridge interpreted Malachi 4 to mean that the Saints would "literally tread upon the ashes of the wicked after they are destroyed from off the face of the earth."[30] Such declarations, though rooted in scripture, would have had little public-relations value. Dualist distinctions coupled with vivid apocalyptic imagery did not augur well for peaceful interaction between Mormons and Gentiles. For the period under study, Mormon millenarianism must be identified as a major source of the animosity felt towards the Saints.

Yet if their millenarianism promoted social stereotyping, their experience in life seemed to validate it. During much of the first sixteen years of Mormon history, the Saints experienced severe persecution and crisis conditions. While apocalyptic attitudes might have been partially responsible for provoking persecution, it is also clear that persecution reinforced their millenarianism by verifying the dualistic analysis of society central to apocalypticism. The Saints knew that as the Second Coming drew nigh, Satan would be waging a war of ever-increasing intensity against them. Therefore, persecution became an assurance, albeit a painful one, that all was proceeding on prophetic schedule.[31] Though physically destructive, such opposition, precisely because it fit into an eschatological drama with a predetermined victory for the Saints, was less than successful in daunting them. Their apocalyptic ideals provided strength in a world turned upside down and allowed them to rationalize otherwise irrational behavior.

As persecution increased, there was a corresponding increase in millenarian rhetoric. Oscillations in the intensity of Mormon millenarianism can often be traced to the treatment they received from their neighbors. This can be seen clearly in the Saints' expulsion from Missouri.[32] Here they were confronted forcibly with the stark inadequacy of their efforts to thwart the onslaughts of the Gentile enemy. As a result, they felt and expressed a heightened dependence upon God, realizing that nothing short of his supernatural intervention could defeat Satan's minions and usher in the long-desired millennial day of rest. A hymn composed by Parley Pratt shortly after the Saints' world had been shattered in Far West, Missouri, is typical:

> How long, O Lord, wilt thou forsake
> The Saints who tremble at Thy word?
> Awake, O Arm, O God! Awake
> And teach the nations Thou art God.
> Descend with all Thy holy throng,
> The year of Thy redeemed bring near,
> Haste, haste the day of vengeance on,
> Bid Zion's children dry their tear.[33]

As the Saints fled Missouri, Joseph Smith and other leaders were taken captive and languished in jail for nearly six months in a Missouri town ironically named Liberty. Their situation was squalid and they were reported to have been fed human flesh. From this crucible of adversity, Joseph Smith himself pleaded that the Lord would avenge the Saints of their wrongs, expressing at the same time abiding faith that "the time soon shall come when the Son of Man shall descend in the clouds of heaven" and shall "have our oppressors in derision" and "will laugh at their calamity, and mock them when their fear cometh."[34]

Especially after subsequent petitions for redress, first in Missouri and ultimately at the White House, fell on deaf ears, it seemed to the Prophet that a cataclysmic conclusion to history was inevitable. "My heart faints within me," he wrote, "when I see, by the visions of the Almighty, the end of this nation, if she continues to disregard the cries and petitions of her virtuous citizens, as she has done, and is now doing."[35] When just such disregard seemed to continue, Smith warned John C. Calhoun in a January 1844 letter that "if the Latter Day Saints are not restored to all their rights, and paid for all their losses, according to the known rules of justice and judgment, reciprocation and common honesty among men, that God will come out of his hiding place and vex this nation with a sore vexation—yea, the consuming wrath of an offended God shall smoke through the nation with as much distress and woe, as independence has blazed through with pleasure and delight."[36]

Similar sentiments were also expressed after Smith's martyrdom in 1844, and again shortly thereafter on the eve of the Saints' exodus to the West. John Taylor spoke for many when he declared, "We owe the United States nothing. We go out by force, as exiles from freedom. The government and people owe us millions for the destruction of life and property in Missouri and in Illinois. The blood of our best men stains the land, and the ashes of our property will preserve it till God comes out of his hiding place, and gives this nation a hotter place than he did Sodom and Gomorrah. 'When they cease to spoil, they shall be spoiled,' for the Lord hath spoken it."[37] The connection between injustices suffered and apocalyptic yearnings is pointed. Earlier a *Times and Seasons* editorial had endeavored to comfort the Saints with this thought: "He that said to the flood 'come' and make an end of wickedness, will say also 'go' to the elements, and sweep the earth with the besom of destruction till it is fit for Paradise again, and then my people shall inherit the kingdom."[38]

Such rhetoric is typical of embattled millenarians. When a people feel the weight of the oppressor's heel, it is understandable that, of all the facets of the eschatological drama, the one they focus on most is the destruction of the wicked. As one scholar explains, the judgments to be poured out "were part of an immutable guarantee that no matter how much the wicked seemed to triumph in the present age, God would supernaturally set the scales of Justice aright at the Day of Judgment."[39] When considering the "great and dreadful day of the Lord" (Malachi 4:5), the Saints' focus was on the attendant destruction of the unbelievers, at least as much as on the salvation of the Saints.

Perhaps the best contemporary analogue for the Saints' apocalypticism was that of antebellum blacks. For them, as well as for the Mormons, the coming of Christ would be a day of deliverance at once liberating and vindicating.[40] The historian Albert Raboteau has shown that the "cornerstone" of black religion was the "idea of a revolution in the conditions of the whites and blacks."[41] Scriptural promises of the ultimate destruction of the wicked at Christ's coming provided a satisfying conclusion to history for the Saints as well. As one early Mormon expressed it, after describing the Saints' hardships and deprivations during the last days at Nauvoo, "we shall have a name and a being on the earth when our enemies are extinct or else the word of the Lord fails" and "we will some day become the head and not the tail."[42] Here was the apocalyptic dream of the "great reversal." Such was the simple yet profound hope of a great many early Mormons.[43]

Eschatological dualism also shaped the Saints' philosophy of missions. The connection is pervasive throughout the early revelations. One example reads,

> Verily, verily, I say unto you, the people of the Ohio call upon me in much faith, thinking I will stay my hand in judgment upon the nations, but I cannot deny my word. Wherefore, lay to with your might and call faithful laborers into my vineyard, that it many be pruned for the last time. And inasmuch as they do repent and receive the fullness of my gospel, and become sanctified, I will stay mine hand in judgment. Wherefore, go forth, crying with a loud voice, saying, The kingdom of heaven is at hand. . . . go forth baptizing with water, preparing the way before my face for the time of my coming.[44]

Since judgment was imminent, the missionaries were not to mince words. "This is not the time to sing lullabies to a slumbering world," advised the *Times and Seasons*.[45] The elders were to "lift a warning voice unto the inhabitants of the earth," and openly "declare . . . that destruction shall come upon the wicked."[46] Or as another revelation expressed it, they were to set forth "clearly and understandingly the desolation of abomination in the last days."[47] Not surprisingly, therefore, Orson Hyde titled his trend-setting tract *Prophetic Warning*. In it he urged, "Pray, therefore, that God may send unto you some servant of his, who is authorized from on high, to administer to you the ordinances of the gospel. Except you do this, you . . . must fall victims to the messengers of destruction, which God will soon send upon the earth."[48]

In what would become a veritable cottage industry among traveling Mormon preachers, Parley Pratt produced the most durable example of this genre with the publication of his *Voice of Warning*. In the first edition, he wrote, "Wo, wo, wo unto the inhabitants of this city; and again wo, wo, wo unto the inhabitants in all this land; for your sins have reached unto Heaven, and God has remembered your iniquities;

and only this once will he call upon you to repent. . . . Behold the sword of vengeance hangs over you and except you repent, the Lord will cause that it shall soon overtake you."[49] Freeman Nickerson's proclamation to the Bostonians nicely sums up both the intent and the content of these declarations: "I request the citizens and authorities of the city of Boston to open a house for the servant of the people, that the Lord hath sent to this city to warn the people of the destruction which will take place in this generation, that is now on the earth, and teach them how they may escape, and come through and abide the day of the second coming of Christ to reign on the earth a thousand years."[50]

In the providential plan, deliverance was always to be proclaimed as a counterpoint to destruction. "When the God of heaven sent a messenger to proclaim judgment on the old world," explained Sidney Rigdon, "he provided an ark for the safety of the righteous: When Sodom was burned, there was a Zoar provided for Lot and his family . . . and in the last days, when the Lord brings judgment on the world, there will be a Mount Zion, and a Jerusalem, where there will be deliverance."[51] Thus, the actual, physical gathering of the elect to revealed places of refuge was the divinely appointed means of escape from coming calamity.[52] After the location for Zion was revealed, Joseph Smith urged all to "embrace the everlasting covenant, and flee to Zion before the overflowing scourge overtake you."[53] Even after the expulsion from Missouri, the doctrine of gathering continued unabated, though the focus was on other settlements of the Saints known as "stakes" of Zion. "This gathering," wrote the First Presidency in an 1841 editorial, "must take place before the Lord comes to 'take vengeance upon the ungodly.'"[54]

If sand in the hourglass was running out, the Saints were nonetheless assured that the "great and dreadful day of the Lord" would not dawn until the elect "shall all have come from one end of heaven to the other, and not one is left in all nations . . . under heaven, and then and not until then will Christ come."[55] Before the Lord rained down his wrath upon the world, all believers would be gathered to the prophetic panoply—Zion and "her stakes."[56] Thus, the Mormons' philosophy of, and motivation for, missions was integrally related to their millenarianism. Because the day of the Lord, as a day of judgment, was at hand, the elders were to traverse the earth to warn the wicked and gather the elect, preaching "nothing but repentance," for truly it was "a day of warning, and not a day of many words."[57]

Though the phrase "voice of warning" carried very literal connotations for early Mormons, it was also balanced by counsel to avoid overzealousness in declaring judgments against the wicked. Mormons in Missouri were told bluntly to "talk not of judgments." And W. W. Phelps advised the elders to "Warn in compassion without threatening the wicked with judgments which are to be poured out upon the world hereafter. You have no right . . . to collect the calamities of six thousand years, and paint them upon the curtain of these last days to scare mankind to repentance; no, you are to preach the gospel . . . even glad tidings of great joy unto all people."[58] Nor was the proclamation to be made without pathos. During the Kirtland temple dedicatory prayer, it was remarked, "O Lord, we delight not in the destruction of our fellow men; their souls are precious before thee; but thy word must be fulfilled."[59] That such a declaration was more than mere rhetoric is obvious from such private disclosures as Orson Hyde's 16 September 1832 diary entry about a visit to his own sister: "Called on sister Laura and her husband Mr. North. They disbelieved. We took our things and left them, and tears from all eyes freely ran, and we shook the dust of our feet against them, but it was like piercing my heart; and all I can say is 'The will of the Lord be done.'"[60]

While all of this may seem foreign to modern sensibilities, it must be remembered that for a people weaned on the Bible and steeped in its literal interpretation, there were simply too many graphic passages predicting woe upon unbelievers to have the notion spiritualized or explained away.[61] Time and again, for instance, one encounters references in early Mormon literature to Acts 3:22–23, which warns that all who will not hearken to Christ will be "cut off from among the people" or to Paul's portrayal of a Savior descending in flaming fire to take vengeance "on them that know not God, and obey not the gospel" (2 Thessalonians 1:8).[62] No Bible verse, however, more effectively bolstered an apocalyptic scenario for the last days than Luke 17:26: "And as it was in the days of Noe, so shall it be also in the days of the Son of man." This scripture told the Saints two things. First, the majority of mankind in their day would reject the message; and second, such people would therefore be destroyed. "Just *precisely* as it was then," wrote the editors of the *Times and Seasons*, "'so shall it be at the coming of the Son of Man.' Revelations shall precede his coming, the whole world shall ridicule them and cast them off, for so it was in the days of Noah, and the consequences were inevitable destruction; and so it will be with this generation, the righteous only, will be saved."[63]

That this would leave few people to enjoy the millennium merely accorded with their understanding of Isaiah's prophecy that "the inhabitants of the earth are burned, and few men left" (Isaiah 24:6). "This destruction," explained Parley Pratt in his *Voice of Warning*, "is to come by fire as literally as the flood in the days of Noah; and it will consume both priests and people from the earth . . . or else we must get a new edition of the Bible, leaving out the 24th of Isaiah."[64] For literalist Latter-day Saints, it was no more difficult to conceive of the earth being swept clean of every single non-Mormon at the Second Coming than it was to accept the fact that the Flood had destroyed all but the eight believers then in existence. Parley Pratt explained to Queen Victoria that "as Noah was a survivor of a world destroyed, and himself and family the sole proprietors of the earth, so will the Saints of the Most High possess the earth, and its whole dominion, and tread upon the ashes of the wicked."[65]

Given its millenarian character, Mormonism consistently moved ahead the traditional saved/damned reckoning of the final judgment, which in their view followed the millennium, to a saved/destroyed outcome apparent at Christ's advent, which preceded it. "In the day of the coming of the Son of Man," explained an early revelation, "cometh an entire separation of the righteous and the wicked; and in that day will I send mine angels to pluck out the wicked and cast them into unquenchable fire."[66] Moreover, as has been shown, there was no middle ground. Only Mormons would survive the second coming of Christ. As Sidney Rigdon put it, all people on the earth during this period would be Saints: "all the rest of the world will without exception be cut off."[67]

That apocalyptic dualism pervaded early Mormon sociology and soteriology is clear. But what about the famous "Vision of the Three Degrees of Glory?"[68] Did it not immediately uproot all the old either/or notions? Was not the early Saints' worldview drastically altered by this vision of a pluralized rather than a polarized afterlife, as has been the outlook of their modern counterparts? The "Vision," as it was commonly called in the early years, portrays a multileveled heaven in which the inevitable variations in earthly behavior are rewarded accordingly. "It appeared self-evident from what truths were left [in the Bible]," wrote Joseph Smith, "that if God rewarded every one according to the deeds done in the body the term 'Heaven,' as intended for the Saints' eternal home must include more kingdoms than one."[69]

The Vision specifies three—the Celestial Kingdom, the Terrestrial Kingdom, and the Telestial Kingdom.[70]

Naturally, the highest degree of glory or salvation—the Celestial Kingdom—is reserved only for those who accept the gospel, receive a legitimate baptism, and endure in faithful obedience to the end of their mortal lives. The next level, the Terrestrial Kingdom, is filled with decent but doctrinally deceived people—the "honorable men of the earth, who were blinded by the craftiness of men." Even blatantly bad people traditionally set aside for everlasting torment, such as liars, adulterers, and whoremongers, will enter the third degree, or Telestial Kingdom, after spending at least a millennium in hell expiating their own sins. Only militantly anti-Mormon apostates will be "doomed to suffer the wrath of God with the devil and his angels in eternity."[71]

Consistent with their apocalyptic dualism and prior perceptions of salvation, however, for years Mormons spoke almost entirely in terms of either being saved in the "Celestial Kingdom" or else being damned, rather than discussing intermediate degrees of salvation. A specific search of published and unpublished sources reveals that throughout the 1830s and on into the early 1840s, the Vision was generally ignored.[72] Though in extant reports of sermons and in the early periodicals the "plan of salvation" and the afterlife were frequent topics of discussion, they almost never included the Vision, even when addressed to a Mormon audience.[73] While there were numerous references to the "Celestial Kingdom," it was understood in the usual way as a synonym for heaven. Discussion, even mention, of the "Terrestrial" or "Telestial" kingdoms, which might have hastened the demise of dualistic thinking, appears to have been almost nonexistent.[74]

The only example of anything like a substantive commentary on the Vision was Joseph Smith's 1843 poetic version, and this may have represented a watershed in Mormon thought on such matters.[75] Perhaps the experience of reissuing the revelation as a kind of epic poem stimulated the Prophet's pondering of the overall significance of the Vision, for in the remaining sixteen months of his life he discussed in new ways the nature of hell and the torment of the damned. Furthermore, he specifically ridiculed the pervasive Protestant rhetoric that in the hereafter there were only two possible destinies—heaven or hell.

Part of the explanation for the absence of an immediate revolution in Mormon soteriology based on the 1832 Vision is the force of tradition. After surveying the religious landscape in America in 1844, the eminent German churchman Philip Schaff remarked that "the reigning theology of the country . . . is the theology of the Westminster Confession."[76] The Westminster Confession, a creedal delineation of faith formulated two hundred years earlier by Reformed divines from England and Scotland, declared that upon death the souls of the "righteous" were received into heaven while the "wicked" were cast into hell. "Besides these two places for souls separated from their bodies," concluded the Confession, "the Scripture acknowledgeth none."[77] For centuries, the polarities of heaven and hell, election and reprobation, had informed the contours of Protestant thought, and this formed an important part of the cultural baggage early converts carried with them into the LDS church. Significantly, such sharply contrasting categories were not explicitly contradicted either in the Book of Mormon or in the new revelations.[78]

One early revelation described the Last Judgment in these familiar terms: "And the righteous shall be gathered on my right hand unto eternal life; and the wicked on my left hand, . . . I will say unto them—Depart from me, ye cursed, into everlasting fire, prepared for the devil and his angels."[79] On another occasion the Lord spoke of the gathering "that the wheat may be secured in the garners to possess eternal life, and be crowned with celestial glory . . . while the tares shall be bound in bundles . . . that they may be burned with unquenchable fire."[80] To portray Judgment Day outcomes as either "Celestial glory" or "unquenchable fire," "eternal life" or "everlasting fire," without mentioning the intermediate glories, appears incomplete from the perspective of later LDS theology.[81] Yet with the exception of the Vision, the early revelations appear to accommodate such traditional polarizations.

Until perspectives on the afterlife expanded in the 1840s, if the Vision was discussed at all, it was done from within an interpretive framework that was still patently polarized. "Men are agents unto themselves," declared W. W. Phelps, "and they can prepare for a kingdom of glory, or, for one without glory"—as much as if to say, though clothed in new terminology, men can prepare for heaven or for hell.[82] Even part of the final quatrain in Smith's poetic version, which in other places offered new insights, summed up the entire revelation in dualistic terms: "The secret of life is blooming in heaven, and blasting in hell."[83]

Telling evidence that the Vision did not immediately force an abandonment of traditional notions of damnation and hell is manifest in the Mormon reaction to the contemporary religious movement known as Universalism. Universalism reflected the optimism of the Age of Enlightenment from which it emerged and, as its name implies, taught that all men would ultimately be redeemed, that damnation would be done away, and that the notion of eternal torment in a lake of sulfurous fire was superstition.[84] Modern Mormons may find much that is appealing in such ideas, believing, as they do, that the vast majority of mankind will ultimately receive some degree of salvation. Early Saints, however, did not react this way. When a Universalist preacher came to Kirtland in 1835, Oliver Cowdery wrote an editorial against his teachings.[85] Among other arguments, Cowdery asked how Universalists could claim there was no postmortal punishment when damnation was specifically provided for in Scripture. "If no such principle exists as damnation, and that eternal," Oliver exclaimed, "[God] certainly has spoken nonsense and folly."[86]

That the Vision was not mentioned in the earliest anti-Mormon works is further evidence of its limited impact initially. Given the tenor of their writings, it is hardly conceivable that such men as Philastus Hurlbut, Origen Bacheler, or La Roy Sunderland would not have eagerly seized the chance to ridicule the Vision had they been aware of it or perceived its eschatological implications.[87] Yet the earliest mention of the doctrine is in the ex-Mormon John Corrill's *Brief History*, published in 1839. Though Corrill had been a leading elder almost from the first, his brief comments evidence little more than simple awareness of the revelation.[88] Furthermore, later anti-Mormon commentators like Henry Caswall or J. B. Turner seem only to be borrowing from Corrill.[89] The question that follows, then, is why did all these early anti-Mormons overlook that which would later become stock-in-trade for such polemicists if the Vision was widely known and its significance generally perceived?

Also significant is the case of the former Mormon William Harris. In his exposé, he claimed that the Saints felt that their idea of heaven "shows the superiority of their system over all others" and that they "ridicule as absurd the notion generally entertained of the location and nature of heaven." Harris promised that as "a matter of curiosity," he would "insert a description of the Mormon Paradise."[90] What followed was not a recapitulation of the Vision, as might be expected from his lead-in, but rather an excerpt from Parley P. Pratt's *Voice of*

Warning showing that heaven would be material, not spiritual, and here on earth, not out in the ethereal blue.[91] This recollection from Harris's seven years in the Church as to what the Saints actually ridiculed about contemporary notions of heaven further confirms the minimal role of the Vision in general LDS thought.[92]

In time, however, this would change. Just four months after the Prophet versified the Vision, he began publicly and repeatedly to denounce the heaven-hell dichotomy. "Says one I believe in one hell & one heaven all are equally miserable or equally happy, but St. Paul informs us of three glories & three heavens."[93] Later, Joseph reiterated that he did not believe the common doctrine of "sending honest men, and noble minded men to hell, along with the murderer and adulterer."[94] In a famous funeral address preached in 1844 at the death of King Follett can be found the culmination of Joseph Smith's thinking about salvation and damnation. In his comments during the preceding months, hell had been acquiring an explicitly nonphysical dimension, and he here announced, "I have no fear of hell fire, that doesn't exist, but the torment and disappointment of the mind of man is as exquisite as a lake burning with fire and brimstone."[95]

Unbelievers would still be damned, but he remarked, "I do not say how long."[96] Though the concept of a terminable hell was provided for in a revelation received even before the Church was organized, not until Joseph led the way interpretively did the Mormon view of hell as a kind of preresurrection purgatory for unrepentant sinners develop.[97] At the same time, he continued to affirm that those who had committed the unpardonable sin "must dwell in hell, worlds without end" and that "they shall rise to that resurrection which is as the lake of fire and brimstone."[98] Only these "sons of perdition" would be damned in the fullest and most traditional sense.[99]

Toward the close of his life, then, Joseph Smith began to emphasize a pluralized rather than a polarized picture of eternity. He interpreted hell symbolically, diminished damnation's domain, and extended the limits of salvation. If in so doing he opened the door for a future break with traditional Protestant views, the old saved/damned dichotomy did not die out immediately. Paradigm shifts take time.[100] As has been shown, the sociological dualism inherent in the Saints' millenarianism prevented significant deviation from the soteriological dualism basic to their Protestant heritage. Though Smith's late Nauvoo teachings did signal the beginning of a slow transformation of Mormon conceptions of the afterlife, the controlling cosmological model for the Saints during the life of the Prophet was still profoundly shaped by millenarian apocalypticism.

4

The Bible, the Mormons, and Millenarianism

More so than today, the early Latter-day Saints were a Bible-oriented people. The messages of Micah and Zephaniah were as familiar to them as the Book of Mormon words of King Benjamin and Alma are to modern Mormons. Their heroes were Abraham, Moses, and Joshua rather than Alma and Captain Moroni. And phrases like "to your tents, O Israel!" (1 Kings 12:16) fell more freely from their lips than "wickedness never was happiness" (Alma 41:10). In part, this was due to cultural context. It has long been recognized that antebellum America was a society saturated with biblicism. The imagery and vocabulary of the King James Version were constantly echoed in the speeches and writings of the era. Expanding what one scholar has said, the Bible was "so omnipresent in the American culture of 1800 or 1820 that historians have as much difficulty taking cognizance of it as of the air the people breathed."[1]

Thus, in certain obvious ways, Mormons were products of their age.[2] On the other hand, the Saints out-Bibled the biblicists. This was so not only because of their marked literalism in scriptural interpretation (there were other literalists as well), but also because in an era that paradoxically was witnessing the decline of the theological influence of the Old Testament and the ascendancy of the New Testament, the Saints' millenarianism caused them to continue to find the Hebrew scriptures central to their self-image. The prophetic books of the Old Testament brimmed with meaning for their understanding of the new dispensation. In their eyes, *they* were the fulfillment of much of what they read about in Isaiah, Jeremiah, and Ezekiel. Moreover, the

historical books provided a veritable treasure trove of types and figures applicable to their day. They could not have agreed more with
the personalization evident in what Thomas Prince said to elected
leaders of Massachusetts a hundred years earlier on the centennial of
the arrival of the *Arabella:* "there never was any People on Earth, so
parallel in their general History to that of the ancient ISRAELITES as this
of NEW ENGLAND. . . . one would be ready to think the greater Part of the
OLD TESTAMENT were written about *us.*"[3]

The Mormons too believed that they would act out Biblical narratives in their own lives. Indeed, students of Mormon history miss or
misconstrue much of the felt significance of the Saints' experiences if
they disregard this pervasive feature of their mental universe. No-
where is this better illustrated than in the writings of the prophet Joseph Smith.[4] It is almost as if the Bible were a script and the Saints
were the actors destined to reenact it on a nineteenth-century stage.[5]
The terms *type* and *typology* are generally associated with the tendency
to view the Old Testament as a book of anticipatory pictures of the
person and work of Christ. While this is a legitimate definition, it is
not the broadest one, and actually the Latter-day Saints almost never
used the Old Testament in this fashion. Anytime an earlier event is
seen to anticipate or foreshadow a later one, or anytime later experience seems to be a recapitulation or fulfillment of an earlier event,
typology or figuralism is at work. Biblical action is felt to take place in
two realms—in antiquity as literal event, but also in the present with
different characters and settings. Significantly, such typological thinking fit hand in glove with Mormon millenarianism.[6]

Immediately after learning of mob actions against the Saints in
Jackson County, Missouri, Joseph Smith wrote to them in words that
make clear his typological or figural thinking. Said he, "all pharohs
host or in other words all hell and the combined powers of Earth are
Marshaling their forces to overthrow us and we like the children of
Israel with the Red Sea before them and the Egyptians ready to fall
upon them to distroy them and no arm could deliver but the arm of
God and this is the case with us."[7] Shortly after his incarceration in
Liberty jail several years later, Smith tried to comfort the scattered
Saints with these words: "those who bear false witness against us do
seem to have a great triumph over us for the present. But we want you
to remember Haman and Mordecai you know that Haman could not
be satisfied so long as he saw Mordecai at the king's gate, and he

sought the life of Mordecai and the people of jews. But the Lord so ordered that Haman was hanged upon his own gallows. So shall it come to pass with poor Haman in the last days. . . . I say unto you that those who have thus vilely treated us like Haman shall be hanged upon their own gallows, or in other words shall fall."[8]

Pursuing a figural understanding of the Old Testament allowed Joseph Smith to make sense out of the opposition he was experiencing from within the household of faith as well. Examples of ancient Israel's backsliding demonstrated that dissension within the modern church was not a sign of its imminent collapse, but rather of its divine sponsorship. When he received a particularly "cutting reproof" from certain brethren in Missouri, Smith recited the story of how the Israelites worshiped the golden calf while Moses was on the mount and asked his supporters, "Therefore, I say, if we should suffer perils among false brethren, should it be accounted a strange thing?"[9] This same Old Testament episode seemed to be relived in 1837 when Smith and other brethren were away tending to business in Michigan. David Whitmer, who had been one of Joseph's earliest and most faithful followers, gradually soured on the prophet's leadership, taking a small group with him. While Smith was out of town, this group of dissenters attempted a coup. The Sunday after his return, Smith occupied the stand and, in the words of notetaker and future church president Wilford Woodruff, "for several hours addressed the Saints in the power of God. Joseph had been absent from Kirtland on business for the church, though not half as long as Moses was in the mount, & many were stir'd up in their hearts & some were against him as the Israelites were against Moses." Fortunately, according to Woodruff, when Smith "arose in the power of God in their midst, as Moses did anciently, they were put to silence for the complainers saw that he stood in the power of a Prophet."[10]

Other episodes of apostasy during Israel's forty years in the wilderness were also typologically linked to contemporary disaffection. In the aftermath of the "extermination order" issued by Governor Boggs to expel the Mormons from Missouri, Smith wrote that the dissenters who aided and abetted the mobbers "like Balaam being greedy for a reward sold us into the hands of those who loved them, for the world loves his own."[11] Singling out W. W. Phelps in a piece of typological satire, he continued, "This poor man who professes to be much of a prophet has no other dumb ass to ride but David Whitmer to forbid his madness when he goes up to curse Israel, and this ass not being of the same kind of Balaams therefore the angel notwithstanding appeared unto him yet he could not penetrate his understanding sufficiently so but what he brays out cursings instead of blessings. Poor ass whoever lives to see it will see him and his rider perish. . . ."[12] But Phelps and Whitmer were not alone. Referring to all the apostates, Joseph remarked, "we classify them in the error of Balaam and in the gainsaying of Core and with the company of Cora and Dathan and Abiram."[13]

Later, when Phelps repented and wished to return to the fold, the Prophet freely forgave him with the line "come on, dear brother, since the war is past, for friends at first, are friends again at last." However, he also tried to convey to him the seriousness of what he had done by making figural application of a pair of verses from Obadiah. Recalling the overwhelming disappointment he felt when Phelps, with whom he "had oft taken sweet council together and enjoyed many refreshing seasons from the Lord," turned against him in the last days of Missouri, Joseph quoted verses 11 and 12: "In that day that thou stoodest on the other side, in the day when Strangers carried away captive his forces, and foreigners entered into his gates and cast lots upon Far West [originally it read "Jerusalem"] even thou wast one of them. But thou shouldst not have looked on the day of thy brother, in the day that he became a stranger neither shouldst thou have spoken proudly in the day of distress."[14]

Types were more than nice figures of speech or clever metaphors, however. They were compelling models for behavior. When John E. Page abandoned Orson Hyde on their mission to the Middle East and the case was brought before the Church, Joseph Smith explained that the problem was that they did not follow Biblical precedent. "He said that no two men when they agreed to go together ought to separate, that the prophets of old would not and quoted the circumstance of Elijah and Elisha [2] Kings 2 chap. when about to go to Gilgal, also when about to go to Jericho, and the Jordan, that Elisha could not get clear of Elijah, that he clung to his garment until he was taken to heaven and that Elder Page should have stuck by Elder Hyde."[15]

Perhaps even more revealing is a single sentence from the Prophet's letter to Gideon Carter: "You quoted a passage in Jeremiah with regard to journeying to Zion; the word of the Lord stands sure, so let it be done."[16] What is noteworthy is the matter-of-fact way in which

Smith took the passage as if it were an actual script delineating exactly how the divine drama was to be played out centuries after Jeremiah spoke. In the figural tradition, the historical meaning and situation of scripture are clearly subordinated to its present significations.[17] Such an approach coincides with the millenarian emphasis on the present as the apex of time, the great and last day anticipated since antiquity. Just as typology permitted Jesus' followers to read the Hebrew Bible from a Christocentric perspective, so a "Restoration-centric" interpretation of the Bible rooted in figuralism made it meaningful for Mormonism. In both ages, the church was the "New Israel," the fulfillment of a typological reading of the scripture.[18]

While the apostle Paul could be highly figural, almost allegorical, in his interpretation of the Hebrew Bible, he could also bring to bear a rigorous literalism. The same held true for the prophet Joseph Smith. A clear example of this was his use of Amos 3:7 to refute speculation about the date of the Second Coming. After one Millerite enthusiast claimed to have seen the "sign of the Son of Man" predicted in Matthew 24, Joseph replied, "he has not seen the sign of the Son of Man, as foretold by Jesus; neither has any man . . . for the Lord hath not shown me any such sign; and as the prophet saith, so it must be—'Surely the Lord God will do nothing but He revealeth His secret unto His servants the prophets.' Therefore, hear this, O earth: The Lord will not come to reign over the righteous, in this world, in 1843, nor until everything for the Bridegroom is ready."[19] Smith found nothing in this literal interpretation of Amos 3:7 which conflicted with the Savior's words about his Second Coming: "of that day and hour knoweth no man" (Matthew 24:36). For, he asked, "Did Christ speak this as a general principle throughout all generations Oh no he spoke in the present tense no man that was then living upon the footstool of God knew the day or the hour But he did not say that there was no man throughout all generations that should not know the day or the hour. No, for this would be in flat contradiction with other scripture for the prophet says the God will do nothing but what he will reveal unto his Servants the prophets consequently if it is not made known to the Prophets it will not come to pass."[20]

Such literalism often fostered doctrinal innovations such as the idea of a premortal existence for all mankind. Smith interpreted "the Lord's question to Job 'where wast thou when I laid the foundation of the Earth'" [Job 38:4] as "evidence that Job was in Existence somewhere at that time."[21] Few examples, though, would have more far reaching effect than the Prophet's reading of Isaiah 2:3 which announces that "out of Zion shall go forth the law, and the word of the Lord from Jerusalem." Smith interpreted "Zion" and "Jerusalem" as two different places, rather than viewing the passage as a manifestation of Hebrew poetic parallelism which would make the terms synonymous. This meant that nearly every mention of "Zion" in Old Testament prophecy was understood as having reference to the New (read "other") Jerusalem to be built in America. This was reinforced for Orson Hyde when he actually visited Mount Zion in Jerusalem. Referring to it and to Calvary, Hyde wrote, "We should not call them mountains in America, or hardly hills; but gentle elevations or rises of land. The area of what was called Mount Zion, I should not think contained more than one acre of ground." This gave him pause, for, continued Hyde, "as I stood upon it and contemplated what the prophets had said of Zion in the last days, and what should be done in her, I could no more bring my mind to believe that the magnet of truth in them which guided their words, pointed to this place, any more than I could believe that a camel can go through the eye of a needle. . . . But on the land of Joseph, far in the west, where the spread eagle of America floats in the breeze and shadows across the land . . . shall Zion rear her stately temples and stretch forth the curtains of her habitation."[22] Thus, the Saints believed that Zion and Jerusalem were two distinct holy cities located in two distinct hemispheres.

For the uniqueness of such a view to be fully appreciated, it must be set against a history of Christian interpretation of prophecy pertaining to Israel's latter-day glory.[23] For a thousand years prior to the Reformation, the Augustinian formulation prevailed, wherein the Christian church was seen allegorically as spiritual Israel and the fulfiller of all Old Testament prophecies. This interpretation obviated the need for any special work among historic Israel. During the Reformation, however, efforts to restore a literal hermeneutic to prophetic interpretation surfaced and occasionally gained center stage. Particularly among some of Calvin's followers, prophecies and statements dealing with Israel and Zion came to be understood at face value.

Thus, the apostle Paul's promise that one day "all Israel shall be saved" (Romans 11:25–26) was taken literally as referring to scattered Jews and the Lost Tribes.[24] Combined with a renewed interest in the prophecies and prophetic numbers of Daniel and Revelation, such approaches led unprecedented numbers of people to expect a national conversion of the Jewish people before the Second Coming.[25] At first, many held to this spiritual "calling" of the Jews but not to a physical return to Israel. The latter smacked too much of the old "carnal millennium" anathematized by early Church fathers.[26] However, voices began to be heard in its favor. One of the earliest was Serjeant Henry Finch, a London lawyer, who found himself in jail for several weeks because he described the future political supremacy of the restored Jewish kingdom a little too enthusiastically for the King's tastes.[27] By the time Increase Mather delivered his famous sermon "The Mystery of Israel's Salvation," the idea of a temporal restoration was commonplace.[28] Later in the eighteenth century, however, and especially in the nineteenth when Christian Zionism mixed with politics, spiritual restoration was no longer considered a prerequisite to territorial restoration.[29]

Of course, not all Christians were persuaded by such views. Fundamentally, it was a matter of hermeneutics. If one thought that the prophecies ought to be interpreted allegorically or figuratively, then no Jewish conversion to Christ was expected, and the church, as "modern" Israel, was felt to fulfill completely God's prophetic promises to Israel. On the other hand, literalists anticipated a wholesale conversion of the Jews and an actual return to their ancestral homeland.[30] Elements of both schools of thought can be found in the early literature of the Latter-day Saints.[31]

Mormons had no problem applying certain prophecies to themselves as spiritual Israel while at the same time vigorously affirming the spiritual and physical restoration of the Jews. As to whether the Jews would gather to the land of Israel as believers in Christ, there were differing opinions. From his earliest days as a missionary, Orson Pratt, for instance, preached that the Jews would return in unbelief to the land of Israel.[32] Wilford Woodruff, on the other hand, wrote on one occasion, "if the Jews ever go to Jerrusalem they will not go as Jews but all Christians as Christ body &c &c."[33]

Generally speaking, though, the Saints' biblicism tilted them toward the former view. A millenarian reading of Zechariah 12–14 in conjunction with Revelation 11 suggested that in the last days the Jews who were gathered to their homeland would be besieged by gentile hordes and ultimately, at the crucial moment in the battle of Armageddon, would be delivered by a Messiah whom they would not recognize until he showed them the wounds in his hands and feet.[34] Any uncertainty as to the identity of this deliverer was swept away in the words of this revelation: "then shall the Jews look upon me and say:

What are these wounds in thine hands and thy feet? Then shall they know that I am the Lord; for I will say unto them: These wounds are the wounds with which I was wounded in the house of my friends. I am he who was lifted up. I am Jesus that was crucified. I am the Son of God. And then shall they weep because of their iniquities; then shall they lament because they persecuted their king."[35]

This meant, of course, that the Mormons saw nothing of value in contemporary efforts to missionize the Jews. Sidney Rigdon was plain in his assessment: "we have no scruple in saying, that Israel will never embrace the gospel, nor the Jews believe in the Messiah as a people, till the Lord *sends* his word to them."[36] Phelps approvingly published comments from a Philadelphia religious periodical entitled *The Reformer* which argued that "the Lord, and not man, will have the glory of bringing about this event, and all the efforts and undertakings of men to accomplish it will prove unavailing, as heretofore has been the case down to the present time." He added that "Neither the house of Joseph in America, nor the Jews among all nations, nor the Ten Tribes which went to that country 'where never mankind dwelt,' can be converted by ministers, though the Gentiles are: for God has said to his Son, in the Psalms, Thy people (Israel) shall be willing in the day of thy power; (that is, when he comes in the clouds of heaven, and all the tribes mourn, they will be ready and willing to receive the Messiah)."[37]

Still, the Saints saw some value in gentile interest in the Jews. As Orson Hyde wrote, "I will here hazard the opinion, that by political power and influence [the Jews] will be gathered and built up; and further, that England is destined in the wisdom and economy of heaven to stretch forth the arm of political power, and advance in the front ranks of this glorious enterprise."[38] His hope was that one day "Israel's banner, sanctified by a Savior's blood, shall float on the walls of old Jerusalem, and the mountains and valleys of Judea reverberate with their songs of praise and thanksgiving to the Lamb that was slain."[39] As impressive as the Jewish territorial restoration would be, and as interested in it as the Saints were, it would always play second fiddle to the Jews' spiritual restoration. This was eloquently summarized in an editorial in the *Times and Seasons:*

But it is not their mere gathering together, that awakens such interest in the bosom of the saint of God, but the glorious events which necessarily grow out of the same. We not only contemplate the ancient covenant people of the Lord, restored to happiness, and in the enjoyment of power, wealth, and immense influence, but the much more sublime and glorious spectacle of the glories of Heaven's King resting down upon them in darkness, for ever rent assunder, the spirit of grace and supplication poured out upon them, the Savior appearing in their midst, shewing his hands, his feet, and side, while twice ten thousand tongues, in one commingling strain and glorious exaltation sing, BLESSED IS HE THAT COMETH IN THE NAME OF THE LORD, HOSANNA, HOSANNA IN THE HIGHEST, AMEN, AND AMEN.[40]

The Saints also believed that Israel's restoration involved more than just the Jews, that the Indians, too, were a "remnant of Jacob." It had long been suspected by others that the Native Americans were as much Israelite as any Jew, but that the whole prophetic scenario of Israel's temporal and spiritual restoration was to be dually enacted—once by the Jews in the Old World and again by the native inhabitants of America—added a new dimension to the drama. As has been shown, throughout this period, the Saints still followed newspaper accounts of Zionist stirrings among the Jews, but they had a local, Indian Israel, as pedigreed as the Jews, to be watched and gathered to a local and new Jerusalem, as real as the ancient Jerusalem. To the common literalist scenario of Jews gathering in the future to Jerusalem and rebuilding David's city, the Saints added the picture of Indians gathering to western Missouri to build Zion, the New Jerusalem.

Nor was the Mormon view merely another variation of the old "lost tribes" theory. For the Latter-day Saints, Indian origins were accounted for in the Book of Mormon history of several migrations from the Kingdom of Judah to the Western Hemisphere around 600 B.C. The ten tribes, lost a century earlier from the Northern Kingdom, were considered a separate group and were usually thought to be sequestered somewhere in the frozen "north countries." They were not to be confused with the "Jewish" Indians.[41]

Like allegorist Christians, the Mormons also viewed the church, consisting overwhelmingly of Anglo-Americans, as "spiritual Israel," but they applied the ancient prophecies to themselves in the same literal way as they did to historic Israel. The need to gather physically, therefore, was just as incumbent upon them as upon the Indians or the Jews. The centrality of this emphasis was illustrated in chapter 2. In essence, then, Mormonism added one more literal gathering spot and several more literal gathering groups to what even literalist Protestants around them had been led to expect.

A good example of how these themes blended together can be found in the Apostolic "Proclamation" of 1845. God's latter-day work involved three groups. It consisted of "restoring, organizing, instructing and establishing the Jews"; of "gathering, instructing, relieving, civilizing, educating, and administering salvation to the remnant of Israel on this continent"; and of "gathering the Gentiles into the same covenant and organization" with Israel. Furthermore, the Lord's work would involve "building Jerusalem in Palestine, and . . . Zion in America." The end result was that "the whole Church of the Saints, both Gentile, Jew and Israel [here meaning Indians], may be prepared as a bride for the coming of the Lord." As for the ten tribes, they will "be revealed in the north country, together with their oracles and records, preparatory to their return, and to their union with Judah."[42] Thus, in the last days, Gentile and Indian Saints would be planted in their American inheritance, Zion, while the Jews and eventually the "lost tribes" of Israel were to be relocated in the renovated land of Canaan with Jerusalem reconstructed as their capital.[43]

So central was the restoration of Israel to the meaning of the Mormon mission that it even influenced what they valued most about their new scriptures. Early Saints stressed that one of the prime purposes for the coming forth of the Book of Mormon and other revelations was to identify Israel and to locate the place of gathering. "If God should give no more revelations," asked Joseph Smith, "where will we find Zion and this remnant?" He added, "take away the Book of Mormon and the revelations, and where is our religion? We have none; for without Zion, and a place of deliverance, we must fall."[44] Note that the sense was not "take away the restoration scriptures, and we shall have none of our distinctive doctrines," but "take away our revelations and we shall not be able to identify Israel in America, nor locate Zion, the city of refuge." The eschatological setting is explicit here and brings into sharp focus the fundamentally millenarian nature of the doctrine of the restoration of Israel.

As its very name implies, the Church of Jesus Christ of Latter-day Saints expected its members to participate in Israel's restoration during their own lifetime. Along with others who held out hope for Israel, this was partially based on their exegesis of Romans 11:25–26. Here Paul associates Israel's future salvation with "the fullness of the Gentiles" being "come in." For centuries, believers in the Jewish restoration had understood this phrase as referring to a great outpouring of the Spirit before the millennium that would result in numerous Gentile conversions and a final flourishing of Christendom before the Lord's return. There was some debate over whether the mass conversion of the Jews or of the Gentiles would take place first, but both were felt to be prerequisites to the Second Coming. The Mormons, of course, anticipated no revival of authentic religion within existing Christian institutions, but they did hope to gather out from among them the full measure of elect Gentiles, their usual understanding of the phrase.

For some, such as Sidney Rigdon, the apocalyptic perception of a world beyond repair overpowered much optimism about Gentile converts and led to an interpretation of the "fullness" of the Gentiles as the *apostasy* of the Gentiles. "When *will* the fulness of the Gentiles be come in?" asked Rigdon, "The answer is again at hand.—That is, when they all shall have ceased to bring forth the fruits of the kingdom of heaven, of all parties, sects, and denominations and not one of them standing in the situation in which God had placed them. . . . then is the time that the world may prepare themselves to see the God of heaven set his hand the second time to recover the remnant of his people."[45] From this perspective, the apostasy was more than just evidence that truth and authority had been lost. It was evidence that the end times were upon them, that the Lord had begun his latter-day work. The prophetic chronology seemed clear—the Gentiles apostatize, the Israelites are gathered, and the millennium is ushered in.

In 1833, Joseph Smith composed his first description of the LDS faith for public consumption in a letter to the *American Revivalist and Rochester Observer.* Referring to Isaiah 11:11, Smith announced that "the time has at last arrived when the God of Abraham of Isaac and of Jacob has set his hand again the second time to recover the remnants of his people which have been left from Assyria, and from Egypt and from Pathros &c. and from the Islands of the Sea and with them to bring in the fulness of the Gentiles and establish that covenant with them which was promised when their sins should be taken away."[46] With the gathering and restoration of Israel under way, there were only two choices for Yankee Gentiles—join the Church, thereby being "adopted" into or "numbered with" Israel, and gather to Zion, or face certain and imminent destruction. As the Prophet expressed it, "Repent ye Repent ye, and imbrace the everlasting Covenant and flee to Zion before the overflowing scourge [alluding to Isaiah 28:15, 18] overtake you."[47] "The City of Zion spoken of by David in Psalms 102," declared Smith, "will be built upon the Land of America" and, in words from Isaiah 35:10, "the ransomed of the Lord shall return and come to it with songs and everlasting joy upon their heads and then they will be delivered from the overflowing scourge that shall pass through the Land."[48] The sobering reality was that "the people of the Lord, those who have complied with the requisitions of the new covenant, have already commenced gathering together to Zion which is in the State of Missouri" and "there are those now living upon the earth whose eyes shall not close in death until they see all these things which I have spoken fulfilled."[49]

A virtual love affair with the restoration of Israel as well as the primitivism it reflected also may have predisposed the Prophet to consider the restoration of such ancient Israelite practices as plural marriage and ritual sacrifice.[50] Though the former has been much discussed elsewhere, it is worth noting here that the revelation commanding polygamy was influenced by restorationist ideals: "Verily, thus saith the Lord unto you my servant Joseph, that inasmuch as you have inquired of my hand to know and understand wherein I, the Lord, justified my servants Abraham, Isaac, and Jacob, as also Moses, David, and Solomon, my servants, as touching the principle and doctrine of their having many wives and concubines. Behold, and lo, I am the Lord thy God, and will answer thee as touching this matter. Therefore, prepare thy heart to receive and obey the instructions which I am about to give unto you . . . an appointment [to] restore all things."[51]

Smith's contemplated restoration of ritual sacrifice was also influenced by a primitivist perspective. Two passages from the New Testament which he cited provide the framework for his comments. Acts 3:19 speaks of the "restitution of all things spoken by the mouth of the holy prophets," and Ephesians 1:10 notes that "in the dispensation of the fulness of time" God would "gather together in one all things in Christ." Since the Saints saw themselves as living in that "dispensation," they expected a full restoration of ancient principles and practices. In particular, Joseph emphasized the uniformity across time of priesthood rights and powers and concluded that "all things had under the Authority of the Priesthood at any former period shall be had again."[52] Malachi 3:3–4 specifically promises a future day in which righteous offerings would be presented by a purified Levitical priesthood. "These sacrifices," explained Joseph Smith, "as well as every ordinance belonging to the priesthood will when the temple of the Lord shall be built and the Sons of Levi be purified, be fully restored and attended to. . . . Else how can the restitution of all things spoken of by all the Holy Prophets be brought to pass."[53]

Understanding exactly what the Prophet had in mind has proved challenging to subsequent Saints. One of the very few church leaders to address the subject during the remainder of the nineteenth century was President John Taylor. In *The Mediation and Atonement,* Taylor quoted Joseph Smith's remarks, but cautioned, "what this offering will be does not distinctly appear." He further added, "the details of those rituals and observances cannot now be fully defined."[54] In the twentieth century, afer the previously serialized "History of Joseph Smith" (which included this sermon) was conveniently published as the *History of the Church,* a few more comments have appeared, but neither elaboration nor consensus is in evidence.

Those who understand the latter-day sacrifices and offerings as the ritual slaughter of animals downplay the practice. Sidney B. Sperry remembers correspondence with the First Presidency in "1921 or 1922" to the effect that "in their opinion sacrifice would be on a more limited scale than formerly."[55] During the same period, Joseph Fielding Smith wrote that "blood sacrifices will be performed long enough to complete the fulness of the restoration in this dispensation. Afterwards sacrifice will be of some other character."[56] And the prolific apostle-theologian Bruce R. McConkie has written that to "complete the restoration of all things, apparently on a one-time basis, sacrifices will again be offered in this dispensation."[57]

Others have not felt that animal sacrifice would be restored at all and instead have offered a figurative reading of the Prophet's comments. Apostle John A. Widtsoe wrote, "It does not seem probable that this offering will be a burnt offering. The coming of Christ ended the Mosaic law." Quoting D&C 124:39, which mentions "memorials for your sacrifices by the sons of Levi" in the context of temple worship, Widtsoe explained, "no provision has been made in the temples for the ancient type of burnt offerings, and the word memorials would seem to exclude such an interpretation."[58] In the semi-official *Priesthood and Church Government* published in 1939, Joseph Smith's remark that "the offering of sacrifice . . . also shall be continued at the last time" elicited this terse footnote: "the coming of Jesus did away with the sacrifices of blood. The offerings to be made by the sons of Aaron in the last days will be of a spiritual nature."[59] However latter-day sacrifice is viewed, all expressions seem cognizant of the words of the

Savior in 3 Nephi: "ye shall offer up to me no more the shedding of blood; yea your sacrifices and your burnt offerings shall be done away . . . and ye shall offer for a sacrifice unto me a broken heart and a contrite spirit" (3 Nephi 9:19–20).

At the same time that Joseph Smith was bringing back polygamy and envisioning a restoration of Old Testament sacrifice, he also restored what he described as the ancient Israelite Temple ceremony.[60] Though some have linked it to Masonic ritual, more satisfying parallels can be drawn with antiquity.[61] What is important here is the fact that the ceremony reinforced in LDS minds the reality of their identity as modern Israel. So did the restoration of the "Aaronic" and "Melchizedek" priesthoods or the reception of one's "patriarchal blessing." The latter was a ritual recreation of Jacob's blessings to his sons wherein Saints were entitled to have one officially designated as "patriarch" lay hands upon their heads, announce their lineage in one of the twelve tribes of Israel (usually Ephraim), and pronounce upon them appropriate words of blessing.

Cursing, as well as blessing, is a common Biblical phenomenon, and the Saints' strong self-identification as part of Israel, as well as their millenarianism, also made them responsive to a recovery of these ancient practices. Early leader Newel K. Whitney was instructed by the Prophet that "when his enemies seek him unto his hurt and distruction let him rise up and curse and the hand of God shall be upon his enemies in Judgment they shall be utterly confounded and brought to dessolation."[62] Joseph Smith himself had been told in the very beginning that "whosoever shall lay their hands upon you by violence, ye shall command to be smitten in my name; and, behold, I will smite them according to your words, in mine own due time."[63] And Jesus' counsel to the ancient apostles was remembered in several revelations which directed the leading elders that "in whatsoever place ye shall enter, and they receive you not in my name, ye shall leave a cursing instead of a blessing, by casting off the dust of your feet against them as a testimony, and cleansing your feet by the wayside."[64]

Particularly during periods of intense persecution the power to curse was invoked as a millenarian mechanism for dealing with what seemed to be beyond the Saints' control. In the aftermath of the expulsion from Zion, at a Pentecostal outpouring in the Kirtland Temple, cursing mingled freely with blessing. Joseph Smith recorded, "the brethren began to prophesy upon each others heads and cursings upon the enimies of Christ who inhabit Jackson county Missouri."[65] Following the Prophet's martyrdom in 1844, "Elder John Taylor bore testimony against those that murdered Joseph and Hyrum Smith; he said they should be cursed and the congregation said, Amen."[66] Moreover, on the eve of the exodus west, as Brigham Young and the Twelve Apostles received word of plans to thwart, if not "obliterate," the Mormons, they "prayed that the Lord would defeat and frustrate all the plans of our enemies, and inasmuch as they lay plans to exterminate this people and destroy the priesthood from off the earth, that the curse of God may come upon them, and all the evil which they design to bring upon us, may befall themselves; and that the Lord would preserve the lives of his servants and lead us out of this ungodly nation in peace."[67]

The related theme of vengeance is both prevalent in the Hebrew Bible and prominent in millenarianism and, therefore, was alive among the Latter-day Saints as well. Yet, as with cursing, it was to be invoked only after patient forbearance and would always be nullified by genuine repentance on the part of the Saints' enemies. "As oft as thine enemy repenteth of the trespass wherewith he has trespassed against thee," directed one early revelation, "thou shalt forgive him, until seventy times seven."[68] And Joseph Smith had this declaration placed in the Church's *Messenger and Advocate:* "Brethren, bear and forbear one with another, for so the Lord does with us. Pray for your enemies in the Church and curse not your foes without: for vengeance is mine, saith the Lord, and I will repay."[69] Ultimately, though, there were circumstances in which defensive action was felt to be legitimate. As tensions mounted in Missouri, a revelation informed the Saints that they were obliged to endure multiple aggressions from their enemies "patiently" and without "reviling against them." However, if after three failed attempts by the Saints to "lift a standard of peace" and prevent conflict, an enemy persisted in coming against them and "if he has sought thy life and thy life is endangered by him, thine enemy is in thine hands and thou are justified" in "going out to battle against" him and "I, the Lord, will avenge thee of thine enemy an hundred-fold."[70] A Book of Mormon prophet reminded his people that "inasmuch as ye are not guilty of the first offense, neither the second, ye shall not suffer yourselves to be slain by the hands of your enemies. And again, the Lord has said that: ye shall defend your families even unto bloodshed."[71]

Such conditions eventually seem to have been met in the Mormon's interactions with the Missourians. An 1834 revelation directed that "inasmuch as mine enemies come against you to drive you from my goodly land, which I have consecrated to be the land of Zion, even from your own lands . . . ye shall curse them; and whomsoever ye curse, I will curse, and ye shall avenge me of mine enemies. And my presence shall be with you even in avenging me of mine enemies, unto the third and fourth generation of them that hate me."[72] At a meeting of leading brethren in the Kirtland Temple, Smith remarked, "I want to enter into the following covenant, that if any more of our brethren are slain or driven from their lands in Missouri by the mob that we will give ourselves no rest until we are avenged of our enemies to the uttermost, this covenant was sealed unanimously by a hosanna and Amen."[73]

Toward the end of a life filled with persecution, and after relentless pursuit by Missouri authorities seeking to convict him of the assassination attempt on Governor Boggs, Smith made it clear that "the time has come when forbearance is no longer a virtue."[74] Just four hours after being acquitted from the third extradition attempt by Missouri officers, Joseph declared, "Before I will bear this unhallowed persecution any longer I will spill my Blood their is a time when bearing it longer is a sin I will not bear it longer I will spil the last drop of Blood I have and all that will not bear it longer say AH And, the Cry of AH rung throughout the Congregation."[75] Though he explicitly counseled the Saints to "be not the aggressor" and to "bear until they strike" both cheeks, he announced that "I this day turn the Key that opens the heavens to restrain you no longer from this time forth."[76] In one memorable statement from the same speech, he exclaimed, "if mobs come upon you any more here, dung your gardings with them."[77] Later that year, he declared, "when the Mobs come upon you, kill them; I never will restrain you again but will go and help you."[78]

All of this, of course, had ample precedent in the Old Testament, precedent that did not go unnoticed by the Prophet. "If oppression comes," he declared, "I will then shew them that there is a Moses and a Joshua amongst us."[79] And yet, consistent with the assumptions of apocalypticism, he also realized that most of the battles would be fought by the Lord and that ultimate victory and recompense would come only with the Savior's advent. Modern revelation picked up on Jesus' parable of the "importunate widow" from Luke 18:1–8 with its concluding query "shall not God avenge his own elect, which cry day and night unto him, though he bear long with them? I tell you that he will avenge them speedily." An 1833 revelation applied this parable to the beleaguered Mormons in Missouri in the following manner:

> Now, unto what shall I liken the children of Zion? I will liken them unto the parable of the woman and the unjust judge. . . . Let them importune at the feet of the judge; and if he heed them not, let them importune at the feet of the governor; and if the governor heed them not, let them importune at the feet of the president; and if the president heed them not, then will the Lord arise and come forth out of his hiding place, and in his fury vex the nation; and in his hot displeasure, and in his fierce anger, in his time, will cut off those wicked, unfaithful, and unjust stewards, and appoint them their portion among hypocrites, and unbelievers; even in outer darkness, where there is weeping, and wailing, and gnashing of teeth.[80]

The Mormons took comfort in the fact that after they had done all they could to rectify the situation, the Lord himself would avenge them of the injustices they had suffered. This, too, Smith frequently called to the Saints' attention through Biblical prophecies. "We rejoice," wrote Joseph, "that the time is at hand when the wicked who will not repent will [invoking a phrase from Isaiah 14:23] be swept from the earth with the besom of destruction."[81] After the expulsion from Jackson County, he wrote to Edward Partridge and leading brethren of Missouri that "we have nothing to fear if we are faithful: God will [in the words of Psalms 110:5] strike through kings in the day of his wrath . . . and what do you suppose he could do with a few mobbers in Jackson County, where, ere long, he will set his feet when earth & heaven shall tremble."[82] From Liberty Jail, Joseph and his prison mates explained why "our harts do not shrink neither are our spirits altogether broken at the grievous yoak which is put upon us." "We know," they declared, "that God will have our oppressors in derision [Psalms 2:4] that he will laugh at their calamity and mock when their fear cometh [Proverbs 1:26]."[83]

In summary, Mormon use of the Bible was at once figural, literal, and allusive. Through it all, the degree to which the prophecies of the last days occupied the Saints' attention is noteworthy, and those passages most congenial with a premillennial eschatology were among the ones most cherished by them. It is also clear that biblicist respect for the social categories of antiquity, such as "Gentile," or the scriptural devices of boundary maintenance, such as cursing, reinforced the dualism of a millenarian mindset. Above all, the Mormon example bears out the observation made earlier that literal interpretation of scripture usually leads to premillennialism. Premillennialism expected extraordinary, even supernatural events to happen in the present and the future. For Mormon millenarians, the God of the latter days was no less powerful or less likely to intervene than he had been in "primitive" times. The Bible stood as an ever present reminder of that fact.

5

The Book of Mormon and
the Millenarian Mind

Some of what has been said about the Saints' use of the Bible merely reflects contemporary patterns of millenarian interpretation; there was little intrinsically "Mormon" about it. The question arises, therefore, if well-worn paths of interpretation had not already existed, would the Saints have seen the same things in the same way? Such a tradition-free approach to the Bible, of course, was impossible, but with the Book of Mormon, a wholly different situation existed. Here there was *no* history of interpretation, no published commentaries, no standard exegesis—only the text itself and the predilections and presuppositions the Saints brought to its interpretation. Thus, the Book of Mormon provides an independent variable against which to test the conclusions of previous chapters, specifically the degree to which its use reflected and reinforced a millenarian worldview.

Before proceeding, a word about methodology is in order. For over a century and a half, students of Mormonism, be they scholars or scribblers, defenders or detractors, have shared a simple assumption: the Book of Mormon can be used as evidence of early Mormon belief. While this is true in many respects, it fails to account properly for that crucial mediating link between the written text and the actual life and teaching of the Church—interpretation. Just as the way in which the Declaration of Independence was understood in the eighteenth century is distinct from how modern Americans have used it,[1] so it cannot merely be assumed that what a modern reader understands by a given passage in the Book of Mormon is what a Latter-day Saint in the 1830s would have understood by the same passage. Nor can it be assumed that what seems significant today is necessarily what Mormons would have found noteworthy in the formative years. To recognize the reality of such interpretive differences, one has only to look at the contrasting uses made of the same Book of Mormon by the RLDS and the LDS church. Thus, the nearly universal procedure of using the unmediated text of the Book of Mormon to articulate early LDS views provides only a plausible reconstruction at best.

Perhaps it is a lingering nineteenth-century belief in the perspicuity of Scripture that leads modern students to assume an identity of understanding between themselves and their subjects.[2] Perhaps they operate on implicit faith that the early Saints literally lived by *every* word that proceeded from the mouth of God. Or perhaps they simply have been unaware of the numerous primary source interpretations from that period which do exist, ranging from passing comment to lengthy exegesis. Whatever the motivation of modern observers, the need exists to ground characterizations of early Mormon thought to sources that actually disclose, rather than merely assume, an early perspective. A search of early Church literature yields several hundred such citations. Table 1 identifies the Book of Mormon chapters and verses most frequently cited by the Saints, and table 2 the topics most commonly developed from those scriptures.[3]

What stands out in bold relief in these tables is the thematic preeminence of that same cluster of concepts—the restoration of Israel—which so engaged the Saints in their use of the Bible. The Book of Mormon was primarily responsible for the insight which allowed the Saints to move beyond a discussion of Israel's identity and destiny that involved the Jews only. As Joseph Smith explained in his letter to the *American Revivalist,* through the Book of Mormon "we learn that our western Tribes of Indians are descendants from that Joseph that was sold into Egypt, and that the land of America is a promised land unto them."[4] Regarding the Gentile converts such as himself who were numbered with this native Israel, W. W. Phelps declared, "The vail which had been cast over the prophecies of the Old Testament was removed by the plainness of the book of Mormon." At last, "that embarrassment under which thousands had labored for years to learn how the Saints would know where to gather was obviated by the book of Mormon."[5] And it was Ether 13:4–8, more than any other passage, which was responsible for these clarifications:

Behold, Ether saw the days of Christ, and he spake concerning a New Jerusalem upon this land. And he spake also concerning the

Table 1.
Most Common Citations from Early Literature

	Number of Times
Chapters	
3 Ne. 21	16
3 Ne. 16	13
3 Ne. 3	10
2 Ne. 29	10
2 Ne. 30	10
2 Ne. 28	9
3 Ne. 20	9
Eth. 13	8
1 Ne. 22	8
Specific Passages	
Eth. 13:4-8	8
3 Ne. 21:1-7	7
2 Ne. 30:3-6	7
2 Ne. 3:4-21	6
2 Ne. 29:3	5
3 Ne. 8:5 - 9:12	5
1 Ne. 22:6-12	4
3 Ne. 15:11 - 16:4	4
Eth. 2:7-12	4
Morm. 8:29-30	4

house of Israel, and the Jerusalem from whence Lehi should come—after it should be destroyed it should be built up again, a holy city unto the Lord; wherefore, it could not be a new Jerusalem for it had been in a time of old; but it should be built up again, and become a holy city of the Lord; and it should be built unto the house of Israel. And that a New Jerusalem should be built upon this land, unto the remnant of the seed of Joseph. . . . Wherefore, the remnant of the house of Joseph should be built upon this land; and it shall be a land of their inheritance; and they shall build up a holy city unto the Lord, like unto the Jerusalem of old.

Table 2.
Principal Themes Based on Classification
of Book of Mormon Passages Cited

Restoration of Israel	
Joseph's descendants (Indians)	16
Jews	6
New Jerusalem	6
Ten Tribes	3
All groups	28
	59
Prophecy Relating to Gentiles	
State of Christendom in 1830	16
America: repent or suffer	15
Fate of all gentiles	6
	37
Archaeological evidences for Book of Mormon	32
Atonement	23
Joseph Smith	14
First Principles of Gospel	13
Concern for Holiness	11
Revelation and Spiritual Gifts	7

Note: Each passage is classified only once.

In the heyday of "manifest destiny," it was not popular to assert, as did the Mormons, that America actually belonged to the Indians and that it would be their millennial inheritance. Yet they took such scriptural declarations at face value. While the Saints frequently pointed out, using portions of 3 Nephi 16, 20, and 21, that all Gentiles who repented would be "numbered among this the remnant of Jacob," such an adopted status, even if it did entitle them to all related blessings, seemed to reverse contemporary caste distinctions. Even more likely to raise hackles was the sharply drawn alternative. Speaking of unrepentant Gentiles, Parley Pratt assured the Indians that "the very places of their dwellings will become desolate except such of them as are gathered and numbered with you; and you will exist in peace, upon the face of this land, from generation to generation. And your children will only know, that the Gentiles once conquered this country, and became a great nation here, as they read it in history; as a thing long since passed away, and the remembrance of it almost gone from the earth."[6]

To say the least, such rhetoric seemed unduly solicitous of the lowly Indian, but the drama only intensified when the "ways and means of this utter destruction" were discussed. On three different occasions during his postmortal ministry in the New World, the Savior applied words from the Old Testament prophet Micah to an American setting. If the Gentiles rejected the new covenant offered to them in the latter days through the Book of Mormon, then "my people who are a remnant of Jacob [Indians] shall be among the Gentiles yea, in the midst of them as a lion among the beast of the forest, as a young lion among the flocks of sheep, who, if he go through both treadeth down and teareth in pieces, and none can deliver. Their hand shall be lifted up upon their adversaries, and all their enemies shall be cut off" (3 Nephi 21:12–13).[7]

Nothing here was figurative to the early Saints. Book of Mormon prophecies, wrote Pratt, "are plain, simple, definite, literal, positive and very express."[8] As for Jesus' words, Pratt explained, "This destruction includes an utter overthrow, and desolation of all our Cities, Forts, and Strong holds—an entire annihilation of our race, except such as embrace the Covenant and are numbered with Israel."[9] Another who believed the passage "very express" was Charles G. Thompson, presiding elder of the Genessee (New York) Conference of the Church. In his "Proclamation and Warning," he intoned,

> wo, wo, wo unto you, O ye Gentiles who inhabit this land, except you speedily repent and obey the message of eternal truth which God has sent for the salvation of his people. . . . Yea, except ye repent and subscribe with your hands unto the Lord, and sir-name yourselves Israel, and call yourselves after the name of Jacob, you must be swept off, for behold your sins have reached unto heaven. . . . The cries of the red men, whom you and your fathers have dispossessed and driven from their lands which God gave unto them and their fathers for an everlasting inheritance, have ascended into the ears of the Lord of Sabaoth.[10]

Even without the "paranoid style" prevalent in antebellum America, it is understandable that such pro-Indian rhetoric caused some outsiders to think there was a treasonous conspiracy against the United States in the offing.[11] Indian agent Henry King's report to the Iowa governor epitomizes the fears common throughout the early years. "It seems evident," he wrote, "from all that I can learn from the leading men among the *Mormons* and from various other sources that a grand conspiracy is about to be entered into between the *Mormons and Indians* to destroy all white settlements on the frontier."[12] Yet the Saints categorically rejected the Mohammedan metaphor. In an editorial published in their British periodical the *Millennial Star* it was explained,

> We wish it distinctly understood that the interpretation given to the Mormon predictions as to the Latter-Day Saints drawing the sword against others who may differ from them in religious belief is without shadow of truth, being contrary to the whole spirit of the Christian religion, which they (the Saints) profess; and however the Lord may see fit to make use of the Indians to execute his vengeance upon the ungodly, before they (the Indians) are converted by the record of their fore-fathers, yet it is certain that if they once become Latter-day Saints they will never more use weapons of war except in defence of their lives, and liberties. The Latter-day Saints never did draw the sword except in defence of their lives and the institutions and laws of their country, and they never will.[13]

That few whites in antebellum America had a more expansive, almost romantic, vision of what lay ahead for the Native American is also made clear from the Saints' exegesis of the popular passage 2 Nephi 30:3–6. Nephi here prophesies that the Book of Mormon would someday come through the Gentiles to the "remnant" of his "seed" and would be the means of restoring them "unto the knowledge of their fathers, and also to the knowledge of Jesus Christ." As a result, his posterity would "rejoice" and the "scales of darkness shall begin to fall from their eyes." In time, they would become "a white and a delightsome people."[14] As might be expected, literalist Latter-day Saints appear to have anticipated an actual blanching of the skin. "The Indians are the people of the Lord," wrote W. W. Phelps in a widely reproduced series of letters to Oliver Cowdery, "and the hour is nigh when they will come flocking into the kingdom of God, like doves to their windows; yea, as the Book of Mormon foretells—they will soon become a white and delightsome people."[15]

Portions of 3 Nephi were read to mean that the Indians would also exercise a prominent role in building and settling the New Jerusalem. Converted white Gentiles "shall come in unto the covenant and be numbered among this the remnant of Jacob [Indians], unto whom I have given this land for their inheritance; and they shall assist my people, the remnant of Jacob . . . that they may build a city, which shall be called the New Jerusalem. And they shall assist my people that they may be gathered in, who are scattered upon all the face of the land, in unto the New Jerusalem" (3 Nephi 21:22–24). The concurrent U.S. government policy of relocating the Indians just west of the revealed Missouri site for Zion, therefore, struck the Saints as too coincidental not to be providential. For those who could read the handwriting on the wall, it was clear that Jehovah was using Andrew Jackson just as he had earlier used Cyrus the Great to facilitate the gathering of his people.

Numerous comments to this effect can be found in the early Church periodicals. "Last week," wrote the editor in the December 1832 *Star*, "about 400, out of 700 of the Shawnees from Ohio, passed this place for their inheritance a few miles west, and the scene was at once calculated to refer the mind to the prophecies concerning the gathering of Israel in the last days."[16] Aware that not all Indians may have been the happy recipients of such assistance, the editor elsewhere commented, "Notwithstanding the Indians may doubt, or even fear the policy of the government of the United States, in gathering and planting them in one place, &c—they may be assured that the object is good, and they will soon be convinced that it is the best thing that has come to pass among them for many generations."[17] Even after the Saints had been driven from Jackson County, Missouri, they still regarded Indian relocation favorably. As late as 1837, in his *Voice of Warning*, Parley Pratt urged the Indians to tolerate the Removal Act "as a kind of reward for the injuries you have received" from the Gentiles.[18]

By the mid-1840s, however, the Mormons were disappointed with the actual results of Indian removal, and the partnership between God and government no longer seemed so apparent. "As to what the missionaries do for the Indians, they have their reward," wrote John Taylor, editor of the *Times and Seasons*, "*they are hirelings*—All they have done, and all they will do, will be as a drop in the bucket." Lest readers get the wrong impression, Taylor continued,

> That we may not be accused of a want of charity, we will state, no doubt, the government officers do what they consider humane and

praiseworthy in removing the Indians; and the christian clergy suppose they are rendering God a little service in preaching to and teaching the rude sons of forest; but from the results . . . it appears he has never given authority to any to act for him without direct revelation, it will be sufficient for our purpose, to say when the deliverer comes out of Zion, he will turn away ungodliness from Jacob.[19]

This was the crux of the issue for Latter-day Saints. "It will be seen," explained Taylor, "that God, and not man, has the power to bring Jacob to his glory again," and then he quoted 2 Nephi 30:3–6.[20]

While the restoration of New World Israel always took precedence in the minds of early Mormons, the traditional millenarian anticipation of the gathering of Old World Israel was also evident in their use of the Book of Mormon. LDS interest was shared by most Protestant denominations and was particularly strong in England. There, by the nineteenth century, religious impulses mingled with political desires to shore up a waning Ottoman empire and generated considerable enthusiasm for the creation of a Jewish state in Palestine.[21] When Mormon apostles arrived in England in 1840, they found themselves in the midst of widespread discussion on the topic. Famed Christian Zionists such as Lord Shaftesbury, as well as the Jewish Sir Moses Montefiore, were prominent in the effort to bring about the restoration of the Jews. The astute Mormon observer of the "signs of the times," Parley Pratt, kept up with the excitement and included occasional reports of it in the *Millennial Star*.[22] In the same way, several years later while editing *The Prophet* in New York City, he reprinted with recommendation "choice" extracts from Mordecai Noah's famed "Discourse on the Restoration of the Jews."[23] The year before Pratt's arrival, Henry Innes, the British Secretary of the Admiralty and a devout millenarian, sent a "Memorandum to the Protestant Sovereigns" on "behalf of many who wait for the redemption of Israel." This document, imploring the European leaders to act as "nursing fathers" and help the Jews return to Palestine, was published in all the prestigious papers of Britain. Pratt called attention to it in the *Millennial Star*, as well as to reports of Jews who allegedly had converted, or who were about to convert, to Christianity, and then remarked, "thus is fulfilling a prediction of Nephi: 'And the Jews shall begin to believe in Christ, and they shall begin to gather in upon the face of the land' (2 Nephi 30:7)."[24]

More so than in the Bible, there were passages in the Book of Mormon, such as the one quoted by Pratt, that could be read to support the necessity of Jewish conversion prior to their prophesied return to the promised land. For example, Nephi predicts that God would scourge the Jews "by other nations for the space of many generations, yea, even down from generation to generation until they shall be persuaded to believe in Christ." Only when "they shall believe in Christ, and worship the Father in his name, with pure hearts and clean hands, and look not forward any more for another Messiah" would the Lord "set his hand again the second time to restore his people from their lost and fallen state" (2 Nephi 25:16–17). During the early years of Mormonism, these passages and the ideas they contain were rarely discussed, but in time they would wield a greater influence on LDS thought. In 1881, Wilford Woodruff attended a meeting of church leaders where "the subject was brought up by Br [George Q.] Cannon [member of the First Presidency] concerning the gathering of the Jews whether they would gather in unbelief or Believe in Christ before they were gathered. Zach 12 ch, 13 & 14 Ch goes to show that the Jews will be in unbelief. Br Cannon read in the Book of Mormon in the late Edition Pages 108, 84, 122, 425, 29 vers Page 488, 489, 558, 12 vers. All went to show that the Jews or some of them would Believe in Christ Before they were gathered."[25]

The Book of Mormon also seemed to include the notion that the book itself would be the key to Jewish national conversion. Mormon explained that his record would "go unto the unbelieving of the Jews; and for this intent shall [it] go—that they may be persuaded that Jesus is the Christ, the Son of the living God; that the Father may bring about, through his most Beloved, his great and eternal purpose, in restoring the Jews, or all the house of Israel, to the land of their inheritance, which the Lord their God hath given them, unto the fulfilling of his covenant" (Mormon 5:14). Commenting on portions of 2 Nephi 29 and 30, Benjamin Winchester, an early Mormon pamphleteer and one-time president of the important Philadelphia branch of the church, remarked that "there are many of the House of Israel that do not believe that Christ is the true Messiah . . . but when the Book of Mormon is presented unto them they will discover that it is the testimony of another nation that was secluded from those of the Eastern continent. . . . This will be a testimony that will not be easily dispensed with [by the Jews]; consequently they will search deep into the matter, and peradventure learn that Jesus is the true Messiah. Hence we see the utility of the Book of Mormon."[26]

The Book of Mormon also alluded to the lost tribes of Israel. Jacob 5, or the parable of the olive tree as it was known in the early years, spoke of "natural branches" being "hid" in the "nethermost part of the vineyard," which also happened to be the "poorest spot." This seemed to coincide perfectly with contemporary notions about the lost ten tribes having been sequestered away to the frozen "north countries." In a letter to Oliver Cowdery, W. W. Phelps postulated,

> The parts of the globe that are known probably contain 700 millions of inhabitants, and those parts which are unknown may be supposed to contain more than four times as many more, making an estimated total of about three thousand, five hundred and eighty million souls; Let no man marvel at this statement, because there may be a continent at the north pole, of more than 1300 square miles, containing thousands of millions of Israelites, who, after a highway is cast up in the great deep, may come to Zion, singing songs of everlasting joy. . . . This idea is greatly strengthened by reading Zenos' account of the tame olive tree in the Book of Mormon. The branches planted in the nethermost parts of the earth, "brought forth much fruit," and no man that pretends to have pure religion, can find "much fruit" among the Gentiles, or heathen of this generation.[27]

As has already been pointed out, the idea that the Gentiles had failed to bring forth "fruit" was actually central to the Saints' Israel-Gentiles-Israel periodization of redemptive history. They read Matthew 21:43 to mean that God originally offered the kingdom to the Jews but in time the Jews ceased to "bring forth the fruits thereof." After their rejection of Christ, the Kingdom was finally taken from them and offered to the Gentiles. According to Romans 11, this was done with the warning that should the Gentiles also cease to produce the fruits of godliness, they too would be "cut off" and the Israelites "grafted" back in. This final shift of divine favor back to the ancient covenant people would culminate in the millennium, the climactic conclusion to the "restoration of Israel." The necessary antecedent, however, was the apostasy of Gentile Christendom. Once that precondition was met, the drama was ready to proceed.

Not surprisingly, therefore, Book of Mormon prophecies dealing with the latter-day waywardness of the Gentiles attracted exegetical attention second only to the theme of Israel's restoration (table 2). Among the relevant scriptures, the prophecy in 2 Nephi 28 was particularly popular. To assist readers of the Book of Mormon, several indexes and reference guides, amounting to extended tables of contents, were prepared in the 1830s and 1840s and offer valuable insight into how the book was understood by early Saints. *References to the Book of Mormon* (or simply *References*) summarized the contents of 2 Nephi 28 as "State of the Gentiles in that day."[28] An index to the 1841 edition of the Book of Mormon amplified this to include three listings: "Their priests shall contend," "Teach with their learning & deny the Holy Ghost," and "Rob the poor."[29] The phraseology of these entries helps pinpoint key verses: "For it shall come to pass in that day that the churches which are built up, and not unto the Lord, when the one shall say unto the other: Behold, I am the Lord's and the others shall say: I, I am the Lord's and thus shall every one say that hath built up churches, and not unto the Lord. And they shall contend one with another; and their priests shall contend one with another, and they shall teach with their learning, and deny the Holy Ghost, which giveth utterance" (2 Nephi 28:3–4).

Remembering Joseph Smith's initial confusion about religion and recognizing that many converts expressed similar concern over the multitude of competing sects, it is easy to see how such verses would have both explained the religious world around them and confirmed the authenticity of the Book of Mormon. As for robbing the poor, that index authors Brigham Young and Willard Richards would have targeted such abuse seems natural. At the time they created the index they were living amidst the abject poverty of the manufacturing district of Manchester, England. Converts and outsiders alike, whose working-class slogan was "We want more bread and less Bibles, more pigs and less parsons," would have resonated with Nephi's description of the oppression exercised by the clerical elite.[30]

The early Mormon indexer Robert Crawford found further evidence for the apostate condition of Gentile Christendom in the contemporary existence of "liberal religion" which he felt was anticipated in 2 Nephi 28:22: "And behold, others [the devil] flattereth away, and telleth them there is no hell; and he saith unto them: I am no devil, for there is none—and thus he whispereth in their ears, until he grasps them with his awful chains, from whence there is no deliverance."[31] Recent studies of nineteenth-century theological controversies concerning hell and eternal punishment as well as the history of popular belief about Satan make clear that such thinking was definitely on the rise at the time the Book of Mormon came forth.[32]

Universalism, in particular, was singled out by the Saints for ridicule. What began in the seventeenth century as a challenge to notions of eternal torment ended up in the latter part of the eighteenth as a positive belief in the universal salvation of all God's moral creations. Deity acquired traits of benevolence rather than vengeance, and his mercy was emphasized more than his justice. Though such liberal views toward God were not held by all, during the final quarter of the eighteenth century, Universalism popularized such liberal notions among the rural folk of northern New England, and by the early nineteenth century the sect had spread across the Yankee belt to Ohio.[33]

In one of the few instances in which Book of Mormon individuals or ideas were explicitly linked to the contemporary religious scene, the first two entries in *References* for the book of Alma were "Nehor the Universalian" and "Amlici the Universalist." One passage, in particular, must have made the connection crystal clear: Nehor "testified unto the people that all mankind should be saved at the last day, and that they need not fear nor tremble, but that they might lift up their heads and rejoice; for the Lord had created all men and had also redeemed all men; and, in the end, all men should have eternal life" (Alma 1:4). In this case, not only the narrative repudiation of Nehor's "Universalism" but also the epithetical characterization of him in *References* as "Universalian" leaves little doubt about how Universalist doctrine was viewed by this Latter-day Saint.

Elsewhere, Corianton, the son of Book of Mormon prophet Alma, also seems to have had Universalist leanings, and it appears that much of that father's message to his son was understood to be a lengthy response to such inclinations. All early Mormon reference guides call the reader's attention to the latter part of Alma 40 and the whole of Alma 41 with the words "the restoration spoken of" or, as Crawford put it, "the restoration of all things." The term *restoration*, of course, was a favorite with nineteenth-century Christian primitivists and denoted the recovery of New Testament principle and practice. But even before that, the phrase had been popularized by Universalists as referring to final, universal salvation or, in the words of their Profession of Faith, to the "restoration" to "holiness and happiness" of "the whole family of mankind."[34] The very verse that Mormons would come to cherish for their own reasons—Acts 3:21, with its reference to the restitution or restoration "of all things"—gave hope to Universalists that biblical prophets had long ago foretold the future salvation of all mankind. In light of such things, Mormon readers would have agreed with Alma's remark that "some have wrested the scriptures, and have gone far astray because of this thing" (Alma 41:1). Alma's subsequent explanation of the term *restoration,* the gist of which was that Judgment Day would bring "back again evil for evil" and "good for that which is good" (Alma 41:13), was probably much appreciated in dealing with Universalism. Particularly pointed, in light of the Universalist slogan about the restoration of all to "holiness and happiness," would have been Alma's warning not to "suppose, because it has been spoken concerning restoration, that ye shall be restored from sin to happiness. Behold, I say unto you, wickedness never was happiness" (Alma 41:10).

Perhaps even more significant than clarifying the meaning of the term *restoration* was Alma's response to the supposed injustice of consigning sinners "to a state of misery" (Alma 42). Young-Richards and Crawford each made two relevant entries for this chapter: "justice in punishment" and "mercy rob justice." The mere fact that they chose to highlight such notions illustrates that liberal religion, with its emphasis on God's love and benevolence, had succeeded in calling such concepts into question. To denigrate eternal punishment, however, was to demean the atonement. "Repentance," explained Alma, "could not come unto men except there were a punishment, which also was eternal as the life of the soul should be, affixed opposite to the plan of happiness, which was as eternal also as the life of the soul" (Alma 42:16). No matter how soothing the thought, mercy, in that striking phrase noticed in the reference guides, could never be allowed to "rob justice" (Alma 42:25).

Beyond liberal religion, hypocritical religion was also felt by the Saints to be graphically foretold in the Book of Mormon. Charles B. Thompson concluded his lengthy volume *Evidences in Proof of the Book of Mormon* with an appendix entitled "A Proclamation and Warning to the Gentiles Who Inhabit America." Declaring "wo unto the inhabitants in all this land," he quoted 2 Nephi 28:11–16 as his justification.[35] These verses describe religionists who "rob the poor because of their fine sanctuaries," "persecute the meek," "wear stiff necks," "are puffed up in the pride of their hearts," "commit whoredoms," "turn aside the just for a thing of naught," and "revile against that which is good." Despite such dismal scenes, *References* did draw attention to the first two verses of 2 Nephi 30 with the interpretive phrase "Mercy yet for the Gentiles." Here Nephi cautions that "because of the words which have been spoken ye need not suppose that the Gentiles are utterly destroyed. For behold, I say unto you that as many of the Gentiles as will repent are the covenant people of the Lord."

Still, a generally dark picture of established religion was fully in keeping with the image of apostasy so common and so essential to apocalyptic millenarianism. In his letter to the *American Revivalist,* Joseph Smith observed, "For some length of time, I have been carfully viewing the state of things as now appear througout our christian Land and have looked at it with feelings of the most painful anxiety." He went on to describe the "vail of stupidity which seems to be drawn over the hearts of the people," and asked, in language reminiscent of the passage just quoted from the Book of Mormon, "has not the pride highmindedness and unbelief of the Gentiles provoked the holy one of Israel to withdraw his holy spirit from them and send forth his Judgments to scourge them for their wickedness; this is certainly the case." "Distruction," he wrote, "to the eye of the spiritual beholder seems to be writen by the finger of an invisable hand in Large capitals upon almost evry thing we behold."[36]

This sobering prophetic analysis stood in sharp contrast to what millenarian Mormons considered the ill-founded optimism of Christendom generally. With the rapid expansion of foreign missions and the spread of domestic revivals during the Second Great Awakening, Gentile churches confidently proclaimed, as Nephi predicted in 2 Nephi 28:21, "all is well in Zion, yea Zion prospereth." But the Latter-day Saints thought they knew better. As the editor of the *Star* expressed it, "There seems to be one error common to all writers on the Millennium, which is that they think that it is to be brought about by converting the Gentiles."[37] Rather than the widespread conversions expected by postmillennialist evangelicals, the Saints found in the Book of Mormon evidence that latter-day apostasy and wickedness among the Gentiles would be such that the true followers of Christ would be relatively "few" and that the "dominions" of his Church would be "small" "upon . . . the face of the earth" (1 Nephi 14:12).

Part of the problem with Gentile Christendom was their dependence on theological tradition. 2 Nephi 28:31 warned, "Cursed is he that putteth his trust in man, or maketh flesh his arm, or shall hearken unto the precepts of men, save their precepts shall be given by the power of the Holy Ghost." Along with other Christian primitivists,

Mormons found the creedalism of the mainline denominations distasteful and saw in this passage a pointed repudiation of such practices. "The world," wrote W. W. Phelps, "endeavors to worship the Lord by wisdom . . . and thousands risk their souls from year to year, on the say-soes, creeds and covenants of men, when it is written 'cursed is he that putteth his trust in man.'"[38]

The nineteenth century witnessed on both sides of the Atlantic a renaissance of what has been called "New Testament restorationism" or Christian primitivism.[39] Under the maxim "No creed but the Bible," a widespread interest in recasting Christianity along biblical lines spawned not only groups like Alexander Campbell's Disciples of Christ and Barton Stone's "Christian" movement in America but the Plymouth Brethren and the Universal Christian Society in England as well. Yet even the primitivist return to scriptural forms and faith alone was insufficient. With their celebration of the Bible as the sole source for theology, primitivists jettisoned centuries of Christian tradition on the assumption that the meaning of Scripture was transparent even to the ploughboy and that neither creeds nor dogmatic expositions were necessary. What resulted, however, was the proliferation rather than the harmonization of doctrinal positions.[40] Amidst the bewildering babel of conflicting voices, something authoritative was needed—modern revelation. To the satisfaction of the early Saints, the Book of Mormon, which presented itself as just such an answer, was felt to "throw greater views upon [Christ's] gospel."[41]

But it was precisely this that so enraged the Christian world around them. On one of his many missionary tours, LDS apostle Heber C. Kimball wrote, "We delivered our testimony to many [ministers] who with one consent said 'we have enough and need no more revelation'; thus fulfilling a prediction of the Book of Mormon."[42] The passage Kimball referred to was 2 Nephi 29:3, which says that because of the Book of Mormon "many of the Gentiles shall say: A Bible! A Bible! We have got a Bible, and there cannot be any more Bible." This passage seemed to be fulfilled at every turn of the corner. "The vanity, the unbelief, the darkness and wickedness of this generation has caused many to fulfill the predictions of Nephi," wrote the editor of the *Messenger and Advocate*.[43]

Above all, the rejection of modern revelation confirmed that Gentile Christendom had become effete and that the stage was thus fully set for that final act in the redemptive drama—the restoration of Israel. Even the very emergence of the Book of Mormon was an unmistakable witness that the "winding-up scenes" were underway. The second most frequently cited series of verses in the early literature was 3 Nephi 21:1–7. Here the Savior promised the Nephites "a sign that ye may know the time when these things shall be about to take place— that I shall gather in from their long dispersion, my people, O house of Israel." That sign, as he went on to explain, was the coming forth of the Book of Mormon itself and "it shall be a sign unto them, that they may know that the work of the Father hath already commenced unto the fulfilling of the covenant which he hath made unto the people who are of the house of Israel." As Parley P. Pratt remarked, this and other similar passages "show, in definite terms not to be misunderstood, that, when that record should come forth in the latter day, and be published to the Gentiles, and come from them to the house of Israel, it should be *a sign, a standard, an ensign* by which they might *know that the time had actually arrived for the work to commence among all nations, in preparing the way for the return of Israel to their own land.*"[44] Thus, the coming forth of the Book of Mormon served as an invaluable prophetic landmark, a millenarian milestone which helped the Saints to locate themselves in the eschatological timetable.

Once located, though, the Saints realized that leadership was essential. Fortunately, the Book of Mormon made clear that a prophet would be raised up in the latter days to assist in this final "work of the Father." 2 Nephi 3 records the prophecy of Joseph who was sold into Egypt that a "choice seer" would be raised up to bless the "fruit of his loins." In verse 15, he identifies the individual quite precisely: "His name shall be called after me; and it shall be after the name of his father. And he shall be like unto me." Such specific prophecy and its fulfillment in Joseph Smith, Jr., obviously appealed to literalist Latter-day Saints. In the church's first hymnbook a song appeared in which this correlation between antiquity and actuality was extolled:

> He likewise did foretell the name,
> That should be given to the same,
> His and his father's should agree,
> And both like his should Joseph be.

The song goes on to encapsulate the essential significance that this popular portion of the Book of Mormon probably held for the average Saint:

> According to his holy plan,
> The Lord has now rais'd up the man,
> His latter day work to begin,
> To gather scatter'd Israel in.
> This seer shall be esteemed high,
> By Joseph's remnants by and by,
> He is the man who's call'd to raise,
> And lead Christ's church in these last days.[45]

All the important elements of Joseph Smith's mission are present—the gathering of Israel, the conversion of the Indians, and the leadership of the restored Church of Christ.

For ages individuals have found refuge from the unknown in the security of prophecy. That Mormons, therefore, discovered comforting scriptural assurances that their leader would be protected and that his work would not be cut short is to be expected. After receiving word of Joseph Smith's 1841 acquittal in Quincy, Illinois, a distant Parley Pratt editorialized in the *Millennial Star,* "Be it known that there is an invisible hand in this matter," and then he quoted 2 Nephi 3:14: "THAT SEER WILL THE LORD BLESS, AND THEY WHO SEEK TO DESTROY HIM SHALL BE CONFOUNDED." As evidence, Pratt cited "some twenty times in succession" in which Joseph's enemies had tried to destroy him legally but had been foiled each time. This, commented Pratt, "is sufficient of itself to establish the truth of the Book of Mormon."[46]

Even more popular than the promised preservation was a pair of passages from 3 Nephi. In his visit to the Americas, the Savior quoted various portions of the Isaiah prophecies. One such segment was the beginning of the "suffering servant" prophecy (Isaiah 52–53), where the servant's "visage" is described as being "so marred, more than any man, and his form more than the sons of men" (3 Nephi 20:43–44). For centuries Christian exegetes had considered this one of the great Messianic prophecies of Christ's scourging and crucifixion. Yet in 3 Nephi it is given another meaning. Speaking of the latter days and of a "servant" who would be instrumental in bringing about the "great and marvelous work," Jesus said, "and there shall be among them those who will not believe it, although a man shall declare it unto them. But behold, the life of my servant shall be in my hand; therefore they shall not hurt him, although he shall be marred because of them. Yet I will heal him, for I will show unto them that my wisdom is greater than the cunning of the devil" (3 Nephi 21:9–10).

References identified this servant as "Joseph the seer," and in a *Nauvoo Neighbor* editorial, John Taylor explained the prophecy thus: "This 'marring' happened near the hill Cummorah, when *Joseph Smith was knocked down with a handspike,* and afterward *healed almost instantly!* The second time he was *marred*" occurred in March 1832 "when his *flesh was scratched off,* and he tarred and feathered. He was agin healed instantly, fulfilling the prophecy *twice*." But to Taylor there was a critical distinction between being "marred" and being martyred, for he also pointed to 1 Nephi 20:19 as evidence that Smith's death had actually been anticipated in prophecy.[47] Thus, the course of Joseph Smith's mortal sojourn at once certified the authenticity of the Book of Mormon and imparted divine significance to what was happening in his life.

Occasionally, parallels between Joseph Smith and Jesus Christ led to novel exegesis. Following the dark days of the Kirtland apostasy, the apostle David W. Patten attempted to curb some of the faultfinding by writing an epistle "to the Saints scattered abroad." His approach was to give a somewhat different twist to the perennial favorite—Romans 11:25–26. Where it speaks of Israel's salvation in the latter days being effected by a "Deliverer" who "shall come out of Sion" and "shall turn away ungodliness from Jacob," Patten claimed that it was referring to Joseph Smith. Despite the fact that other Mormon commentators such as Parley Pratt followed the traditional interpretation of the "Deliverer" as Christ, Patten used 2 Nephi 3 and 3 Nephi 20, along with numerous Biblical passages, to argue that this "Deliverer" was in reality Joseph Smith.[48]

If apologetics produced apotheosis, so did the enthusiasm of converts. While Patten's interpretation was unusual, a more common mixing of the roles of Jesus and Joseph occurred when explaining the identity of the "prophet" spoken of by Moses in Deuteronomy 18:15–19 and quoted again by Peter in Acts 3:22–23. On two occasions it was deemed worthwhile to print clarifications in Church periodicals. In both instances, passages from the Book of Mormon were invoked. The *Star* published a letter asserting that the problem lay in "not knowing the scriptures, on the subject, especially the book of Mormon. For Christ said, when he showed himself to the Nephites, Behold I am he of whom Moses spake, saying: A prophet shall the Lord your God raise up."[49] In Nauvoo, the editor of the *Times and Seasons* cited a similarly clear passage from 1 Nephi 22 "where the matter is fully set at rest" as to the Messianic identity of the "prophet." Nonetheless, the high regard in which Joseph Smith was held among the Saints caused the editor to tread lightly: "If any are fearful lest we, by our interpretation, wrest a gem from the crown of our beloved prophet, let them remember, that we place it in the royal diadem of him who is more excellent than Joseph; and where even Joseph will be pleased to have it remain and shine. That God hath exalted him to a station of great dignity and responsibility, we do not doubt, but the truth of it rests on other testimony than the above."[50]

The Book of Mormon could also be read to support other individuals and events essential to their eschatology. As the Church's general conference convened at Nauvoo in April 1840, Orson Hyde, obviously anxious to hasten the restoration of Israel, announced that the Spirit was whispering to him to "take up a mission" to the Jews and Jerusalem. The expression was heartily seconded from the floor and approved by Joseph Smith. Thus began one of the most famous missions in Mormon history, culminating two years later in a special apostolic prayer offered on the Mount of Olives to dedicate the Holy Land for the return of the Jews.[51] Shortly after he set out, Hyde wrote a letter commenting on a Zionist movement then being reported in the newspapers. This recalled to his mind the words of Isaiah that there would be "none to guide [Israel] among all the sons she hath brought forth; neither that taketh her by the hand but these two *things* which are come unto thee."[52] Noting that in the 2 Nephi 8 recapitulation of Isaiah, *things* appeared as *sons*, "this is better sense, and more to the point," declared Hyde. It also allowed him and his missionary companion, John E. Page, to step into the pages of prophecy: "As Jerusalem has no sons to take her by the hand and lead her among all the number whom she hath brought forth, Bro. Page and myself feel that we ought to hurry along and take her by the hand; for we are her sons but the Gentiles have brought us up."[53]

In the fall of 1845, the church decided to evacuate Nauvoo. Rather than engage enraged vigilantes from Hancock County in what seemed to be an inevitable civil war, church leaders decided to make the previously contemplated move west the following spring. Again, Book of Mormon prophecy helped to explain current events and did so from a decidedly apocalyptic point of view. According to 3 Nephi 16:10, "At that day when the Gentiles shall sin against my gospel, and shall be lifted up in the pride of their hearts above all nations, and above all the people of the whole earth, and shall be filled with all manner of lyings, and of deceits, and of mischiefs, and all manner of hypocrisy, and murders, and priestcrafts, and whoredoms and of secret abominations; and if they shall do all those things, and shall reject the fulness of my gospel, behold, saith the Father, I will bring the fulness of my gospel from among them." Some found literal fulfillment of these words in the church's exodus from Nauvoo. In a circular entitled "Message from Orson Pratt to the Saints in the Eastern and Midland States," Pratt declared,

> This wholesale banishment of the Saints from the American republic will no doubt, be one of the grandest and most glorious events yet witnessed in the history of this church. It seems to be a direct and literal fulfilment of many prophecies, both ancient and modern. Jesus has expressly told us, (Book of Mormon), that if the "Gentiles shall reject the fulness of my gospel, behold, saith the Father, I will bring the fulness of my gospel from among them." Now, what could the Gentiles further do to reject the "fulness of the Gospel"— the Book of Mormon? Is there one crime that they are not guilty of? I speak of them in a national capacity. . . .
>
>   If then, all these crimes do not amount to a national rejection of the "fulness of the gospel," I know not what more they can do to fully ripen them in crime and iniquity. Therefore, is not the time at hand for the Lord to bring the "fulness of the gospel" from among the Gentiles of this nation? If we are banished to the western wilds among the remnants of Joseph, is it not to ripen the wicked and save the righteous? Is it not to save us from the impending judgments which modern revelation have denounced against this nation? How could the gospel be brought from among the Gentiles while the priesthood and the Saints tarried in their midst.[54]

Clearly, then, LDS use of the Book of Mormon demonstrated a definite preoccupation with prophetic descriptions of the last days. Just as Christians in their use of the Bible, the Saints, too, with regard to the Book of Mormon, have had a canon within the canon. Mosiah, Alma, and Helaman, three of the largest and most historically oriented books, constitute approximately half of the Book of Mormon. Yet only 15 percent of the citations in the early literature were drawn from them. On the other hand, 3 Nephi and Ether represent just over 15 percent of the total volume of the book and account for nearly 45 percent of all citations. When content is considered what is clear is that the prophetic portions of the Book of Mormon—parts of 3

Nephi, 2 Nephi, and Ether—received significantly greater attention than the historical books—Mosiah, Alma and Helaman. Prophecies relating to the restoration of Israel and the fate of the Gentiles were by far the principal interests of the early Saints. Though the Book of Mormon has since been used in the LDS community as a source for a uniquely Mormon anthropology, soteriology, and even Christology, its earliest uses were primarily eschatological and reflected as well as reinforced a millenarian worldview.

6

Moderate Millenarians

It used to be the conventional wisdom that millenarianism was directly related to social and economic deprivation and often constituted a kind of prepolitical, working-class radicalism. Further study of millenarian groups, however, has led to the caution that scholars "should be especially reluctant to conclude that prophetic and millennial theorizing arose from tensions in the lives of individuals and in their society."[1] In the case of the Latter-day Saints, it is important to keep in mind the caution of the anthropologist David Aberle: "the discovery of what constitutes serious deprivation for particular groups or individuals is a difficult empirical problem [requiring] careful attention to the reference points that people employ to judge their legitimate expectations, as well as to their actual circumstances."[2] Close examination of where Mormons did articulate a sense of deprivation, as well as a review of what they criticized and supported in antebellum America, allows a more accurate identification of their place on the cultural map of the period. It also illustrates how some millenarian groups can raise outspoken opposition to various aspects of society and still be very much a part of the dominant culture.

Near the top of the Mormon list of concerns was the contemporary absence of spiritual gifts. Here was deprivation as keenly felt as any lack of physical sustenance, and it was at the heart of what millenarian Mormons found wrong with society. Referring to several New Testament descriptions of spiritual gifts, Joseph Smith declared, "By the foregoing testimonies we may look at the Christian world and see the apostasy there has been from the apostolic platform."[3] A Book of

Mormon prophet reasoned, "if there were miracles wrought then, why has God ceased to be a God of miracles, and yet be an unchangeable Being?" The answer was simple: "the reason why he ceaseth to do miracles among the children of men is because that they dwindle in unbelief and depart from the right way, and know not the God in whom they should trust" (Mormon 9:19–20). Christendom had framed the excuse that the age of miracles was past simply to camouflage its own impotence. As another Book of Mormon prophet put it, "if these things have ceased, . . . awful is the state of man" (Moroni 7:38). Christ, after all, in his famous commission in Mark 16:16–18 had singled out certain gifts as "signs" that should invariably follow the faithful. "I wish the reader never to pass this commission," remarked Parley Pratt, "until he understands it, because, when once understood, he never need mistake the kingdom of God, but will at once discover those peculiarities, which were forever to distinguish it from all other kingdoms or religious systems on earth."[4]

Not surprisingly, the Saints freely proclaimed their spiritual giftedness as prime evidence that the primitive church had been restored.[5] This included "the gift of tongues, prophecy, revelation, visions, healing, interpretation of tongues &c."[6] As the perceptive Shaker poet John Greenleaf Whittier noted,

> They contrast strongly the miraculous power of the Gospel in the apostolic time with the present state of our nominal Christianity. They ask for signs of divine power, the faith, overcoming all things which opened the prison doors of the apostles, gave them power over the elements, which rebuked disease and death itself, and made visible to all the presence of the Living God. They ask for any declaration in the Scriptures that this miraculous power of faith was to be confined to the first confessors of Christianity. They speak a language of hope and promise to weak, weary hearts, tossed and troubled, who have wandered from sect to sect, seeking in vain for the primal manifestations of the divine power.[7]

The pervasiveness of spiritual gifts among the Latter-day Saints testifies to the fact that in early Mormonism many searching souls found a legitimate outlet for pentecostal proclivities.

The proclamation of widespread spiritual apostasy and the assumption that only a new dispensation of divine grace could rectify it also provided the lens through which the Saints looked at other aspects of nineteenth-century America. Given their moral values, one might expect them to have seen in the various reform movements of the day a kindred spirit, but this was not so. Even if reform had been the right answer, its association with the apostate ecclesiastical establishment condemned it as unauthorized. With obvious satire, the *Messenger and Advocate* remarked, "God has done his work and we don't need any more prophets. We have Bible societies, missionary societies, abolition of slavery societies and temperance societies to convert the world and bring in the Millennium."[8] Such groups were superfluous at best and sinister at worst. "As to so many appendaged societies to the gospel, we must say," remarked the editor of the *Star* in standard "antimission" rhetoric, "that neither the Savior, nor his apostles, nor the Scriptures, have taught any thing more necessary, than to repent and believe on the Lord Jesus, and be baptized for the remission of sins; to receive the gift of the Holy Ghost; and continue faithful to the end, to inherit eternal life."[9] Moreover, such efforts ignored a millenarian eschatology. "Though they were ten times as vigilant and their reformations ten to one," explained the *Star,* "still when the Savior comes the people will be as they were in the days of Noah."[10]

It is important to point out, however, that a millenarian judgment against the spiritual legitimacy of establishment Christianity and its various programs did not mean that the Latter-day Saints rejected the basic moral sensibilities of the religious world around them. In words that might have come from any contemporary Christian preceptor, Joseph Smith declared, "we believe in being honest, true, chaste, benevolent, virtuous, and in doing good to *all men.* . . . If there is anything virtuous, lovely, or of good report, or praiseworthy, we seek after these things."[11] Mormons championed temperance and healthful living in their now legendary "Word of Wisdom," an 1833 revelation proscribing tobacco, liquor, coffee and tea, and prescribing a generous diet of grains, fruits, and vegetables in season, along with the sparing use of meat.[12] And, for a time during the earliest years, strict evangelical standards influenced their ideas of proper recreation and diversion as well. In 1835, for instance, an editorial in the Church newspaper renounced "the frivolous practice of playing ball" as something liable to "bring reproach upon the glorious cause of our Redeemer."[13] Two years later, a group of Church leaders resolved, "That we discard the practice of ball-playing, wrestling, jumping and all such low and degrading amusements."[14]

Even dancing was initially proscribed. All of the early reference guides to the Book of Mormon cite an episode in 1 Nephi in which during their transoceanic voyage to the promised land, several family members "were lifted up unto exceeding rudeness," singing, dancing, and making merry. Each guide had only to reference the episode as simply "dancing in the ship" (1 Nephi 18:9) to identify the evil. On one occasion in the 1830s, nineteen members of the church were disciplined for "attending a ball."[15] In the 1840s, apostle-editor John Taylor wrote, "As an abstract principle . . . we have no objections to it; but when it leads people into bad company and causes them to keep untimely hours, it has a tendency to enervate and weaken the system and leads to profligate and intemperate habits. And so far as it does this . . . it is injurious to society, and corrupting to the morals of youth."[16] In time, however, the Saints would warm to dancing, and it became a favorite diversion in pioneer Utah.[17]

Another contemporary corrupter was the novel. As pointedly as any Protestant periodical, the *Messenger and Advocate* warned that novel reading led to "lightness and lechery."[18] As with most evangelicals, the Mormons liked their literature moralistic and didactic. An 1832 revelation had admonished them to seek "words of wisdom" out of the "best books,"[19] and novels never seemed to qualify. In the words of editor Taylor, they were "as destitute of truth, true science and practical knowledge as Satan's promises were to Eve." "Why," exclaimed Taylor, "read the fancied brains of disappointed men and women, and then go the theatre; and ten to one, but you will be just like them."[20]

Antebellum evangelicals also warned about the pride-engendering dangers of "costly apparel," and, consciously or unconsciously, certain of them sought "boundary maintenance" through the regulation of dress. Early Mormon scripture was not one whit behind in inveighing against conspicuous consumption. In a particularly stinging indictment, a Book of Mormon prophet charged that "ye do love money, and your substance, and your fine apparel, and the adorning of your churches, more than ye love the poor and the needy, the sick and the afflicted" (Mormon 8:37). "And again, thou shalt not be proud in thy heart," a revelation directed, "let all thy garments be plain, and their beauty the beauty of the work of thine own hands."[21] Not only did costly apparel promote pride, it prevented the allocation of resources for things that really mattered. "Every yard of ribbon that I buy that is needless," declared Brigham Young, "every flounce, every gewgaw that is purchased for my family needlessly, robs the Church of God."[22]

"Needlessly," of course, was the operative word, and it allowed the Saints a degree of breathing room in the matter of fashion. Sidney Rigdon once asked the Saints how they ever contemplated fulfilling their prophetic destiny to become the showplace of the earth if they wore "apparel untastefully arranged."[23] The Saints were sympathetic to the plain style, but they hesitated to make too much of the matter. "Indeed among some that would be called wise," wrote Rigdon, "they think that the cut of their coat and shape of their hat is of great importance and has a considerable to do with their salvation; hence we have to this day the broad brimmed hat and the long tailed coat, and the vest with skirts, worn as a badge of righteousness; but let the Saints know assuredly that their righteousness does not consist in putting on some old antiquated dress, but in enterprise in accomplishing the will of God."[24]

Acceptance of prevailing mores also helps explain why early reference guides were quick to cite the prohibition of polygamy found in the Book of Mormon (Jacob 2, 3). This may seem ironic in light of subsequent history, but the guides were written in the period *before* plural marriage was introduced.[25] Not surprisingly, therefore, it was the condemnation of polygamy that was noticed, not the phrase, later to become so popular in polygamy defenses, which indicated that if the Lord wished to "raise up seed" unto himself, he could command his people to practice plural marriage; "otherwise they shall hearken unto these things" (Jacob 2:30). The earliest Saints wanted to make clear that they stood squarely within traditional Christian morality when it came to domestic arrangements. "Inasmuch as this church of Christ has been reproached with the crime of fornication, and polygamy," noted an article on marriage appended to the first (1835) edition of the *Doctrine and Covenants*, "we declare that we believe that one man should have one wife; and one woman, but one husband."[26]

As for the cultural deviance of later polygamists, extant studies indicate that their morals and mores were sufficiently close to those of evangelical America that they entered plural marriage only amidst the most profound psychological anxiety and practiced it more as a multiplication of monogamy than as a radical new social arrangement. "The Mormons," remarked the historian Lawrence Foster, "were considerably closer to the family ideals and practices of the larger society than either the Shakers or the Oneida Perfectionists. In fact, Mormon literature of the polygamy period, whether for internal or external consumption, frequently sounds more Victorian than the writings of the Victorians."[27]

Social conservatism was also apparent in their response to slavery and race. It is true that several passages in the Book of Mormon interdict slavery, or "bondage" as it was called. King Benjamin prides himself on not having permitted his people to "make slaves one of another" (Mosiah 2:13), and when the Anti-Nephi-Lehies offer to become Nephite slaves, Ammon responds that "it is against the law of our brethren, which was established by my father, that there should be any slaves among them" (Alma 27:9). The latter passage was singled out by Brigham Young and Willard Richards in their index with the words "slavery forbidden" and by Crawford with "prohibition of slavery." Yet in a lengthy 1836 discussion on the topic, Joseph Smith condemned abolitionism and cited commonly invoked Biblical sanctions for, rather than Book of Mormon proscriptions against, the "peculiar institution."[28] Particularly ironic is the fact that Brigham Young, a decade after calling attention in his 1840 index to the Nephite law prohibiting slavery, signed into effect a Deseret law that permitted it.[29]

How is this to be explained? Perhaps, in light of seeming Biblical sanctions, the Saints did not view the Book of Mormon prohibitions as universally normative. On the other hand, they may have viewed the Nephite practice as ideal, but, as loyal Jacksonians and avowed antiabolitionists, felt it impolitic to push the point.[30] Most likely, they were not troubled at all by the matter. For centuries, individuals had distinguished between whites and blacks when it came to civil liberties and human rights. During the Revolution, for example, the Founding Fathers denounced in grandiloquent terms the specter of bondage to Britain, and yet at the same time justified, even demanded, the perpetual involuntary servitude of black Americans.[31] This distinction was widespread until the Civil War and helps explain how Joseph Smith could, with cultural consistency, denounce abolition and uphold slavery after having received a revelation that "it is not right that any man should be in bondage one to another."[32] The simple insertion of the word "white" before "man" provides the key.

The common racial assumptions of antebellum America may also help explain why the Saints took literally the several Book of Mormon references to the Lamanites becoming "white and delightsome."[33] Like many others, they probably just assumed a direct relationship between skin color and moral purity. W. W. Phelps expressed it thus:

Is it not apparent from reason and analogy as drawn from a careful reading of the Scriptures that God causes the saints, or people that fall away from his church to be cursed in time, with a black skin? Was not Cain, being marked, obliged to inherit the curse, he and his children, forever? . . . Are or are not the Indians a sample of marking with blackness for rebellion against God's holy word and holy order? And can we not observe in the countenances of almost all nations, except the Gentile, a dark and sallow hue, which tells the sons of God, without a line of history, that they have fallen or changed from the original beauty and grace of Father Adam?[34]

If the Saints were not radicals in the realm of race or even marital relations, did they not, nonetheless, epitomize utopian radicalism when it came to the economic order? Such a perception has long been a cornerstone of the argument that nineteenth-century Mormonism was thoroughly countercultural in both aspiration and aspect. Mormonism has been described as "a radical critique of the American economy and class structure" and "the very epitome of an antibourgeois mentality."[35] However, even a cursory reading of more recent scholarship pertaining to Mormon communitarianism reveals sufficient behavioral evidence to allow the view that at any given point in the nineteenth century, most Latter-day Saints seem to have imbibed the prevailing ethos of economic liberalism a little too fully to fit the description of being antibourgeois or radically communitarian. In the 1830s, for example, one is struck not by the abortive attempt to live the utopian Law of Consecration, but by the typically Jacksonian acquisitiveness displayed in Kirtland by mid-decade Mormons.[36] In the 1840s, Joseph Smith seems to have been merely echoing the conventional wisdom when he sermonized against the "folly" of the "common stock" principle,[37] and Nauvoo, the "City of Joseph," certainly followed the contemporary midwestern pattern of boosterism and boom.[38] Even decades later in Utah, when the Saints again attempted to implement the Law of Consecration through the United Orders, the reality was that where Mormon congregations did not resist communalism altogether, most opted for a significantly less formal arrangement than was found in the legendary Orderville.[39]

Even this brief review, then, points up problems in allowing communitarian rhetoric to represent behavioral reality. Studies of seventeenth-century New England village life demonstrate that the notion of a "closed, corporate, Christian commonwealth," which stood for

years as the stereotypical New England town, can now be countered
by studies of Puritan communities "where modern privatism and in-
dividualism are said to have prevailed from the start."[40] So the Mormon record can also be read from a different angle that makes indi-
vidualism and liberalism more apparent. LDS attitudes and behavior
in the nineteenth century seem less countercultural, and communitarianism and theocracy more superficial, than has often been assumed. Indeed, it may be that the oft-romanticized theocratic communalism of the Saints was doomed from the start precisely because
Mormons had always been too American at heart. For the ordinary
Saint, Adam Smith and Joseph Smith may not have been antithetical
after all.

The Saints also participated in the "common cultural revolution"
taking place in the new American republic "against what was perceived as 'King-craft, Priest-craft, Lawyer-craft, and Doctor-craft.'"[41]
What seems to have been at issue was a common mistrust among ordinary citizens of mediating elites. Such populist sentiment abounds
in the Book of Mormon and in early LDS literature. With rhetorical
flourish, Joseph Smith declared that he would strike "with accelerat-
ed force against religious bigotry, priestcraft, lawyercraft, doctorcraft,
lying editors, suborned judges and jurors, and the authority of per-
jured executives, backed by mobs, blasphemers, licentious and corrupt men and women."[42] Given the nearly constant Mormon experience of both religious and legal persecution, it is hardly surpising that
some of their most vigorous denunciations were reserved for priests
and lawyers. "As long as I have a tongue to speak," vowed Joseph
Smith, "I will expose the iniquity of the lawyers and wicked men. I fear
not their boiling over nor the boiling over of hell, their thunders, nor
the lightning of their forked tongues."[43] The connection between
democratic impulses and LDS opposition to the established ministry
is clear in a statement entitled "The Political Motto of the Church."
"Exalt the standard of Democracy!" it urged. "Down with that of
priestcraft, and let all the people say Amen!"[44]

As for medicine, Latter-day Saints cited a passage in the Book of
Mormon which mentions the "excellent qualities of the many plants
and roots which God had prepared to remove the cause of diseases"
(Alma 46:40). They agreed with Samuel Thomson, the best-known
proponent of herbalist opposition to orthodox medicine and in
whose system both Mormon "doctors" Frederick G. Williams and Wil-

lard Richards were licentiates, when he wrote that Americans "should in medicine as in religion and politics, act for themselves."[45] After reading about the life and labors of Thomson, Wilford Woodruff wrote, "I have no doubt but that his invention theory & practice of administering roots barks & herbs as medicine, is a great blessing to mankind & is one of the greatest improvments of the last days & is causing a great revolution throughout America in the mode of practice, by which means he has drawn down a flood of persecution & slander upon his head."[46]

Another aspect of the great democratic revolution underway in antebellum America was the popular revulsion against predestination. The belief in election, or God's extension of saving grace only to a predestined few, had been a hallmark of Calvinist or Reformed Protestant thought for nearly three centuries by the time the Book of Mormon was published, and Calvinism was the dominant theological orientation of Americans at least until the Revolution. At issue was the proper relationship between grace and nature, that is, between how much salvation depended on God and how much it depended on man, as well as whether Christ's atonement was limited or universal in scope. By the second quarter of the nineteenth century, the "new measures" revivalism of the Second Great Awakening had combined with the earlier Enlightenment-spurred celebration of human potential to tip the scale decisively to the side of man and an unlimited opportunity for saving grace. For many Americans, predestined election had come to symbolize in religious terms an issue that exercised the entire nation—the propriety of inherited versus achieved status. In the wake of the democratic revolution, *election* took on a pejorative connotation for all but orthodox diehards and became a catchword for an increasingly unpopular Calvinism.[47]

Mormons shared this antipathy. Under the heading "The Zoramites preach election," *References* cited these words: "We believe that thou hast elected us to be thy holy children; and . . . thou hast elected us that we shall be saved, whilst all around us are elected to be cast by thy wrath down to hell" (Alma 31:16–17). In the mind of the author of *References*, this passage paralleled the detested doctrine of "double predestination." It is the only place in the entire Book of Mormon where the word *elect* or its cognates, so commonly associated with Calvinism, are used. Brigham Young and Willard Richards, on the other hand, discovered the "true" doctrine of election in the early part of Alma 13. That they were making an interpretive judgment as to what election meant is clear from the fact that their reference reads "election spoken of," despite the absence of the term in the text. The particular passage they had in mind can be pinpointed with reasonable certainty since about the same time that they prepared their index, they also wrote an article entitled "Election and Reprobation" in which they quoted Alma 13:3–7. The passage says that those ordained to the High Priesthood were called "on account of their faith, while others would reject the spirit of God on account of the hardness of their hearts and blindness of their minds, while, if it had not been for this they might have had as great privilege as their brethren. Or, in fine, in the first place they were on the same standing with their brethren; thus this holy calling being prepared from the foundation of the world for such as would not harden their hearts."[48] Calvinism had been stood on its head.

Much has also been written about Mormon involvement with American popular culture in the realm of magic and treasure hunting.[49] Such a participation would have been consistent with both their primitivism and their millenarianism, since, in part, folk magic represented a reaction against clerical elites and the established order, and the millenarian worldview has a fundamental sympathy for thaumaturgy or wonder-working.[50] However, the LDS case should not be overstated. Mormon literature itself actually has relatively little to say about magic or buried treasure, and even when it does, it may be reflecting the particular background of certain converts rather than the essence of the new religion.

Few Book of Mormon passages, for instance, discuss topics related to magic, and those that do were rarely noted by early Mormon readers.[51] Brigham Young and Willard Richards, in their extensive index, make no reference to any such passage. The principal commentary on buried treasure is found in Helaman 13 as part of Samuel the Lamanite's prophecy of the Nephites' last days, and *References* alone calls attention to the early portion of that discussion with the words "the hiding of riches in the earth." The passage noted warns that because of wickedness a "curse" will come upon the land such that "whoso shall hide up treasures in the earth shall find them again no more." The righteous were to be spared, of course, but "he that hideth not up his treasures unto me, cursed is he, and also the treasure, and none shall redeem it because of the curse of the land" (Helaman 13:16–20).

Later in the Book of Mormon it is recorded that "the inhabitants thereof began to hide up their treasures in the earth; and they became slippery, because the Lord had cursed the land, that they could not hold them, nor retain them. And it came to pass that there were sorceries, and witchcrafts, and magics; and the power of the evil one was wrought upon all the face of the land, even unto the fulfilling of all the words of Abinadi, and also Samuel the Lamanite" (Mormon 1:18–19). Both *References* and Crawford cite the beginning of this passage with the words "treasures become slippery."

The important issue is *why* these scriptures were referenced to begin with. Was it because the principles and experiences involved were considered normative and relieveable in the American republic, or exotic and bound in time and space to ancient America? Unfortunately, the phrasing of the references alone allows no certain evaluation of motive. As for evidence of any tie-in with the magic lore discussed in Quinn's study, the Book of Mormon text makes no mention of "clever spirits" protecting treasure, nor of seerstones or hazel sticks locating it, nor indeed of any power other than God's as the cause for its becoming "slippery." The most likely explanation for the inclusion of these citations relates to the Saints' previously demonstrated preoccupation with manifestations of divine or supernatural power. Individuals impressed by trees and mountains being removed by faith or by Nephi being transported from place to place by the Spirit would likewise find noteworthy that God made hidden treasures become "slippery."

In any case, it seems unnecessary to disengage magic from either religion or millenarianism. Each espouses a belief in the supernatural and each proposes a method of control.[52] Similarities are more noticeable than the old Frazerian distinctions, long since discarded by most anthropologists, that magic is manipulative and religion supplicative, or that magic seeks to influence forces while religion deals with beings.[53] Nor are any of them inherently antithetical to rationalism. As one anthropologist remarked about even modern individuals, "People, be they Azande [African tribe] or Americans, can act under the influence of their magical beliefs in some contexts and in a rational-technical manner in others. When things go wrong in an uncontrollable and unforeseeable way, the Azande will attribute it to witchcraft, the American perhaps to bad luck."[54] Ultimately, magic should be viewed from the supernaturalistic, even spiritual, perspective of the nineteenth century rather than the naturalistic perspective of the twentieth century. Despite the advance of mechanistic philosophy and technology, for many early nineteenth-century Americans, Mormons included, the world had not yet been fully stripped of the attributes of personality that make magic, religion, or millenarianism untenable and unnecessary.[55]

Whether considering the Saints' evangelical mores or their enthusiastic participation in various aspects of the popular culture of the day, Mormons are best classified as moderate millenarians whose critique of society focused primarily on its spiritual rather than structural deficiencies. As the theorist Antonio Gramsci argued long ago, thought systems which attempt to counter the dominant or hegemonic ideology usually end up incorporating the very structures, categories, and premises of the hegemonic discourse itself. A simple linguistic example would be the statement "black is beautiful." It still partakes of racist categories, merely inverting the hierarchy, rather than radically altering the whole framework of discussion. Similarly, while the Saints wished to invert the spiritual hierarchy, they rarely sought to restructure the society around them. What Mormonism found wrong with antebellum America was that a hireling ministry and centuries of theological traditions had led humanity astray. That had to be rectified, and was, in part by the Mormon restoration. Ultimately, however, the transformation of the world awaited the supernaturally inaugurated millennium.

This realization also mutes the connection between Mormon millenarianism and revolution. From the earliest years, Latter-day Saints have been accused of being subversive to the United States government. To be sure, early Mormon literature is replete with ringing affirmations of the reality of Christ's and the Saints' reign on earth, but they are almost always set in a millennial context. Like many other Christians, the Mormons did expect the eventual fulfillment of scriptural promises that God would make a "full end of all nations" (Jeremiah 30:11) and that "the kingdoms of this world" would become the kingdom of "our Lord and of his Christ" (Revelation 11:15). The crucial question was how and when. At times, LDS writers were not explicit, and this, combined with their definite anticipation of imminent fulfillment, has led some observers to think that Mormons expected to do more before Christ returned than merely be prepared to reign. Still, their fundamental eschatology was clear. The Saints would not be presenting the returning Lord with a political kingdom to rule. Rather, it would be the other way around, though they certainly felt they should do all they could to prepare themselves for that rule. Thus, it is just as likely that the legendary Mormon Council of Fifty, a nineteenth-century governing body set up in anticipation of managing the millennial kingdom and often considered the epitome of Mormon subversiveness, was a symbolic formality more than an actual revolutionary agency prepared to seize secular power.[56]

Far from the Mormon Council of Fifty's moving in to take over the world's citizenry, Christ himself would personally establish "a seat of government among them" which would "put an end to jarring creeds and political wranglings, by uniting the republics, states, provinces, territories, nations, tribes, kindreds, tongues, people, and sects of North and South America in one great and common bond of brotherhood." In the end, "truth and knowledge shall make them free, and love cement their union." Christ, not the Mormon prophet, would "be their king and their lawgiver; while wars shall cease and peace prevail for a thousand years."[57] This proclamation from the Quorum of the Twelve Apostles hardly sounds like a Mormon jihad or coup d'état. On the contrary, it predicts conversion, not coercion, to Christ's millennial standard. As Joseph Smith remarked, "I will not seek to compel any man to believe as I do, only by the force of reasoning, for truth will cut its own way."[58] Those seeking to portray the Prophet as a revolutionary quote his remark "I calculate to be one of the instruments in setting up the Kingdom of Daniel" but leave out the qualifying phrase "by the word of the Lord." They cite his claim "I intend to lay a foundation that will revolutionize the whole world" but omit "it will not be by Sword or Gun that this Kingdom will roll on—the power of truth is such that—all nations will be under necessity of obeying the Gospel."[59]

But what about Smith's candidacy for President of the United States? Was that not clear evidence of theocratic intent? Did it not raise the specter of an un-American marriage of church and state? The *Times and Seasons* replied,

> We . . . shrink from the idea of introducing any thing that would in the least deprive us of our freedom, or reduce us to a state of religious vassalage. . . . No one can be more opposed to an unhallowed alliance of this kind than ourselves, but while we would deprecate any alliance having a tendency to deprive the sons of liberty of their

rights, we cannot but think that the course taken by many of our politicians is altogether culpable, that the division is extending too far, and that in our jealousy lest a union of this kind should take place, we have thrust out God from all of our political movements. . . . Certainly if any person ought to interfere in political matters it should be those whose minds and judgments are influenced by correct principles—religious as well as political.[60]

The issue for the Saints, before Christ returned to set up the millennial monarchy, was not the legitimacy of the government so much as the suitability of the governors. Mormons cherished the Constitution and saw it as part of that perfect primordium untainted by profane history.[61] The same, however, could not be said of subsequent laws and leaders. Like the Abolitionists, the Saints found politicians unsympathetic to their deeply held convictions. As a result, the Abolitionists felt the need to create an independent political party—the Liberty party—dedicated to implementing their ideals; the Latter-day Saints ran Joseph Smith for President. Other high-toned reformers likewise turned from moral to political persuasion in an attempt to legislate their beliefs. One scholar has observed of Yankee Whigs that wherever they "went in their westward migration, they carried with them a righteous and confident urge to use the secular government to create a morally unified society."[62]

While willing to use political power or worldly wealth to preserve or promote their spiritual enterprise, these were far from ends in themselves. The idea that the Saints were basically victimized outcasts, soured on a society that had cut them out of their fair share, misrepresents their motives. Their primary concern was to see the kingdom of God fully established on earth. Consistent with this outlook, the Holy Book tended to be a greater motivator for them than either the pocketbook or the ballot-box. Millenarian Mormons knew that soon enough a new world order would prevail. They would patiently do their part to prepare the way for the Lord's return and their millennial reign with him. From this perspective, they were more interested in the bursting open of graves than in the breaking down of institutions. They were a people whose figuralism linked them to Moses in esteeming "the reproach of Christ greater riches than the treasures of the earth" (Hebrews 11:26). "Viewed in this light," writes the religious historian Timothy Smith, "the Saints perceived themselves to have caught hold of the little end of the biggest thing in the universe—a cornucopia of unimaginable blessings promising 'the riches of eternity.'" One did not have to feel marginal to, or be seeking to subvert, "the existing social and economic order to opt for such an inheritance. Yeomen and craftsmen, captains and queens could recognize the infinite value of this 'pearl of great price.'"[63]

7

Apocalyptic Adversaries:
Mormonism Meets Millerism

In his diary for Sunday, 12 February 1843, Joseph Smith recorded that "seven or eight young men came to see me, part of them from the city of New York. They treated me with the greatest respect. I showed them the fallacy of Mr. Miller's *data* concerning the coming of Christ and the end of the world, or as it is commonly called, Millerism, and preached them quite a sermon."[1] Perhaps the two most successful millenarian groups in mid-nineteenth-century America were the Mormons and the Millerites. They flourished at roughly the same time and in roughly the same area, and a close comparison of the two can produce a more nuanced understanding of *Mormon* millenarianism.[2]

William Miller was an upstate New York farmer old enough to be Joseph Smith's father. At about the same time that young Joseph Smith was undergoing his religious turmoil, Miller also came to the conclusion that "there are but few who walk the narrow path."[3] While Smith was learning new truths through visions and revelations, Miller felt that, by careful study of the Bible, he was discovering the keys to prophetic interpretation. What he discerned was a symbolic uniformity throughout Biblical prophecy whereby if in one passage a beast symbolized a kingdom, or a day a year, then such should *always* be the case, unless otherwise specified in the text. Focusing particularly, but not exclusively, on the books of Daniel and Revelation, he discovered through a complex method of symbolic and typological interpretation that the Second Coming of Christ would occur "about the year 1843."[4]

Miller arrived at this insight around the same time that Joseph Smith had his "First Vision," but he did not publicize it beyond a small circle of family and friends until 1831. That year a neighboring Baptist congregation invited him to preach in their meetinghouse, and his public ministry began. For the rest of the decade he preached throughout northeastern New York and western Vermont. Somewhat to his frustration, he was appreciated more for his successful revivals than for his adventism. In 1836, he published his foundational work, *Evidence from Scripture and History of the Second Coming of Christ about the Year 1843; Exhibited in a Course of Lectures,* known simply as *Lectures,* and continued to gather new recruits.

It was not until 1840, however, when Joshua V. Himes, veteran evangelical reformer and friend of William Lloyd Garrison, took up the crusade, that Millerism really became an independent and self-conscious movement. Himes alone did for Millerism what Sidney Rigdon with his pulpit eloquence, Parley Pratt with his pamphleteering zeal, and Brigham Young with his organizational ability did for Mormonism. Under Himes's aggressive leadership, Millerite newspapers—the *Signs of the Times* in Boston and the *Midnight Cry* in New York—were started; regional and general conferences were convened; "Second Advent libraries" were established; separate adventist prayer meetings and Bible studies were inaugurated; and more extensive, better organized lecture tours were carried out.

Unlike Joseph Smith, Miller founded no new church. Just as Wesley originally intended Methodism to be a reinvigorating movement within the Anglican church, so Miller felt that belief in the "near advent" of Christ was something that could vitalize all denominations. In a way, Millerism was simply one more of the numerous nineteenth-century reform movements like Temperance or Abolitionism that focused on a single issue, a single crusade, and drew devotees from a wide variety of churches. This contributed to its doctrinally diverse character. As one historian has noted, "The Millerites varied greatly. Millerism was many things to many people, with little consensus of belief or practice, a 'movement' rife with disputes and contradictions."[5]

There was, of course, the common doctrinal core centered on belief in the personal, literal, and imminent return of Jesus Christ. This Miller stressed frequently. In a synopsis of his beliefs published in 1841 (with which most premillennialists would have had few quibbles), he declared,

> I believe that the Scriptures do reveal unto us in plain language that Jesus Christ will appear again on this earth, that he will come in the

glory of God, in the clouds of heaven, with all his Saints and angels; that he will raise the dead bodies of all his Saints who have slept, change the bodies of all that are alive on the earth that are his, and both these living and raised Saints will be caught up to meet the Lord in the air. There the Saints will be judged and presented to the Father, without spot or wrinkle. . . . Then will the Father give the bride to the son Jesus Christ; and when the marriage takes place, the church will become the "New Jerusalem," the "beloved city." And while this is being done in the air, the earth will be cleansed by fire, the elements will melt with fervent heat, the works of men will be destroyed, the bodies of the wicked will be burned to ashes, the devil and evil spirits with the souls and spirits of those who have rejected the gospel will be banished from the earth, shut up in the pit or place prepared for the devil and his angels, and will not be permitted to visit the earth again until 1000 years. This is the first resurrection and first judgment. Then Christ and his people will come down from the heavens, or middle air, and live with his Saints on the new earth in a new heaven, or dispensation, forever, even forever, and ever. After 1000 years shall have passed away . . . the sea, death and hell will give up their dead. . . . The Saints will judge them, the justice of God will drive them from the earth into the lake of fire and brimstone, where they will be tormented day and night, forever and ever. "This is the second death." After the second resurrection and second judgment, the righteous will then possess the earth forever.[6]

As late as 1842, despite Miller's long-standing belief that the end would occur "about the year 1843," the matter of a definite time had been subordinated to acceptance of the more general premillennial scenario set forth above. A general conference in December 1841 announced that it was necessary only for Millerites to believe in the "near" advent of Christ rather than a definite time. However, leading Millerites soon pressed for acceptance of 1843 as a test of fellowship. As a result, some left the movement. With time drawing to a close, Miller refined his prediction. In a synopsis of his views published in the *Midnight Cry*, he wrote, "I believe the time can be known by all who desire to understand and to be ready for his coming. And I am fully convinced that some time between March 21st, 1843, and March 21st, 1844, according to the Jewish mode of computation of time, Christ will come."[7]

Almost as important as belief in a definite time was rejection of the popular notions of a temporal millennium and the literal return of the Jews to Jerusalem. By "temporal millennium," Miller meant the postmillennial doctrine that Jesus would personally come only after the thousand years and that the world would gradually be turned into a millennium as people turned to Christ. From Miller's perspective, individuals who taught such a doctrine fulfilled the Matthean prophecy of people who would say, "My lord delayeth his coming."[8] Miller read the Bible to the effect that immediately before Christ's coming the world would be "as it was in the days of Noah," not in a condition of Christian harmony. This, of course, was the standard premillennialist position.

In denying the literal restoration of the Jews to their homeland, however, the Millerites parted company with other millenarians, including the Latter-day Saints. The concept even caused problems within the Millerite fold and is one example of the diversity among believers in the near advent of Christ. For Miller, the matter was quite clear. Old Testament prophecy regarding Israel would be fulfilled symbolically in the Christian church, not literally in the Jewish nation.[9] But, as one historian has noted, "The issue actually fractured adventism in New York City where a group of 'judaizers' who believed that the Jews must return to Palestine before the end of the world seceded from the Millerites' General Conference, established their own meeting, and adopted Jewish customs and clothing."[10]

As 1843 wore on, the tempo of the "midnight cry" was stepped up. Tent meetings, camp meetings, and the famous Millerite chart, a visual aid filled with horned beasts and prophetic numbers, were seen in major population centers throughout the Northeast. There was also a radicalizing tendency within the movement. By fall, a new cry was being raised—"Come out of Babylon." To the chagrin of former pewmates, all nonadventists came to be regarded as corrupt apostates and the entire Christian world, not just Roman Catholicism, was labeled Babylon, "the great whore." Of course, Latter-day Saints, while holding freedom of worship in high regard and striving to maintain friendly relations with their unbelieving neighbors, all along had expressed a theologically similar denunciation of the salvific validity of any church in Christendom. For the Millerites, though, what led to their distinct "come-outer" phase from mid-1843 on was both increasing persecution and their own insistence on belief in an 1843 advent as the litmus test for true Christianity.[11]

As the predicted year elapsed and 22 March 1844 dawned, Millerites faced their first disconfirmation. Apparently most responded as A. N. Bentley did when he wrote to Miller, "As God has lengthened out our day, I for one, feel thankful."[12] This reaction is not as surprising as it might seem given the Festinger theory that where belief is strong, social reinforcement pronounced, and commitment irreversible, belief actually increases rather than decreases in the wake of disconfirmation.[13]

Spring of 1844 brought new hope, and the summer new campaigns. Most significantly, veteran adventist Samuel Snow reexamined the prophecies and announced his discovery that a specific day, the Jewish Day of Atonement—the "seventh month and tenth day"— which he calculated to be 22 October 1844, would be the actual date of Christ's return.[14] This was just what eager adventists were hoping for, and the new "cry" readily caught on. Himes, more concerned with the movement than the moment, enthused, "'43 never made so great and good an impression as this has done . . . for ought I know he may come on the 7th month & 10th day."[15] Miller was not so sure. Despite claims to the contrary, he never felt he had violated the Savior's words that "the day and hour knoweth no man." He had specified only the year. Now here was an actual date being put forward. Not until two weeks before the set time did he change his mind. Finally, and to the great delight of all Millerites, he wrote to Himes, "I see a glory in the seventh month which I never saw before. . . . Thank the Lord. I am almost home. Glory! Glory! Glory! . . . I am strong in the opinion that the next will be the last Lord's day sinners will ever have in probation."[16]

Without ascension robes and not on hill tops, Millerites gathered quietly on the designated day to preach, pray, and await the advent.[17] During their vigil, they watched the hours tick by "until a faint glow in the east, for ages the sign of renewal, brought not cheer but despair" to these anxious adventists.[18] The story, of course, does not end with the "Great Disappointment," as it was called, for in time the Seventh-day Adventists, the Christian Advent church, and several other smaller, more ephemeral groups rose out of the ashes of Millerism. Nonetheless, against this backdrop the Mormon-Millerite encounter of the early 1840s can be properly evaluated.

Since the Millerites were also Baptists, Methodists, and Congregationalists, it comes as no surprise to learn that they shared the usual

Protestant antipathy to Mormonism as unscriptural, unevangelical, and even diabolical. Mormons were perceived as being outside the religious mainstream and thus aroused deep-seated suspicion in an identity-anxious antebellum America.[19] Most of the relatively few comments Millerites made about Mormonism could have come from any sector of American Christianity and consisted of the usual bombastic denunciation and caricature.[20] Only one full-scale attempt was made to refute the Mormons—Joshua V. Himes's 1842 pamphlet, *Mormon Delusions and Monstrosities*—and it, admittedly, was merely a pastiche of other anti-Mormon attacks. The first half consisted of a reprint of Alexander Campbell's 1831 attack on the Book of Mormon, and the latter half was excerpted from La Roy Sunderland's *Mormonism Exposed*, published several years earlier in New York.[21] Even Himes's own preface, in which he outlined particular objections to Mormonism, was borrowed material. The point is that Millerites mounted no independent attack on Mormonism.[22] With others, they deplored the temporal involvements of LDS church leaders, which they took to be too authoritarian and monetarily motivated. Above all, though, they denounced the possibility of extra-biblical Scripture and the Mormon claim to modern prophecy.

The Millerite view of revelation was the one which had held sway in majoritarian Christianity since the days of the Montanist controversy late in the second century. Montanus, like Joseph Smith, believed that the Spirit would continue to speak anew in each age, even at times to the superseding of previous prophets and apostles. For the early Catholic fathers, as for later believers, this seemed to lay Christianity at the mercy of the prophets of each new generation. The Johannine promise that the Spirit would lead into all truth, therefore, was redefined to mean that the Spirit *had* uniquely *led* the original apostles into all truth as they composed the books of the New Testament and would lead subsequent generations of Christians to that same truth only through their writings, not through direct personal communications from God. As Tertullian graphically summarized it, "The Holy Spirit was chased into a book."[23] Thus, even though Mormons and Millerites, or Mormons and almost any other religious group, shared a belief in revelation, the term was understood quite differently.

If Millerites were distracted from examining Mormon eschatology by more objectionable elements in the Latter-day Saint faith, the Mormons, on the other hand, had little else to notice in Millerism. Intent on discrediting each other, neither group acknowledged what they had in common. It is important, therefore, to pause and identify what they did share. Contrary to the prevailing postmillennialism of the day, both groups taught the literal, personal return of Christ to inaugurate the millennium. Both groups believed that at Christ's coming he would destroy the wicked (which they each characterized as everyone but themselves), raise the faithful dead as the first resurrection, renew the earth, and reign with the believers for a thousand years of bliss. In the end, heaven would not lie beyond the bounds of time and space, but would be located on a changed earth. In substance, these were beliefs held in common by all premillennial thinkers of the day.[24]

On other matters, however, the Saints felt they had to take exception to Millerism. Though the satirical tone of their responses differed little from the Millerites' or from polemics of the period generally, they did, in a number of articles, sermons, and pamphlets, deal with significant eschatological issues.[25] Most LDS commentary comes from the early months of 1843, as the advent year was about to commence, and then again the next winter as it was about to end. Traveling elders had earlier encountered and mentioned Millerite lecturers, and the Boston-based Mormon John Hardy had written a noneschatologically oriented rebuttal to Himes's *Mormon Monstrosities* the year before, but 1843 marks the intensification of the discussion.[26]

A major Latter-day Saint objection to Millerism, and one peculiar to the Mormons, was their claim that Miller and his followers were "running where they had not been sent," that they were unauthorized to raise the "midnight cry." To do so would require modern, plenary revelation and a prophet to receive it, both of which the Millerites vigorously eschewed. As Noah Packard expressed it in his tract *Millerism Exposed,* "[Matthew 25:6] shows plainly that someone will receive a revelation and command to give the Midnight Cry; and it cannot be the Millerites, for they do not believe in modern revelation." Packard also read Matthew 24:25—"who then is a faithful and wise servant whom his Lord hath made ruler over his household to give them meat in due season"—as evidence that there must be a divinely commissioned representative on earth to help usher in the millennium. Said he, "Here we find a single servant spoken of whom the Lord, and not man, will set over his household, to give them meat before his coming, or in due season."[27]

In substance, this was the same criticism that Mormons leveled against all Christian denominations. If God had an authorized servant on earth, then, as Amos pointed out and Joseph Smith himself recognized, the Lord certainly would not circumvent him. Responding to the claims of Hiram Redding that he had seen the "sign of the Son of Man," Joseph retorted, "He has not seen the sign of the son of man as foretold by Jesus, neither has any man . . . for the Lord hath not shown me any such sign, and, as the prophet saith, so it must be: Surely the Lord God will do nothing, but he revealeth his secret unto his servants the prophets [Amos 3:7]. Therefore, hear this, O earth, the Lord will not come to reign over the righteous, in this world, in 1843, nor until everything for the bridegroom is ready."[28]

Whether or not Redding was a Millerite or Joseph Smith was referring to Miller's prediction, the press took it that way. Less than two months after Smith's comment first appeared in the *Times and Seasons*, it was quoted in the Millerite newspaper *Midnight Cry* with this editorial comment: "One day the world represents Mormonism and Millerism as twin brothers. The next, they hear that 'Joe Smith' has wiped all the stain from his pure skirts which a belief in Christ's near coming would attach to it, and they seem disposed to fondle him as their favorite pet. [This prophecy] from the Mormon imposter is going the rounds as if it afforded great relief."[29]

This was not the last time Joseph Smith would wipe from his garments the "stain" of belief in what by then was an almost immediate advent, nor was Amos 3:7 his only rationale for doing so. A month later at General Conference on 6 April 1843, he remarked, "Were I going to prophesy I would prophesy the end will not come in 1844 or 5 or 6 or [for] 40 years." And his reason was clearly stated: "I was once praying earnestly upon this subject and a voice said unto me, My son, if thou livest till thou art 85 years of age, thou shalt see the face of the son of man."[30] Several days earlier he had made the same disclosure to a private gathering with this additional commentary, "I was left thus without being able to decide wether this coming referred to the beginning of the Millennium, or to some previous appearing, or wether I should die and thus see his face. I believe the coming of the son of man will not be any sooner than that time."[31]

For the moment, this seemed to calm concerns about an imminent advent, but in the early months of 1844, Millerism again became an issue. John Taylor noted in the *Times and Seasons* that "the proselytes of Miller are also holding forth in this city, as well as in all the principal cities of the west."[32] In late January, Sidney Rigdon debated one such Millerite itinerant, and the discussion reportedly "excited a good deal of interest."[33] On March 10, with only days remaining before the expiration of the appointed year, Joseph Smith again took up the matter. John Fullmer recorded his message thus: "The Revelation of the Son of Man from Heaven would not be in this year, nor the next; and he would say to his Millerite friends, that it *would not in* forty *years to come*. He uttered all this in the *name of the Lord,* and said we should go home and write it."[34]

Smith's reasoning for so declaring grew out of another answer to prayer: "I have asked of the Lord concerning his coming, & while asking, the Lord gave me a sign & said in the days of Noah I set a bow in the heavens as a sign & token that in any year that the bow should be seen the Lord would not come, but there should be seed time—harvest during that year, but whenever you see the bow withdraw, it shall be a token that their shall be famine pestilence & great distress among the nations." Thus, he declared, "I take the responsibility upon myself to prophesy in the name of the Lord that Christ will not come this year as Miller has prophecyed, for we have seen the bow."[35]

Direct, divine revelation was ultimately the most reliable reason for rejecting Millerism, but there were other reasons as well. One of the most common was that the Millerite calculation left insufficient time for all the necessary precursor events to take place. The gist of Rigdon's argument against Millerism was that "the prophecies which are to be fulfilled before the Savior's coming would not allow of so short a time as is specified."[36] Or, as Joseph Smith told his young visitors from New York, "The prophecies must be fulfilled; the sun must be darkened and the moon turned into blood, and many more things take place before Christ would come."[37]

Of that list of essential antecedents, the most unmistakable was the gathering of the Jews to Jerusalem. In one of the earliest references to Miller, and one that set the tone for what would follow, Parley Pratt and Elias Higbee, in their 1840 "Proclamation to the World," declared that "as to the signs of the times, we believe that the gathering of Israel and the second advent of Messiah, with all the great events connected therewith, are near at hand. . . . But we disclaim all fellowship with the predictions of the Rev. Mr. Miller, Rev. Joseph Wolff, and others— such as that the Lord will come in 1840, 1841, 1843, 1847, and so on." Their reasoning was simple: "We do not believe that he will come until the Jews gather to Palestine and rebuild their city."[38] George J. Adams delivered a series of lectures in Boston in June 1842, which included the same attack on Millerism. His principal argument was that "the Jews must be gathered home from their long dispersion, and rebuild their city on its own heaps of ruins, even Jerusalem itself, before Christ should come."[39] Joseph Smith later elaborated: "Jerusalem must be rebuilt & Judah must return & water come out from under the temple—the waters of the dead sea be healed.—it will take some time to build the walls & the Temple. &c & all this must be done before the Son of Man will make his appearance."[40] The conclusion was obvious. "As this cannot be done in one year," wrote early Mormon pamphleteer, Moses Martin, "Mr. Miller's words must fall to the ground, or else those of the holy prophets of old."[41]

In August 1843, while in Philadelphia on a mission to the East, Wilford Woodruff and several other apostles went to hear leading Millerite Josiah Litch lecture on the Millerite view of the gathering of the Jews. Litch taught that when the Lord promised the land of Canaan to Abraham's "seed," he meant it singularly as having reference to Christ, "not to seeds. . . . So the land belongs to Jesus Christ & not the Jews." Moreover, it was destined to be occupied "not [by] the Jews the natural seed, but [by] those that are Baptised into Jesus Christ & his spiritual Children." This would occur when Christ "comes with his Church & Body & will then take Jerrusalem."[42] Woodruff responded to Litch's lecture thus: "I will admit," he wrote, "that . . . if the Jews ever go to Jerrusalem they will not go as Jews but all Christians as Christ body &c &c." He added that this, however, did not "do away with the literal fulfillment of the Bible concerning the return of the Jews and the rebuilding of Jerrusalem."[43] On that point, the Saints could not compromise. Moses Martin considered it "consummate ignorance" to "suppose that prophecy has any allusion to spiritual gathering" and declared that "it would take a larger and more powerful spiritualizing machine than Mr. Miller" to make him believe it.[44]

Indeed, it was precisely here, in the matter of how literally to interpret Scripture, and prophecy in particular, that another reason is discernible for why Mormons found Millerism intolerable. "Prophecy," wrote Miller is "highly figurative," and requires a consistent system of symbolic and typological interpretation.[45] Actually, this was a premise shared by Biblical commentators at least since the days of the Reformation.[46] But it was not satisfactory to the Latter-day Saints. After reading Miller's *Lectures,* Woodruff wrote, "he has made out as much of a whole sail business in spiritualizing the scriptures & trying to make out the fulfillment of all predictions of the old & new Testiment by refering to the French Government & other afairs which was as foreign from the subject as Heaven is from Hell."[47]

Joseph Smith's hermeneutics, however, were simpler. "What is the rule of interpretation?" he asked: *"Just no interpretation at all."* It should be "understood precisely as it reads."[48] While he accepted the traditional historicist view of Daniel wherein Daniel's visions of beasts were matched with successive empires in ancient history, Joseph did not agree that the book of Revelation could be read that way. "John," he declared, "only saw that which . . . was yet in futurity."[49] Furthermore, instead of Daniel's symbolic images of worldly kingdoms, John saw real animals, "strange beasts of which we have no conception" that "had been saved from ten thousand times ten thousand earths like this."[50] These beasts, continued Joseph, "were actually living in heaven, and were actually to have power given to them over the inhabitants of the earth precisely according to the plain reading of the revelations."[51] As an example, he cited the beast with seven heads and ten horns mentioned in Revelation 13. Admitting that it had been interpreted as everything from Nebuchadnezzar to Catholicism, he declared, "The beast John saw was an actual beast to whom power was to be given . . . to destroy the inhabitants of the earth."[52]

Miller, on the other hand, had no place for making distinctions between prophets. For him, all the inspired authors acted "in union, speaking the same things, observing the same rules, so that a Bible reader may almost with propriety suppose, let him read in what prophecy he may that he is reading the same prophet, the same author."[53] This premise was fundamental to his whole system of prophetic numerology and allowed him, by its uniformly applicable principles, to range across the entire Bible and find united testimony to 1843 as the year of Christ's coming. Since the Lord told Ezekiel, "I have appointed thee each day for a year" (Ezekiel 4:6), Miller felt justified in applying that equation, known as the day-year theory, to *all* prophecy wherein numbers of days were specified. For instance, Daniel 8:13–14 foretells that after "two thousand and three hundred days; then shall the sanctuary be cleansed." Converting the days to years and dating it from 457 B.C., the year he believed Ezra returned to rebuild Jerusalem, Miller calculated that in 1843 the "sanctuary," which he interpreted spiritually as God's people, would be cleansed, or "justified," as part of Christ's coming.[54]

Such prophetic numerology was the final area of Mormon disagreement with Millerite teaching. A very detailed rebuttal of it appeared in the *Times and Seasons* in February 1843. The author appears to have been fully acquainted with the various Millerite calculations and took issue with a number of them, including the example cited above. Predictably, in that case, he opposed the symbolic rendering of "sanctuary," arguing that it referred to the temple sanctuary which was actually "cleansed under Judas Maccabees in B.C. 165."[55] Throughout the article, his purpose was "to show the total failure of days being symbols of years in all cases in the scriptures." For him, "counting prophetic numbers" was "manifest folly."[56]

While editor John Taylor published the rebuttal, he felt the need to qualify it. He was leery of throwing out the baby with the bathwater. Regarding prophetic numbers, he said, "we believe that there is a certainty in them when they are understood; (or why did the prophets give them?) but we do not think that either Mr. Miller or his followers understand them."[57] The trouble with the Millerite computations was that they applied the day-year theory straight across the board without being sensitive to what Taylor called the "different rules of calculation." If Miller would just petition God for revelation, "he may, perhaps, get to know what a prophet's time is . . . and having the spirit of prophecy to know the circumstances under which the numbers were given, and their application, he will be able to arrive at more just conclusions than to believe that the end of the world will be this year, or next."[58]

Of course, anyone could dabble with prophetic numerology, and some Latter-day Saints tried putting it to their own use. In his *Dissertation on Nebuchadnezzar's Dream,* William Appleby expressly applied the day-year theory to Revelation 12:6 where a woman—which he took to be genuine Christianity—is described as having "fled into the wilderness" for "a thousand two hundred and three score days." After reading Mosheim's *Ecclesiastical History,* Appleby decided that "the gifts and blessings of Christ," which he believed characterized the true church, "began to decline in the days of Constantine, and about the year A.D. 570, they were all fled." Then, "by adding the 570 to the 1260," he wrote, "we have 1830, which is the *year* she must be organized" and come forth out of the wilderness.[59]

Franklin D. Richards included in the front of his "Scriptural Items" notebook several pages of numerological calculations. First, he placed the removal of the "daily sacrifice" in 720 B.C. coincident with the traditional date for the carrying away of the 10 tribes. Then he added the 1290 day-years mentioned in Daniel 12:11 to arrive at A.D. 570. Thus by a path different from Appleby's, Richards arrived at the same point in time for the "woman" being "driven into a State of disorganization or into the Wilderness where she dwelt 1260 days or years" according to Rev 12:6, 14. "The Amount of the above numbers (1260 + 570 = 1830) is the Year of our Lord in which the Time would expire that the Woman should dwell in the Wilderness and in which we infer that she left her place of obscurity and again dwelt among men which she did on the 6th day of the 4th month of A.D. 1830."[60] In 1829, a revelation had announced the "beginning of the rising up and the coming forth of my church out of the wilderness—clear as the moon, and fair as the sun, and terrible as an army with banners."[61]

While agreeing with those who identified the organization of the LDS church with the emergence of the woman from the wilderness of apostasy—an idea implicit in the use of the term "restoration"— Smith was less sanguine about the overall system of prophetic numerology. Yet he did not dismiss it out of hand. In his April 1843 Conference address he evidenced both familiarity with, and skepticism of, prophetic numerology and used it against the Millerite timetable. Turning to Revelation 14:6–7, where the angel announces that "the hour of [God's] judgment is come," Joseph interpreted the word *hour* in terms of the apostle Peter's equation of "1000 [human] years as 1 [divine] day." Thus, by his calculation, the "hour of judgment" would last "41 years 8 months." The Prophet wasn't clear on when the period began, but he did say that "the coming of the Son of man never will be, never can be till the judgments spoken of for this hour are poured out, which judgments are commenced."[62] Appleby was more definite: "14 years has passed since the Gospel was committed: take 14 from 41 leaves 27 years for the winding up scene."[63] Whatever the starting point, the "hour" still left many years before the Second Coming, thus negating Miller's computation. Moreover, Joseph cited one prophecy commentator to the effect that there would still be "45 years according to Bible reckoning" left before the end of time.[64]

Another passage popular among prophetic numerologists, to which Joseph Smith also referred, was Hosea 6:2: "After two days will he revive us; in the third day he will raise us up, and we shall live in his sight." This seemed to be a clear description of the first resurrection and millennial reign of the Saints in the presence of Christ. Miller interpreted the two "days" as two thousand-year periods prior to the millennium and dated their commencement from a "league" the Jews supposedly made with the Romans in 158 B.C., which he felt was being discussed in Hosea 5. This, of course, led to 1843 as the year of millennial dawning.[65] The other common prophetic calculation was the "seven times" of Leviticus 26:28 which, by the day-year theory, totaled 2520 years. For reasons left unexplained, Smith dated both prophetic equivalencies from an unstated event in 630 B.C. "which," he said, "brings it to 1890."[66]

How serious about prophetic numerology Joseph Smith really was, or whether he was simply humoring the Millerites, is uncertain.[67] What is clear is that the Saints were more involved with the larger prophetic community of discourse than has generally been assumed.[68] They understood the issues and could reason with the best of the prophecy commentators. Even if Joseph Smith himself was not much given to such matters, the frequency with which the elders were counseled to avoid the topic, and the evidence that they did not, suggests that it was a popular pastime.[69]

Several key insights into Mormonism can be gleaned from the LDS encounter with the Millerites. Prominent in the Mormon response to Millerism was the frequent reference to revelation—revelation to give the "midnight cry," revelation to solve the prophetic numbers, revelation to gather the Jews, and revelation to explain the imagery of prophecy. Dealing with Millerism made revelation's fundamental importance to Mormon millenarianism all the more apparent. Most important, though, was the way in which the Millerite encounter provided impetus for the eventual abatement of the sense among Latter-day Saints that the Second Coming was imminent. As has been shown repeatedly in this study, though neither Joseph Smith nor his followers were given to date-setting, many of their expressions evidence an acute expectation of the impending advent. The early years were heady times for the Saints. Revelations were announced at a breathtaking rate, and the drama of unfolding events convinced many Mormons that they were living on the eve of the Second Coming. Even later in the nineteenth century, during critical times such as the Utah War, the Civil War, and the persecution of the 1880s, the Saints read the "signs of the times" with great anticipation.[70] Nonetheless, for Joseph Smith, responding to Millerism during the final eighteen months of his life appears to have helped him lay aside ideas of an imminent end. His clear and repeated denunciations of a near advent, uttered in reaction to Millerism, suggest that a permanent modification occurred in his thinking at this time. Still, it would not be until the twentieth century that general familiarity with, and reflection on, such comments led the bulk of the Saints away from a belief that the Second Coming was very near. Modern church leaders regularly make calming and qualifying statements which provide a counterpoint to undue anxiety about the nearness of the millennium.

8

The Millenarian Appeal of
Mormonism in England

If millenarianism seems pervasive in Mormonism, it might still be argued that such was merely an American phenomenon, a particular manifestation of the broader democratic revolt underway in the early nineteenth century. Insight can therefore be gained by comparing American Mormons with Latter-day Saints outside the United States. In 1837, the first Mormon missionaries landed in Liverpool. Less than a decade later, one out of every three Latter-day Saints in the world was British, and the vast majority of those were English.[1] Mormonism in early Victorian England, therefore, provides an excellent test case for exploring the essentiality of millenarianism to early Mormonism.[2]

While England and America share a common language and, to a large degree, a common culture, their religious development has been significantly different. The most obvious contrast is that, unlike America, England, since the days of Henry VIII, has had a state religion—Anglicanism.[3] Its Civil War, fought two hundred years before America's, was in large measure a religious war. At that time Puritanism, which sought to "purify" the Church of England of its "popish" precepts and practices, gained the upper hand, but with the subsequent Restoration of scepter and mitre, non-Anglicans became "Dissenters" and were sorely persecuted. Even after the Glorious Revolution in 1688–89, toleration for dissenting religion was limited, and political power continued solely in Anglican hands.[4] By the nineteenth century, the winds of reform were blowing, stimulated in part by the American and French revolutions and the accompanying advance of democracy, and in part by the international Evangelical movement. Still, coming from a country where disestablishment had been accomplished several generations earlier and where ministers as such did not wield political power, Mormon missionaries, despite the transformation underway, saw the religious landscape of England as marred by government-sponsored priestcraft.

At the time of their arrival two out of every three English citizens were members of the Church of England. As might be expected of a church numbering in the millions, all was not well in the Anglican household. For centuries there had been complaints and attempts at reform, and the period just before the coming of the Mormons was no different. While the Church of England in the nineteenth century was actually making improvements in pastoral performance, Mormonism profited from the popular image of its corrupt and disorganized state and drew converts from the disenchanted among the large nominal sector of early Victorian Anglicanism.[5]

A second major branch of English religion at the time of the Saints' arrival consisted of the Dissenters.[6] Though they often tended to dissent from the pro-crown politics of the Tories as well, they acquired the name because of their dissent from the established Church of England. Also known as Nonconformists, they included such groups as the Presbyterians, Congregationalists (or Independents, as they had been called in England since the days of the Civil War), Baptists, and Quakers. Though nationally less significant in number, it appears that more Nonconformists joined the LDS Church than did Anglicans.[7] Aside from occasionally shared political perspectives and similar socioeconomic circumstances, religious sympathies were of primary importance. Nonconformists tended to be responsive to the transatlantic wave of revivalism that had been sweeping both England and America since the mid-eighteenth century.[8]

This connection is typified in an 1838 episode involving Mormon missionaries and a Baptist congregation in Barnoldswicke. Hearing of the profound interest in the Mormon message manifest in the nearby north Lancashire villages of Chatburn and Downham, Barnoldswicke Baptists sent for the Mormon elders. According to the prominent British missionary Joseph Fielding, "six or seven hundred" crowded into the chapel in eager anticipation. Orson Hyde preached on the millenarian theme of the first resurrection and Heber Kimball followed with a discourse on "the first principles of the gospel." As Kimball reported it, "the congregation was overjoyed, tears ran down their cheeks, and the minister could not refrain from frequently clapping his hands together while in the meeting for joy." The service concluded at 10 P.M., but the preacher and some of the people followed the elders to their quarters where discussion continued until four the next morning. So great was the interest that later that morning "a number of influential men suspended operation in their factories to allow their workmen the privilege of hearing us preach."[9]

The leading source of converts to Mormonism, however, seems to have been the Methodists. According to the only statistical study to date, more Methodists were baptized into the church than either Anglicans or Dissenters. This is significant when it is recognized that at the time of the earliest Mormon missions, there were four Anglicans for every one Methodist in England.[10] Methodism began as a renewal movement within the Anglican Church and focused on evangelism and spirituality.[11] "Like Quakerism in the preceding century," explains one historian, "'methodism' was as much a style of spirituality and an affirmation of the possibility of the immediate experience of divinity as it was an organized religious body. It was the most visible sector of a broad movement of popular piety that affirmed that the age of miracles was not past and that Christianity would regain the purity and vitality of its beginnings."[12]

As time passed, however, Methodism followed the sociological model of movement from sect to denomination. Renewal rigidified into regimentation, and the initial outpouring of the spirit was subordinated to institutional concerns. Even before Wesley's death in the final decade of the 1700s, cries were heard that "primitive" Methodism had been lost. Within a few years, splinter groups began to break away, and by the turn of the century it was no longer possible to talk of Methodism as a single entity. In nineteenth-century England, it is necessary to distinguish Wesleyan Methodism or, more simply, Wesleyanism from Primitive Methodism, Independent Methodism, New Connexion Methodism, and a host of others.[13]

This is an important distinction sometimes overlooked in Mormon studies but valuable precisely because it points to the source of a disproportionate number of early English converts. The most obvious example of this was the conversion of hundreds of the United Brethren by apostle Wilford Woodruff. The United Brethren had broken away from the Primitive Methodists who in turn had earlier broken away from the Wesleyans not only for the usual reasons of ecclesiological localism but also on the grounds that the original spirituality had been lost and that a proper understanding of eschatology was lacking.[14] In striving to recapture the early spirit of Methodism in the face of a definite establishmentarian drift in the nineteenth century, non-Wesleyan Methodists were questing for some of the very same values heralded as immediate and available by Mormon missionaries.[15]

Interestingly enough, the kinship with early Methodism did not go unnoticed by the Saints. Parley Pratt reprinted one of John Wesley's sermons in the *Millennial Star* under the heading "JOHN WESLEY A LATTER-DAY SAINT, in Regard to the Spiritual Gifts and the Apostasy of the Church!!"[16] But not all Methodists seeking a charismatic religion were "come-outers." Some, including a number who later converted to Mormonism, could not bring themselves to formally dissociate with Wesleyanism.[17] Therefore, it may be more helpful to look at Methodism as encompassing a spectrum of religious attitudes and ideas rather than one particular set of beliefs and behaviors. Toward one end of the spectrum would be found those individuals, whatever their denominational affiliation, who were interested above all else in enjoying a vital, gifted Christianity and who often espoused a millenarian eschatology. Given the tendency of early Mormon missionaries to stress both the "signs following belief" and the "signs of the times," it is not surprising that a greater percentage of Methodist converts, who themselves were the single most statistically significant group, came from that end of the spectrum.

As in America, the pursuit of the primitive gospel, especially the quest for charisma, was intimately connected with millenarianism. Numbers of searching souls had "pondered long over the scriptures, especially the prophecies and promises of the coming of Christ's kingdom." Many of them "had already had some form of inner-light experience, and all were ready to be influenced by visions and dreams."[18] "I was earnestly looking out," wrote one such individual, "for some one to be visited by the Spirit, to revive the work, and raise up the cause of God. . . . I went everywhere that I heard of any one being visited by the Spirit of God to prophesy, in hopes of finding the truth."[19] Searching souls often made their way to the site of a Mormon sermon and then made their way into the church. Postulating the dismal and "dead" state of institutional Christianity, their millenarian faith was, as another put it, that "something would turn up, either the gospel would be introduced, or afflictions would come upon the nation."[20]

The English had had a long history of interest in eschatology, and the half-century before the Latter-day Saints arrived was to be their most prolific period.[21] As huge armies marched across the European continent and regimes toppled, events triggered by the French Revolution excited an atmosphere of millennial prophecy and expectation unparalleled since the Civil War.[22] Serious study of the prophecies reached high tide in England in the late 1820s and 1830s and was symbolized by the 1835 publication of Joshua Brooks's massive *Dictionary of Writers on the Prophecies.* The Saints, of course, were deeply interested in such matters. In July 1840, apostle Willard Richards made note in his journal that he had picked up "a new work on the dispersion & history of the Jews, cleansing of the Sanctuary, 2nd coming of Christ Reign with his Saints and End of the World by Samuel Kent," from which he proceeded to fill several pages of his diary with notes.[23] The flurry of millenarian interest on both sides of the Atlantic at this time was so pronounced that it has caused the historian Ernest Sandeen to ask, "Is it only a coincidence that the excitement over the imminent second advent and the dawning millennium broke out in both Britain and America during 1828–32? Is it only a coincidence that a return to apostolic simplicity and power was being sought in both countries just at this time or that speaking in tongues and healing should become local sensations?"[24]

Whatever the explanation, a more conducive setting for the spread of Mormonism could hardly be imagined. These were crucial themes in the Mormon message, and the Saints did not hesitate to capitalize on the eschatological excitement they encountered. Exactly how English millenarianism helped serve as midwife to Mormonism becomes more clear through specific examples. One apparently significant source of early English converts was the Christian Society of Robert Aitken.[25] The group was based in Liverpool and was not yet two years old when the Mormons arrived in 1837. Aitken was a disappointed Anglican who sought ordination in the Wesleyan Connexion, was rebuffed, mingled temporarily with the schismatic Wesleyan Methodist Association, and eventually broke away to create his own society. He had moved steadily toward the evangelical, almost pentecostal, end of the religious spectrum, and had therefore earned the usual caricature of "ranter." He also became an avid student of the prophecies and a premillennialist. As Mormon convert Edward Tullidge remembered, "his themes on the ancient prophecies and their fulfillment in 'these latter days' were very like" those of "eloquent Sidney Rigdon" and included "glorious outbursts of inspiration when he dwelt upon the prospect of a latter-day church rising in fulfillment of the prophets."[26]

In a published sermon entitled "The Second Coming of Christ," Aitken declared that "the doctrine of our Lord's second advent is a key to the prophetical Scriptures both of the Old and New Testament." To those who chided his interest in prophecy, he remarked, "There is life or death, destruction or salvation, in the taking heed to, or in the despising of unfulfilled prophecy."[27] What it showed him, in standard millenarian fashion, was the overwhelmingly apostate condition of "Gentile Churches." In reasoning that resonated for Mormons, Aitken remarked,

> And now, if we want a standard whereby to judge of the apostasy of the present churches, we must take the church of Christ when the apostatizing spirit was least manifested—that is to say, in the apostolic age. With this pattern in our eye, where, I ask, are the gifts of the spirit—where the miraculous power—where the gift of healing—where the gift of prophecy—where the signs that were appointed to follow them that believed? What has become of the angel messengers, who so frequently appeared to the primitive Christians? . . . Where is the persecution that all that live godly in Christ Jesus shall endure—and where is the being hated of all men for Christ's name's sake? Alas! alas! my brethren, the gifts of the Spirit are gone, and, I fear, most of the graces have gone with them; and, as to suffering and reproach, to which the Church is called, such things have long been mere matters of history.[28]

By the end of the decade, Aitken's Christian Society had expanded to a number of urban centers, including London, where Wilford Woodruff first heard him. Woodruff readily recognized a doctrinal kinship and wrote that Aitken had "presented some of the most sublime truths that I had ever heard delivered by a sectarian priest." He was delighted that Aitken had "come out against the sexts" but noted that "he has got as far as he can." Woodruff later reported that "there was some little prospect of the Rev. R. Aitken's A.M. receiving & embracing the work which will open doors to many souls so I felt to rejoice."[29]

Actually, "Aitkenism" had already opened doors, though Aitken himself never joined the LDS Church and eventually returned to Anglicanism. In the published journal of his 1837–38 mission, Heber C. Kimball wrote, "Soon after our arrival in England, great many of the

AIKENITES embraced the gospel."[30] The nucleus of the first branch in Liverpool raised up by John Taylor and Joseph Fielding in early 1840 were converts from Aitken's Hope Street Chapel.[31] A prominent English convert and one-time president of the Staffordshire Conference, Alfred Cordon, had previously been an Aitkenite class leader and was responsible for the conversion of other Aitkenites, including an entire congregation in Doncaster, Yorkshire, during his missionary labors. And John Greenhow, president of the large Liverpool Conference, told of his former experience as an elder in the Christian Society, describing how there was a "general consciousness prevailing" among the Aitkenites "that something was wanting."[32] When the Mormon elders arrived, that something was discovered.

Another adventist sect from which English Mormonism may have drawn a small contingent was the Christian Israelites.[33] John Wroe, an eccentric zealot from Bowling, managed to convince a number of former Southcottians in the 1820s that he should be regarded as prophet and successor to Joanna Southcott. A generation earlier, prophet Southcott had gathered around herself a significant lower-class movement which was both millenarian and charismatic.[34] Wroe added a Judaizing attempt to revive Old Testament law, liturgy, and priesthood, and called his group the Christian Israelites. Mosaic codes were to be fulfilled to the letter, including circumcision, the eating of kosher food, the wearing of beards, and even the learning of Hebrew. He also accepted the "British-Israel" notion that the English were actually the lost tribes of Israel but did not know it. He promptly assigned converts an Israelite lineage, and called these "invisible," as well as the "visible" (historic), Jews to gather to the New Jerusalem to be built in Ashton, a little town just outside of Manchester. There they constructed a lavish "Sanctuary" able to hold several thousand. The biblically prescribed walls around the Holy City, however, were never completed since Wroe was run out of town in 1831 for indiscretions with young virgins, given, as Abishag to David, to "cherish" him.

The movement continued for a while, but by 1842 the Sanctuary had been sold and, according to William Cooke Taylor, on a tour that year of Lancashire manufacturing districts, some Ashton Israelites had been absorbed into Mormonism.[35] The case of James Wood is perhaps typical of the ideological connection. Wood lived in Wroe's new headquarters in Wakefield, Yorkshire, and had been impressed with Wroeite sermons on the "second advent." This in turn heightened his receptiveness to the "Restored Gospel," for when he received from Ashton friends a copy of Parley Pratt's apocalyptic *Letter to the Queen,* he wrote to Pratt that the LDS church, "if I am not greatly mistaken," is "that Church I have long wished to see established in the earth."[36]

One group that approached Mormonism in its pronounced blend of primitivism and millenarianism was the Catholic Apostolic Church, or, more popularly, the Irvingites.[37] Joseph Smith once remarked that the Irvingites "counterfeited the truth perhaps the nearest of any of our modern sectarians," though he might have said that they *anticipated* the truth closer than any others.[38] In the 1820s, Edward Irving, a Scot, was ministering to a Scottish Presbyterian congregation in London and had attracted considerable attention with the eloquence of his sermons. His interest in biblical prophecy brought him into contact with Henry Drummond, who invited him to a series of prophetic study conferences held annually during the late 1820s at Drummond's palatial estate in Albury. These conferences resulted in the publication of the three-volume *Dialogues on Prophecy,* which represents the pinnacle of premillennial discourse in England.[39]

The Albury group believed that England had become an "apostate nation." In Irving's analysis, as in Mormon thought, the deaths of the Apostles resulted in the apostasy of the Church, and if ever Christianity were to be restored to its original faith and unity, it would again require a foundation of twelve apostles. "We cried unto the Lord," declared Irving, "for apostles, prophets, evangelists, pastors, and teachers . . . because we saw it written in God's Word that these are the appointed ordinances for the edifying of the body of Jesus."[40] The first apostle was called by prophecy in 1832, and by 1835, the same year the LDS Quorum of the Twelve was reconstituted in Kirtland, the full number of twelve Irvingite apostles had been commissioned. This apostolate and a never fully constituted quorum of "seventies" exercised leadership over the whole Catholic Apostolic Church. The rest of the Irvingite ministry was essentially episcopal—a supervising bishop, or "angel" as he was called, who presided over a local church or region, a council of elders, and a group of deacons to assist with temporal affairs.

Spiritual gifts were the experiential aspect of primitive Christianity that the Irvingites sought in prayer. When various gifts were manifested in Scotland in 1830, it caught the attention of Irving and his London congregation. At the final prophetic conference in Albury that year, the chairman made it clear that not only did they have the "responsibility" to "inquire into the state of those gifts said to be now present in the west of Scotland" but that "it is our duty to pray for the revival of the gifts manifested in the primitive Church."[41] Within a year, tongues and prophecy were prominent in Irving's congregation, and healings occurred as well. This prompted the actual break in 1832 with the Presbyterian Church and the formation of the new Catholic Apostolic Church.

Though Irvingites tended to be solidly middle class and more prosperous than most English Mormon converts, primitivist and millenarian similarities led to several contacts between the two groups. There was, for example, the episode involving the Irvingite envoy John Hewitt and the LDS brethren in Kirtland. In June 1835, only a few months after the Mormon Quorum of the Twelve had been organized, Hewitt arrived in Ohio, ostensibly to "examine the work." From what the Irvingites had been able to read in a Mormon periodical, they considered themselves and the Saints united in "the Apostolic cause," and they promised much-needed temporal assistance from affluent emigrants if Hewitt brought back a favorable report. However, despite a follow-up effort on the part of the Kirtland brethren, Hewitt never completed his mission and instead settled down in the neighboring town of Painesville to teach school.[42] The next year, two men from Scotland paid a call on the Prophet "to make inquiry about the work of the Lord in these last days" and spoke to him about the "prophesies" of Edward Irving.[43]

It was as a precursor, however, especially in Canada and to a degree in Scotland, that Irvingism played its most important role in the Mormon drama.[44] Canadian convert Joseph Fielding described thus his state of mind prior to hearing the Mormon elders: "I had for some time been much interested in the subject of the millennium, etc., which had been revived by Edward Irving, a Scotch minister in London, and partly from his writings, etc., and partly by reading the Word of God, I was fully convinced the Christian world as it is called was in a very different state to what (it was) supposed. As to the second coming (of) Christ it (was) almost entirely denied or misunderstood."[45] When he finally agreed to listen to Parley Pratt, he wrote, "I soon discovered that he had the spirit and power of God and such Wisdom as none but God himself could have given to man, by which he could

explain those prophecies of which the Preachers of the Day were ignorant, showing the great design and connection of the Scriptures
throughout."[46] Fielding joined. His neighbor, John Taylor, who also
appears to have imbibed Irvingite doctrine, had already been converted by Pratt.[47] The trajectory into the LDS church in either case seems
clear. Primitivist impulses, both experiential and ecclesiastical, coupled with a pronounced millenarianism—Fielding wrote, "I could not
but speak of the Second Coming of Christ"—were given impetus by
Irvingism and fulfillment in Mormonism.

Pratt himself acknowledged the preparatory influence of the Catholic Apostolic Church on his Canadian converts. "I have gotten access
to the writings and publications of the people called 'Irvingites,' in
Scotland and England," he reported in a letter to headquarters, "and
I find they have searched deep into the gathering of Israel; the coming of Christ to reign on the earth; the apostasy of the Gentile church,
and the need of an organization by authority from God, and of the
restitution of the gifts of the Spirit."[48] Taylor and Fielding had been
exposed to Irvingite writings through their participation in a group
of disenchanted Methodists meeting to search the scriptures at the
home of William Patrick, clerk of the House of Assembly and former
treasurer of the Toronto Temperance Society. It was to this group that
William Caird, the Catholic Apostolic evangelist and husband of
famed Scottish charismatic Mary Campbell, had been sent in 1834.
The group's hospitableness to Irvingite doctrine led shortly thereafter to several of their number, including Taylor, who was a lay preacher, having their pulpit privileges withdrawn for heterodoxy by the local Methodist conference.[49]

Shortly before Pratt was to leave Upper Canada, word came that
Caird was returning. The Toronto band of truth seekers "were all expectation, and very anxious that [Caird] should arrive in time to meet
me before I should return home," reported Pratt. The similarities
between Irvingism and Mormonism were perplexing. "Some of those
who had heard both of us, tried to think that both systems were one
and would run together," explained Pratt. "Others said they would
wait and see which serpent swallowed the other before they would join
either." Given his appreciation for the way in which Irvingism had
prepared his hearers for the Mormon message, Pratt had formed a
favorable impression of Caird and even hoped that "he would be an
instrument in the hands of God to receive and spread the truth."[50]

Unfortunately, Caird not only refused to hear Pratt but com-

menced a public slander of Mormonism. This was more disappoint-
ing to Pratt, however, than it was damaging to the LDS cause. Pratt issued a handbill entitled "Doth Our Law Judge a Man Before it Hear
Him?" refuting Caird's personal attacks and inviting the public to listen to a series of lectures contrasting Irvingism and Mormonism. The
well-advertised meeting filled the hall to overflowing on the designated nights, and ultimately, according to Pratt, "the truth prevailed over
the counterfeit, while the people's minds were settled as to which was
the Moses and which was the magician."[51]

Since Irvingite teachings had helped prepare the way for such a
bounteous harvest in Canada, it is little wonder that Pratt expected
them to do likewise in England. "Tens of thousands are awakened in
that land to these subjects," he enthused. And Pratt was hopeful, in
particular, that from his Canadian converts, "many" of whom were
"late from England," would come "access to many names in that country," since they were "already beginning to express desires for their
friends in that country to hear these things."[52] This indeed proved to
be the case in the years ahead; though, as has been shown, the widespread interest in millenarianism and primitivism so important to the
establishment of Mormonism in England came from more sources
than just the writings of Edward Irving and his fellow laborers.

In sum, the religious milieu of early Victorian England was highly
conducive to the transatlantic establishment of the Church of Jesus
Christ of Latter-day Saints. During the Quorum of the Twelve's 1840
mission to England, Brigham Young and Willard Richards wrote to
the First Presidency, "We find the people of this land much more
ready to receive the gospel than those of America."[53] A major share of
the credit must go to the pronouncedly primitivist, charismatic, and
millenarian nature of early Mormonism, which acted as a magnet for
similar interests in England. One student, recognizing the conducive-
ness of that religious culture, went so far as to remark that "there was
nothing in [Mormonism] that had not been anticipated over the preceding half-century."[54] The appeal of earliest Mormonism was not its
foreignness, but its familiar spirit. From its own perspective, what it
did was to unite into "the fulness of truth" those scattered and isolat-
ed insights embedded in the English environment.

Unfortunately, some could not see beyond the fragments:

When we arose to preach unto the people repentance, and baptism
for the remission of sins, the cry of "Baptist, Baptist," would be run

in our ears. If we spoke of the Church and body of Christ being composed of Prophets and Apostles, as well as other members, "Irvingites, Irvingites," would immediately dash into the mind. If in the midst of our remarks, we even once suffered the saying to drop from our lips, "The testimony of Jesus is the spirit of prophecy," "O you belong to Johanna Southcote," would be heard from several places at once. If we spoke of the second coming of Christ, the cry would be, "Aitkenites." If we made mention of the Priesthood, they would call us "Catholics." If we testified of the ministering of angels, the people would reply, "The Irvingites have their angels, and even the Duke of Normandy is ready to swear that he has the ministering of angels every night."[55]

And yet, for those thousands who thought they perceived something grander in Mormonism, the religious environment of England was felt to pave the way. "We know," wrote editor Thomas Ward, "that the minds of many of our elders were prepared for the work through the belief and reception of many of the principles propagated by [Alexander] Campbell" (and, it might be added just as appropriately, the numerous other primitivist, millenarian, and charismatic groups in early nineteenth-century England). "It was our own case, and we shall not cease to be grateful for being permitted to come in contact with them, which as far as we received them, we believe still; and we will even go further and acknowledge that the Lord permitted the propagation of those principles as a forerunner to the fulness of the gospel, though its advocates knew it not."[56] As the apostle Orson F. Whitney summed it up, such individuals and movements "shed the lustre of advanced thought over the pathway soon to be brightened by the beams of eternal truth."[57] That the beloved LDS hymn "The Morning Breaks, the Shadows Flee" was actually a millenarian adaptation by Parley Pratt of a century-earlier Charles Wesley hymn by the same title, therefore, is merely symbolic of the numerous ways in which Mormonism capitalized on, and was influenced by, the charismatic millenarianism within English religion which made it ripe for the establishment of Mormonism.[58] From the LDS perspective, whereas Wesley and countless other seekers, prophets, and millenarians wrote in hope and foretaste, Pratt and thousands of English converts, in the words of their beloved hymn, actually lived to see the "dawning of a brighter day majestic rise upon the world," English as well as American.

Epilogue:
Mormonism, Millenarianism,
and Modernity

In the end, the brighter day majestically rising upon the world was to take longer than enthusiastic Latter-day Saints first expected. Indeed, it has yet to arrive in full splendor. Nonetheless, it is impossible to understand the dynamics of early Mormonism without acknowledging the pervasive way in which eschatology helped the Saints make sense of the world around them and their place in it. Since that time, one of the great themes in religious history has been the confrontation with modernity. Of interest to this exploration of the millenarian world of early Mormonism is how within the LDS community modernity has influenced, and been influenced by, millenarianism.

An important initial distinction is the difference between institutional and intellectual modernization. The former has been described as the "permeation of religious institutions by techniques and procedures developed in other sectors of [modern] society" that seem institutionally advantageous yet intellectually innocuous.[1] From statistical reports and time management to telecommunications and computerization, from the bureaucratic rationalism symbolized by its now insufficient 26-story headquarters building to its public relations typified by BYU athletics and the Mormon Tabernacle Choir, Mormonism, as an institution, has taken on the coloration of modernity.[2]

When it comes to the world of thought, to beliefs and values, however, modernity has been met with a different mindset. In important ways, this has been due to the mutually reinforcing persistence of primitivism and millenarianism. Both maintain a similar philosophy of history which, in spirit, is antimodern. The march of time is not upward; history is actually a long downward spiral of spiritual decay. It is the story of apostasy. Not surprisingly, severe judgments are proclaimed against a present considered to be the faint and fallen image of a distant golden age. Both millenarianism and primitivism see resolution only in restoration, by a dramatic return to pristine purity. Primitivism focuses on *what* is to be restored, while millenarianism emphasizes *when* and *how* the former glory will be recovered. The link between primordium and millennium is well illustrated in Mormonism.

The rise of modernism, however, has been antagonistic to such ideals. Two important consequences of this dramatic paradigm shift in Western consciousness are of particular relevance—the creation of secularism and the emergence of "scientific" history. "Modernization is in many ways a secularizing process," writes Peter Williams, "and generally results in what we might call the 'desacralization' of the world." Its impact on religion is that "the role of the supernatural as a direct, tangible force is downplayed considerably."[3] A second and related ramification is that a sense of profane time supplants the mythic realm of sacred time so elegantly portrayed by Mircea Eliade as central to millenarianism.[4] John Dwyer has noted that "the subjection of man to [non-mythical] history is the insight which, more than any other, characterizes the modern age."[5] Such subjection, however, is precisely what is absent in the "historylessness" of primitivism and millenarianism. While the more celebrated clashes between modernism and traditionalism have dealt with conceptions of creation, compared to the social sciences, the challenge presented by the physical sciences has been "relatively mild."[6] Notions of doctrinal rather than biological evolution, and of cultural and ethical relativism, have been far more threatening to primitivist millenarians.[7]

Latter-day Saints have responded, and continue to respond, to these influences in much the same way that conservative religionists do generally—by rejecting them for a universe thoroughly grounded in absolutes and the supernatural. As much as any other factor, what makes this possible for Mormons today is their core conviction that they are led by a living prophet and living apostles. Admittedly, their modern Moses may be dressed in a three-piece suit, but he still provides a symbolic connection with the mythic world of the sacred past. Through a living prophet and continuing revelation, Mormonism is prepared to respond to change without succumbing to desacralization. The overarching issue from the LDS perspective is not whether the church is abandoning traditional ways for modern ideas, but whether God's hand is in it.

While current prophets may theoretically supersede their predecessors, ancient or modern, in reality they are restrained by a primitivist respect for an additional primordium—the corpus of modern prophetic pronouncement. The speeches and writings of apostles and prophets throughout the history of the church provide a large body of material generally regarded as on par with Scripture. Where particular comments stray too far, their noncanonical status can be invoked, but by and large Latter-day Saints, leader and layman alike, are as loath to contradict what an apostle in the 1800s declared as they are to challenge the writings of Paul.

Thus, the millenarianism of earlier years tends to be preserved by respect for previous prophetic declarations. During the 1980s, LDS apostle and theologian Bruce R. McConkie published the longest work ever written by a Latter-day Saint on eschatological matters. What is striking is how little McConkie's millennial treatise differs from those written during Mormonism's first generation. The same supernatural biological and geological changes anticipated then are expected today, including the abolishment of infant mortality, the herbivorization of carnivores, the unification of continental landmasses, and the commingling of mortals and resurrected immortals. That such views seemed plausible in the early nineteenth century is perhaps not surprising. That they are still maintained today provides dramatic testimony of the degree to which LDS millenarianism in particular and Mormonism in general have resisted the encroachments of modernity.[8]

The pendulum, however, should not be swung too far in the opposite direction. A study of leaders' discourses at the church's general conferences over the past 150 years reveals that millenarian rhetoric "diminished drastically after 1920." Thus, "even though an apocalyptic scenario of the last days is still a central Mormon doctrine, it is no longer enunciated by modern conference speakers with anything like the emphatic fervor of nineteenth-century leaders."[9] Though Latter-day Saints still talk about the end times, for many Mormons these doctrines have a detached and textbookish quality. The social ramifications of their eschatology are rarely if ever discussed today, and soteriological dualism is disparaged. The term "wicked," for instance, no longer refers to all unbelievers. Today, it is applied only to the morally corrupt, and the good and honorable of all religions are expected to be alive during the millennium. As people make their peace with the world, the dream of the "great reversal" diminishes. In short, the more abrasive features of millenarianism which served LDS needs in an earlier period have been quietly, perhaps unwittingly, laid aside in recent years.

Still, on the eve of the twenty-first century, though Mormonism has acquired the institutional accouterments of modernization, its persistent supernaturalism keeps it intellectually insulated from the acids of modernity. It has gone far towards modernizing without becoming secularized. Key has been its conviction of continuing revelation. Primitivism produced living prophets and, in turn, has been preserved by them. So has millenarianism. But the door is always open to change. Shrouded in the "sacred canopy" of modern revelation, Mormons are free to pick and choose their way into modernity. Inspired guidance from living prophets gives them the confidence to feel that they can truly live "in" the modern world and yet be "of" it only to a degree not harmful to their sacred enterprise. Whichever path they are counseled to pursue, Latter-day Saints continue to expect that it will lead them to an actual thousand years of paradisiacal peace and prosperity which they call the millennium.

Notes

Introduction

1. The founding of the Mormon History Association is detailed in Leonard J. Arrington, "Reflections on the Founding and Purpose of the Mormon History Association," *Journal of Mormon History* 10 (1983): 91–103. Significant scholarly work produced before this period is outlined in Marvin S. Hill, "The Historiography of Mormonism," *Church History* 27 (Dec. 1959): 418–26; and Leonard J. Arrington, "Scholarly Studies of Mormonism in the Twentieth Century," *Dialogue: A Journal of Mormon Thought* 1 (Spring 1966): 15–32; hereafter, *Dialogue.* Also valuable but more specialized are Rodman W. Paul, "The Mormons as a Theme in Western Historical Writing," *Journal of American History* 54 (1967): 511–23; and Thomas G. Alexander and James B. Allen, "The Mormons in the Mountain West: A Selective Bibliography," *Arizona and the West* 9 (1967): 365–84.

2. These developments are discussed at greater length in Leonard J. Arrington, "The Writing of Latter-day Saint History: Problems, Accomplishments, and Ambitions," *Dialogue* 14 (1981): 119–29; Davis Bitton, "Ten Years in Camelot: A Personal Memoir," *Dialogue* 16 (1983): 9–33; and James B. Allen, "Since 1950: Creators and Creations of Mormon History," in *New Views of Mormon History,* ed. Davis Bitton and Maureen Ursenbach Beecher (Salt Lake City: University of Utah Press, 1987), 407–38.

The results of the "explosion" have yet to be comprehensively detailed, but a good place to start is with the 90–page bibliography at the back of James B. Allen and Glen M. Leonard, *The Story of the Latter-day Saints,* 2d ed. (Salt Lake City: Deseret Book, 1992), which was quite complete at the time of publication. Readers may also consult the "Mormon Bibliography" published annually in *BYU Studies* and "Among the Mormons: A Survey of Current Literature" published periodically in *Dialogue.* Selective historiographical articles include Thomas G. Alexander, "Toward the New Mormon History: An Examination of the Literature on the Latter-day Saints in the Far West," in *Historians and the American West,* ed. Michael P. Malone (Lincoln: University of Nebraska Press, 1983), 344–68; and Marvin Hill, "The 'New Mormon History' Reassessed in Light of Recent Books on Joseph Smith and Mormon Origins," *Dialogue* 21 (Autumn 1988): 115–27. Historians should not overlook Armand L. Mauss and Jeffrey R. Franks, "Comprehensive Bibliography of Social Science Literature on the Mormons," *Review of Religious Research* 26 (1984): 73–115.

3. To date, the best one-volume surveys reflecting the "new Mormon history" are Leonard J. Arrington and Davis Bitton, *The Mormon Experience: A History of the Latter-day Saints* (New York: Knopf, 1979); and James B. Allen and Glen M. Leonard, *The Story of the Latter-day Saints,* 2d ed. (Salt Lake City: Deseret Book, 1992).

4. This literature is ably reviewed in Leonard I. Sweet, "Millennialism in America: Recent Studies," *Theological Studies* 40 (1979): 510–31; and in Hillel Schwartz, "The End of the Beginning: Millenarian Studies, 1969–1975," *Religious Studies Review* 2 (1976): 1–15. The quotation is from Sweet, p. 511.

5. Leonard I. Sweet, "The Evangelical Tradition in America," in *The Evangelical Tradition in America,* ed. Leonard I. Sweet (Macon: Mercer University Press, 1984), 23.

6. James H. Moorhead, "Searching for the Millennium in America," *Princeton Seminary Bulletin* 8 (1987): 17–33. This view is also shared in Dietrich G. Buss, "MEETING OF HEAVEN AND EARTH: A Survey and Analysis of the Literature on Millennialism in America, 1965–1985," *Fides et Historia* 20 (Spring/Summer 1988): 5–28.

7. Marvin S. Hill, "The Role of Christian Primitivism in the Origin and Development of the Mormon Kingdom, 1830–1844," (Ph.D. diss., University of Chicago, 1968); Leonard J. Arrington, Feramorz Y. Fox, and Dean L. May, *Building the City of God: Community and Cooperation Among the Mormons* (Salt Lake City: Deseret Book, 1976); and Jan Shipps, *Mormonism: The Story of a New Religious Tradition* (Urbana: University of Illinois Press, 1985).

8. R. H. Charles, *Eschatology: The Doctrine of a Future Life in Israel, Judaism, and Christianity* (1899; New York: Schocken, 1963).

9. Mark R. Grandstaff and Milton V. Backman, Jr., "The Social Origins of Kirtland Mormons," *BYU Studies* 30 (Spring 1990): 47–66.

10. Sweet, "Millennialism in America," 513.

11. While the terms *premillennialism* and *postmillennialism* would not enter theological vocabulary until the nineteenth century, scholars have tended to use them for earlier periods as handy labels to distinguish contrasting tendencies in millennialist eschatologies. There are problems

with this, however. As with scholarly constructs generally, the distinctions inevitably make a somewhat ill-fitting coat in which to clothe the thought of any given group or individual. The following studies illustrate why various eschatologies cannot always be neatly pigeonholed by such classifications. For the seventeenth century, see Richard Cogley, "Seventeenth-Century English Millenarianism," *Religion* 17 (Oct. 1987): 379–96. For the eighteenth century, see James W. Davidson, *The Logic of Millennial Thought: Eighteenth Century New England* (New Haven: Yale University Press, 1977). And for the nineteenth century, see James H. Moorhead, "Between Progress and Apocalypse: A Reassessment of Millennialism in American Religious Thought, 1800–1880," *Journal of American History* 71 (Dec. 1984): 524–42.

12. Robert G. Clouse, ed., *The Meaning of the Millennium: Four Views* (Downers Grove, Ill.: Intervarsity Press, 1977), 7.

13. George Marsden, *The Evangelical Mind and the New School Presbyterian Experience: A Case Study of Thought and Theology in Nineteenth-Century America* (New Haven: Yale University Press, 1970), 185. Marsden also sheds valuable light on the subsequent history of millennial ideologies in *Fundamentalism and American Culture: The Shaping of Twentieth-Century Evangelicalism, 1870–1925* (New York: Oxford University Press, 1980).

14. Ernest R. Sandeen, "Millennialism," in *The Rise of Adventism: Religion and Society in Mid-Nineteenth-Century America*, ed. Edwin S. Gaustad (New York: Harper & Row, 1974), 113.

15. W. H. Oliver, *Prophets and Millennialists: The Uses of Biblical Prophecy in England from the 1790s to the 1840s* (Auckland: Auckland University Press, 1978), 18–19.

16. Ibid., 21.

17. The millenarian model used above is found in the publication of conference papers entitled *Millennial Dreams in Action: Essays in Comparative Study*, ed. Sylvia L. Thrupp (The Hague: Mouton, 1962), 31. The model has been used by students of Christian millenarianism in particular. See, for instance, Norman Cohn, *The Pursuit of the Millennium: Revolutionary Millenarians and Mystical Anarchists of the Middle Ages*, rev. ed. (New York: Oxford University Press, 1970), 15.

18. David E. Smith, "Millenarian Scholarship in America," *American Quarterly* 17 (1965): 542.

19. Ernest Lee Tuveson, *Redeemer Nation: The Idea of America's Millennial Role* (Chicago: University of Chicago Press, 1968), 175–86.

20. A noteworthy exception to this generalization is Timothy Smith, "The Book of Mormon in a Biblical Culture," *Journal of Mormon History* 7 (1980): 17–18. While recognizing similarities to postmillennialist evangelicals, he also realizes that the Saints were fundamentally premillennialist.

21. The idea was first articulated in Klaus Hansen, *Quest for Empire: The Political Kingdom of God and the Council of Fifty* (East Lansing: Michigan State University Press, 1967); and in Louis G. Reinwand, "An Interpretive Study of Mormon Millennialism During the Nineteenth Century with Emphasis on Millennial Development in Utah" (M.A. thesis, Brigham Young University, 1971).

With respect to its grasp of Christian eschatology, Sandeen, *Roots of Fundamentalism: British and American Millenarianism, 1800–1930* (Chicago: University of Chicago Press, 1970), 302, notes that *Quest for Empire* was "not entirely competent." In the absence of other contenders, however, Hansen's 1967 publication tended to become the accepted source on Mormon millenarianism. Similar views can be found in Hansen, *Mormonism and the American Experience* (Chicago: University of Chicago Press, 1981), and Keith E. Norman, "How Long O Lord?: The Delay of the Parousia in Mormonism," *Sunstone* 8 (Jan. 1983): 59–65. The "transformation" of the Mormon "millennial vision" is approached from a different angle in Shipps, *Mormonism.*

22. Hansen, *Quest for Empire;* Reinwand, "Interpretive Study of Mormon Millennialism," 43–48, 153–60.

23. The most recent historiographical pieces are Buss, "MEETING OF HEAVEN AND EARTH"; and Moorhead, "Searching for the Millennium in America." Sweet, "Millennialism in America," 510–31; and Schwartz, "The End of the Beginning," 1–15, should also be consulted.

24. Sweet, "Millennialism in America," 522

25. James H. Moorhead, *American Apocalypse: Yankee Protestants and Civil War, 1860–1869* (New Haven: Yale University Press, 1978), 8. The difficulty in classifying people's eschatologies is well illustrated in the case John Wesley. Kenneth O. Brown surveyed a century's worth of studies on Wesley and found that scholars were almost equally divided in their characterization of him as either premillennialist or postmillennialist. See Brown, "John Wesley: Post or Premillennialist?" *Methodist History* 28 (Oct. 1989): 33–41.

26. Sandeen, *Roots of Fundamentalism,* 183–86; Timothy P. Weber, *Living in the Shadow of the Second Coming: American Premillennialism, 1875–1925* (New York: Oxford University Press, 1979), 65–81.

27. Weber, *Living in the Shadow,* 67.

28. Cited in Marsden, *Evangelical Mind,* 194.

29. *Messenger and Advocate* 2 (July 1836): 344. Hyde seems to have adapted earlier verses from Parley Pratt, *The Millennium, a Poem, to which is added Hymns and Songs on Various Subjects, New and Interesting, Adapted to the Dispensation of the Fulness of Times* (Boston, 1835), 52:

Shall we behold the nations doomed
To sword and famine, blood and fire,
Yet not the least exertion make,
But from the scene in peace retire.
No; while his love for me extends,
The pattern makes my duty plain—
I'll sound, to earth's remotest end,
The gospel to the sons of men!

30. Smith, "Millenarian Scholarship in America," 539.
31. Weber, *Living in the Shadow,* 69–70.
32. Cited in Paul E. Johnson, *A Shopkeeper's Millennium: Society and Revivals in Rochester, New York, 1815–1837* (New York: Hill and Wang, 1978), 3–4.
33. Robert K. Whalen, "Millenarianism and Millennialism in America, 1790–1880" (Ph.D. diss., State University College of New York at Stony Brook, 1971), 134n.

Chapter 1:
The Eschatological Background of Early Mormonism

1. Information in this and subsequent paragraphs is drawn from Klaus Koch, "What is Apocalyptic: An Attempt at a Preliminary Definition," in *Visionaries and Their Apocalypses,* ed. Paul D. Hanson (Philadelphia: Fortress, 1983), 16–36; John J. Collins, ed., *Apocalypse: the Morphology of a Genre,* vol. 14 of *Semeia* (1979); Collins, "Apocalyptic Literature," in *Early Judaism and its Modern Interpreters,* ed. R. Kraft and G. W. Nickelsburg (Chico, Calif.: Scholars Press, 1986), 345–70; Paul D. Hanson, "Apocalypticism," in *Interpreter's Dictionary of the Bible, Supplementary Volume,* ed. Keith Crim (Nashville: Abingdon, 1976); Hanson, "Apocalyptic Literature," in *The Hebrew Bible and its Modern Interpreters,* ed. Douglas H. Knight and Gene M. Tucker (Chico, Calif.: Scholars Press, 1985), 465–88.
2. Material in this and subsequent paragraphs is drawn from John J. Collins, *The Apocalyptic Imagination: An Introduction to the Jewish Matrix of Christianity* (New York: Crossroad, 1984); Bernard McGinn, "Early Apocalypticism: The Ongoing Debate," in *The Apocalypse in English Renaissance Thought and Literature,* ed. C. A. Patrides and Joseph Wittreich (Manchester: Manchester University Press, 1984), 2–39; Paul D. Hanson's work, including *The Dawn of Apocalyptic: The History and Sociological Roots of Jewish Apocalyptic Eschatology,* rev. ed. (Philadelphia: Fortress Press, 1979), *Visionaries and Their Apocalypses* (Philadelphia: Fortress, 1983), and *Old Testament Apocalyptic* (Nashville: Abingdon Press, 1987); and Christopher

Rowland, *The Open Heaven: A Study of Apocalyptic in Judaism and Early Christianity* (New York: Crossroad, 1982).

3. Here scholars notice a sort of determinism, not the kind related to that view of salvation which predestines particular individuals to a given place in the afterlife, but the kind that sees history as moving inexorably toward a predetermined future. One can push this distinction between historical determinism and personal determinism too far, but it does help separate apocalyptic determinism from Augustinian or Calvinist determinism.

4. Some of the early apocalypses include numerological components which allowed the faithful to calculate the exact date, but most simply impress with a sense of nearness.

5. Albert Schweitzer, *The Quest for the Historical Jesus: A Critical Study of its Progress from Reimarus to Wrede* (1906; New York: Macmillan, 1961).

6. As James Dunn expressed it, "Christianity began as an apocalyptic sect within Judaism." Dunn, *Diversity and Unity in the New Testament: An Inquiry into the Character of Earliest Christianity* (Philadelphia: Westminster Press, 1977), 325. See also John J. Collins, "The Apocalyptic Context of Christian Origins," *Michigan Quarterly Review* 22 (Summer 1983): 250–64; Howard Clark Kee, *Christian Origins in Sociological Perspective* (Philadelphia: Westminster, 1980); Kee, "The Social Setting of Mark: An Apocalyptic Community," *SBL Seminar Papers* 23 (1984): 245–55; Marion L. Soads, "Paul: Apostle and Apocalyptic Visionary," *Biblical Theology Bulletin* 16 (Oct. 1986): 148–50; and Soads, *The Apostle Paul: An Introduction to His Life, Letters and Theology* (Philadelphia: Fortress, 1986).

7. Jewish apocalyptic had, in turn, been influenced by Persian ideas. See George W. Nickelsburg, *Resurrection, Immortality, and Eternal Life in Inter-Testamental Judaism* (Cambridge: Harvard University Press, 1972); Gerhard Hasel, "Resurrection in the Theology of Old Testament Apocalyptic," *Zeitschrift für die Alttestamentliche Wissenschaft* 92 (1980): 267–84; Bernhard Lang, "Afterlife: Ancient Israel's Changing Vision of the World Beyond," *Bible Review* 4 (Feb. 1988): 12–23; Mary Boyce, *A History of Zoroastrianism* (Leiden: Brill, 1975); Boyce, "On the Antiquity of Zoroastrian Apocalyptic," *Bulletin of the School of Oriental and African Studies* 47 (1984): 57–75; W. E. Davies and Louis Finkelstein, *The Cambridge History of Judaism, Volume I: The Persian Period* (Cambridge: Cambridge University Press, 1984), particularly chapter 12, "Iranian Influence on Judaism"; and Reginald H. Fuller, *The Formation of the Resurrection Narratives* (Philadelphia: Fortress, 1980).

8. Robert H. Spivey and D. Moody Smith, *Anatomy of the New Testament: A Guide to its Structure and Meaning*, 3d ed. (New York: Macmillan, 1982), 33. See also David Flusser, *Judaism and the Origins of Christianity* (Jerusalem: Magnes Press, 1988).

9. Norman Perrin and Dennis Duling, *The New Testament: An Introduction* (New York: Harcourt Brace & Jovanovich, 1974). A more recent introduction to the New Testament which acknowledges the pervasiveness of apocalypticism in its overall approach is Christopher Rowland, *Christian Origins: From Messianic Movement to Christian Religion* (Minneapolis: Augsburg, 1985).

10. A. L. Moore, *The Parousia in the New Testament* (Leiden: Brill, 1966); Richard H. Hiers, *Jesus and the Future* (Atlanta: John Knox Press, 1981); W. D. Davies and D. Daube, eds., *The Background of the New Testament and Its Eschatology* (Cambridge: Cambridge University Press, 1956); H. M. Shires, *The Eschatology of Paul in the Light of Modern Scholarship* (Philadelphia: Westminster, 1966).

11. John G. Gager, *Kingdom and Community: The Social World of Early Christianity* (Englewood Cliffs: Prentice-Hall, 1975). Evaluating evidence for an earlier transformation is Paul J. Achtmeier, "An Apocalyptic Shift in Early Christian Tradition: Reflections on Some Canonical Evidence," *Catholic Biblical Quarterly* 45 (Apr. 1983): 231–48.

12. A comprehensive history of chiliasm is D. H. Kromminga, *The Millennium in the Church: Studies in the History of Christian Chiliasm* (Grand Rapids: Eerdmans, 1945). For the early period, Jean Danielou, *The Theology of Jewish Christianity* (Chicago: University of Chicago Press, 1964), 377–404, is the standard work. A recent study of relevance is Samuele Bacchiocchi, "Sabbatical Typologies of Messianic Redemption," *Journal for the Study of Judaism* 17 (Dec. 1986): 153–76.

13. M. O'Rourke Boyle, "Irenaeus' Millennial Hope: A Polemical Weapon," *Recherches de théologie ancienne et médiévale* 36 (1969): 5–16. On Gnosticism generally, see Kurt Rudolph, *Gnosis: The Nature and History of Gnosticism*, trans. R. McL. Wilson (San Francisco: Harper & Row, 1983).

14. Brian E. Daley, *The Hope of the Early Church: A Handbook of Patristic Eschatology* (Cambridge: Cambridge University Press, 1991). Of related interest, though pursuing an eschatological debate among modern Evangelicals, is Thomas D. Lea, "A Survey of the Doctrine of the Return of Christ in the Ante-Nicene Fathers," *Journal of the Evangelical Theological Society* 29 (June 1986): 163–77.

15. There are, of course, verses in the Bible which promise "a new heaven and a new earth" and numerous passages which describe the restored glory of Israel. While they would be interpretively linked to Rev. 20 by later Christian eschatologists seeking to elaborate on the nature of the millennium, it should here be recognized that from the beginning such harmonization of diverse texts has been an exercise in interpretation and elaboration.

16. Most twentieth century scholarship on the Montanists has been produced in French and German. Effective, brief distillations of this Eu-

ropean scholarship can be found in W. H. C. Frend, *The Rise of Christianity* (Philadelphia: Fortress, 1984); and Jaroslav Pelikan, *The Emergence of the Catholic Tradition, 100–600* (Chicago: University of Chicago Press, 1971). The latest comprehensive treatment in English is B. W. Goree, "The Cultural Bases of Montanism" (Ph.D. diss., Baylor University, 1980).

17. Bernard McGinn, *Visions of the End: Apocalyptic Traditions in the Middle Ages* (New York: Columbia University Press, 1979); McGinn, "Apocalypticism in the Middle Ages: An Historiographical Sketch," *Mediaeval Studies* 37 (1975): 252–86; McGinn, *Apocalyptic Spirituality* (New York: Paulist Press, 1979); Marjorie Reeves, "The Development of Apocalyptic Thought: Medieval Attitudes," in *Apocalypse in English Renaissance,* ed. Patrides and Wittreich, 40–72; Robert E. Lerner, "The Black Death and Western European Eschatological Mentalities," *American Historical Review* 86 (June 1981): 537–38; and Paul J. Alexander, *The Byzantine Apocalyptic Tradition* (Berkeley: University of California Press, 1985).

18. Cohn, *Pursuit of the Millennium;* and Werner Verbeke et al., eds., *The Use and Abuse of Eschatology in the Middle Ages* (Leuven: Leuven University Press, 1988).

19. Howard Kaminsky, "Chiliasm and the Hussite Revolution," *Church History* 26 (Mar. 1957): 43–71; Kaminsky, *A History of the Hussite Revolution* (Berkeley: University of California Press, 1967); Jarold K. Zeman, *The Hussite Movement and the Reformation in Bohemia, Moravia, and Slovakia* (Ann Arbor: Michigan Slavic Publications, 1977).

20. Richard K. Emerson, *Antichrist in the Middle Ages: A Study of Medieval Apocalypticism, Art, and Literature* (Seattle: University of Washington Press, 1981).

21. Robin Bruce Barnes, *Prophecy and Gnosis: Apocalypticism in the Wake of the Lutheran Reformation* (Stanford: Stanford University Press, 1988), 2–3.

22. Barnes, *Prophecy and Gnosis* makes this point at length. The standard work on the Radical Reformation is George Huntston Williams, *The Radical Reformation* (Philadelphia: Westminster, 1962). See also Williams, "The Radical Reformation Revisited," *Union Theological Seminary Quarterly Review* 39 (1984): 1–24; Donald F. Durnbaugh, "Characteristics of the Radical Reformation in Historical Perspective," *Communio Viatorum* 29 (Autumn 1986): 97–118; Richard G. Bailey, "The 16th Century's Apocalyptic Heritage and Thomas Muntzer," *Mennonite Quarterly Review* 57 (Jan. 1983): 27–44; Eric W. Gritsch, *Thomas Muntzer: A Tragedy of Errors* (Minneapolis: Fortress Press, 1989); and James M. Stayer, "The Revolutionary Origins of the 'Peace Churches': The Peasants' War and the Anabaptists, the English Civil War and the Quakers," *Brethren Life and Thought* 30 (Spring 1985): 71–80.

23. Information in this and subsequent paragraphs is drawn from Bry-

an W. Ball, *A Great Expectation: Eschatological Thought in English Protestantism to 1660* (Leiden: Brill, 1975); Richard Bauckham, *Tudor Apocalypse: Sixteenth-Century Apocalypticism, Millenarianism, and the English Reformation* (Appleford: Courtenay Press, 1978); Paul Christianson, *Reformers and Babylon: English Apocalyptic Visions from the Reformation to the Eve of the Civil War* (Toronto: University of Toronto Press, 1978); Katharine R. Firth, *The Apocalyptic Tradition in Reformation Britain, 1530–1645* (Oxford: Oxford University Press, 1979); and George Kroeze, "The Variety of Millennial Hopes in the English Reformation, 1560–1660" (Ph.D. diss., Fuller Theological Seminary, 1985).

24. In *Tudor Apocalypse*, Bauckham discusses a "trend toward optimism" which developed in English eschatological thought, especially after the defeat of the Spanish Armada.

Exhaustive study of the abbot Joachim and his influence has been done by Marjorie Reeves in *The Influence of Prophecy in the Later Middle Ages: A Study in Joachimism* (Oxford: Oxford University Press, 1969) and *Joachim of Fiore and the Prophetic Future* (New York: Harper & Row, 1977).

25. Deok Kyo Oh, "The Church's Resurrection: John Cotton's Eschatological Understanding of the Ecclesiastical Reformation" (Ph.D. diss., Westminster Theological Seminary, 1987).

The phrase "a glimpse of Syon's glory" is taken from a popular pamphlet by that name published in 1641. Its authorship is uncertain. Those who have argued in favor of Thomas Goodwin as author include John F. Wilson, "'A glimpse of Syon's glory,'" *Church History* 31 (1962): 66–73; and A. R. Dallison, "The Authorship of the 'Glimpse of Syon's Glory,'" in *Puritans, the Millennium, and the Future of Israel: Puritan Eschatology 1600–1660*, ed. Peter Toon (Cambridge: James Clark: 1970), 131–36. Paul Christianson contends Jeremiah Burroughs was the author in *Reformers and Babylon*, 212–19, 251–52.

26. On the views and influence of Thomas Brightman, see Bauckham, *Tudor Apocalypse*, 212–29; Peter Toon, "The Latter Day Glory," in *Puritans, the Millennium, and the Future of Israel*, ed. Toon, 23–41; and the chapters on Puritan eschatology in Theodore Dwight Bozeman, *To Live Ancient Lives: The Primitivist Dimension in Puritanism* (Chapel Hill: Institute of Early American History and Culture, 1988), 193–262.

Brightman's major work was a commentary on Revelation. It was published posthumously first in Latin in 1609 and 1612, and then in several expatriate English editions (due to Anglican censorship) in 1611, 1615, and 1616. In English, its title is variously translated as *A Revelation of the Revelation* or *A Revelation of the Apocalypse*. The first approved editions in England did not appear until the 1640s.

27. Robert E. Lerner, "Refreshment of the Saints: The Time after An-

tichrist as a Station for Earthly Progress in Medieval Thought," *Traditio* 32 (1976): 97–144.

28. See Robert G. Clouse, "The Rebirth of Millenarianism," in *Puritans, the Millennium, and the Future of Israel,* ed. Toon, 42–56. Alsted's contribution to the history of eschatology is also discussed in Clouse, "Johann Heinrich Alsted and English Millenarianism," *Harvard Theological Review* 62 (1969): 189–207.

29. Joseph Hall, *The Revelation Unrevealed Concerning the Thousand-Yeares Reigne of the Saints with Christ upon Earth* (1650), cited in A. R. Dallison, "Contemporary Criticism of Millenarianism," in *Puritans, the Millennium, and the Future of Israel,* ed. Toon, 109–10.

30. Bernard Capp, "The Fifth Monarchists and Popular Millenarianism," in *Radical Religion in the English Revolution,* ed. J. F. McGregor and B. Reay (Oxford: Oxford University Press, 1984), 165–89; Capp, "The Political Dimension of Apocalyptic Thought," in *The Apocalypse in English Renaissance Thought and Literature,* ed. Patrides and Wittreich, 93–124; Christopher Hill, *The World Turned Upside Down: Radical Ideas During the English Revolution* (New York: Viking, 1972); Hill, *Antichrist in Seventeenth-Century England* (Oxford: Oxford University Press, 1971); William L. Lamont, *Godly Rule: Politics and Religion, 1603–1660;* and Christianson, *Reformers and Babylon.*

31. Cited in Capp, "The Fifth Monarchists," 186, 187.

32. Ibid., 189.

33. Paul J. Korshin, "Queuing and Waiting: The Apocalypse in England, 1660–1750," in *The Apocalypse in English Renaissance Thought and Literature,* ed. Patrides and Wittreich, 240–65. The notion that millenarianism disappeared among intellectuals in the early eighteenth century is dispelled in Harry M. Bracken, "Bishop Berkeley's Messianism," and George S. Rousseau, "Mysticism and Millenarianism: 'Immortal Dr. Cheyne,'" both in *Millenarianism and Messianism in English Literature and Thought, 1650–1800,* ed. Richard H. Popkin (Leiden: Brill, 1988), 65–126. Berkeley's impact on intellectual life in the Colonies is described in Edwin S. Gaustad, *George Berkeley in America* (New Haven: Yale University Press, 1979). See also Margaret C. Jacob, "Millenarianism and Science in the Late Seventeenth Century," *Journal of the History of Ideas* 37 (Apr.–June 1976): 335–41; Jacob, *The Cultural Meaning of the Scientific Revolution* (Philadelphia: Temple University Press, 1988); Arthur Quinn, "On Reading Newton Apocalyptically," in *Millenarianism and Messianism,* ed. Popkin, 176–92; and Frank E. Manuel, *The Religion of Isaac Newton* (Oxford: Clarendon, 1974).

34. Hillel Schwartz, *The French Prophets: The History of a Millenarian Group in Eighteenth Century England* (Berkeley: University of California Press, 1980), 290, 8.

35. David S. Lovejoy, *Religious Enthusiasm in the New World: Heresy to Revolution* (Cambridge: Harvard University Press, 1985); James W. Davidson, *The Logic of Millennial Thought: Eighteenth-Century New England* (New Haven: Yale University Press, 1977).

36. See Susie I. Tucker, *Enthusiasm: A Study in Semantic Change* (Cambridge: Cambridge University Press, 1972); Michael Heyd, "The Reaction to Enthusiasm in the Seventeenth Century: Toward an Integrative Approach," *Journal of Modern History* 53 (1981): 258–80; and George Rosen, "Enthusiasm, 'a dark lanthorn of the spirit,'" *Bulletin of the History of Medicine* 42 (1968): 393–421.

37. Korshin, "Queuing and Waiting," 258.

38. Ronald Knox, *Enthusiasm: A Chapter in the History of Religion* (Oxford: Oxford University Press, 1950); Clarke Garrett, *Spirit Possession and Popular Religion: From the Camisards to the Shakers* (Baltimore: Johns Hopkins University Press, 1987); Philip F. Gura, *A Glimpse of Sion's Glory: Puritan Radicalism in New England, 1620–1660* (Middletown: Wesleyan University Press, 1984). The linkage between religious heterodoxy, including millenarianism, and irrational behavior dates to the Civil War period. That the connection also existed in medieval Judaism is made clear in Ithamar Gruenwald, *Apocalyptic and Merkavah Mysticism* (Leiden: Brill, 1980); and Moshe Idel, *Kabbalah: New Perspectives* (New Haven: Yale University Press, 1988).

39. Korshin, "Queuing and Waiting," 260. Deborah Valenze details the rising popularity of chapbooks dealing with eschatological themes in "Prophecy and Popular Literature in Eighteenth-Century England," *Journal of Ecclesiastical History* 29 (Jan. 1978): 75–92.

40. Garrett, *Spirit Possession and Popular Religion,* 10–11. In some ways, the standard treatment of this phenomenon is still Knox, *Enthusiasm,* though it is marred by the author's orthodox bias against the legitimacy of special, personal inspiration.

41. John F. C. Harrison, *The Second Coming: Popular Millenarianism, 1780–1850* (New Brunswick, N.J.: Rutgers University Press, 1979); Oliver, *Prophets and Millennialists;* Garrett, *Spirit Possession and Popular Religion;* James K. Hopkins, *A Woman to Deliver Her People: Joanna Southcott and English Millenarianism in an Era of Revolution* (Austin: University of Texas Press, 1982); G. A. Rawlyk, *Ravished by the Spirit: Religious Revivals, Baptists, and Henry Alline* (Kingston: McGill-Queens University Press, 1984); Ruth H. Bloch, *Visionary Republic: Millennial Themes in American Thought, 1756–1800* (Cambridge: Cambridge University Press, 1985); and Stephen G. Marini, *Radical Sects of Revolutionary New England* (Cambridge: Harvard University Press, 1987).

42. Cited in Marini, *Radical Sects,* 52.

43. An early detailed account of Meacham's life is Calvin Green, "Bio-

graphical Account of the Life, Character, and Ministry of Father Joseph Meacham," ed. Theodore E. Johnson, *Shaker Quarterly* 10 (Spring, Summer, Fall 1970): 20–32, 51–68, 92–102. Secondary accounts can be found in Stephen J. Stein, *The Shaker Experience in America: A History of the United Society of Believers* (New Haven: Yale University Press, 1992); Garrett, *Spirit Possession and Popular Religion;* Marini, *Radical Sects;* and Lawrence Foster, *Religion and Sexuality: Three American Communal Experiments of the Nineteenth Century* (New York: Oxford University Press, 1981).

44. The quoted portion is from Marini, *Radical Sects,* 54.

45. Rutland County, Vermont, tradition has it that the parents of Oliver Cowdery and Joseph Smith, the two principals in organizing the Church of Jesus Christ of Latter-day Saints, were involved with this group, at least during their "rodsmen" phase. The evidence for and against this is analyzed in D. Michael Quinn, *Early Mormonism and the Magic World View* (Salt Lake City: Signature, 1987), 30–35, 84–97.

Discussion of other charismatic millenarians in Vermont can be found in Donal Ward, "Religious Enthusiasm in Vermont, 1761–1847" (Ph.D. diss., Notre Dame University, 1980).

46. James H. Moorhead, "Between Progress and Apocalypse: A Reassessment of Millennialism in American Religious Thought, 1800–1880," *Journal of American History* 71 (Dec. 1984): 524–42.

47. The numerous studies that have either implicitly accepted or explicitly demonstrated this thesis are reviewed in Leonard I. Sweet, "The Evangelical Tradition in America," in *Evangelical Tradition,* ed. Sweet, 14–46.

48. John F. Wilson, *Public Religion in American Culture* (Philadelphia: Temple University Press, 1979), 108; and William G. McLoughlin, *Revivals, Awakenings, and Social Reform: An Essay in Religion and Social Change in America, 1607–1977* (Chicago: University of Chicago Press, 1978), xiv.

The melding of millennialism and nationalism is briefly discussed in James F. Maclear, "The Republic and the Millennium," in *Religion in American History: Interpretive Essays,* ed. John M. Mulder and John F. Wilson, (Englewood Cliffs: Prentice-Hall, 1978), 181–98. The standard book-length treatment is Ernest Lee Tuveson, *Redeemer Nation: The Idea of America's Millennial Role* (Chicago: University of Chicago Press, 1968). Timothy Smith, however, argues for the universalist rather than nationalist character of nineteenth-century postmillennialism in "Righteousness and Hope: Christian Holiness and the Millennial Vision in America, 1800–1900," *American Quarterly* 31 (Spring 1979): 21–45.

49. Lewis O. Saum, *The Popular Mood of Pre–Civil War America* (Westport, Conn.: Greenwood Press, 1980), 26.

50. John B. Boles, "John Hershey: Dissenting Theologian of Abolitionism, Perfectionism, and Millennialism," *Methodist History* 14 (July 1976): 215–34.

51. Nathan O. Hatch, "Millennialism and Popular Religion in the Early Republic," in *Evangelical Tradition,* ed. Sweet, 130. For a fuller discussion, see Hatch, *The Democratization of American Christianity* (New Haven: Yale University Press, 1989).

52. Gordon S. Wood, "Evangelical America and Early Mormonism," *New York History* 61 (Oct. 1980): 368.

53. Michael Barkun, *Crucible of the Millennium: The Burned-Over District of New York in the 1840s* (Syracuse: Syracuse University Press, 1986), 148.

54. Mormons bore this title until 1834, when the High Council—the Church's "board of directors" at that time—voted to name it the "Church of the Latter Day Saints." Four years later, in 1838, a revelation decreed: "thus shall my church be called in the last days, viz, The church of Jesus Christ of Latter Day Saints." *Elders' Journal of the Church of Latter Day Saints* 1 (Aug. 1838): 52; hereafter, *Elders' Journal.*

The earliest years of Mormonism, especially the foundational experiences of Joseph Smith, are best detailed in Richard L. Bushman, *Joseph Smith and the Beginnings of Mormonism* (Urbana: University of Illinois Press, 1984).

55. Mario De Pillis, "The Quest for Religious Authority and the Rise of Mormonism," *Dialogue* 1 (Spring 1966): 68–88.

Chapter 2
Mormons as Millenarians

1. Dean C. Jessee, ed., *The Papers of Joseph Smith: Volume 1, Autobiographical and Historical Writings* (Salt Lake City: Deseret Book, 1989), 6–7. See also *The Personal Writings of Joseph Smith,* ed. Jessee (Salt Lake City: Deseret Book, 1984), 6. Jessee retains the original spelling and syntax. A similar literal adherence to the original will also be followed in this book for other quotations from early Mormon sources.

2. Sandeen, *Roots of Fundamentalism,* 22.

3. The standard biography of Rigdon is F. Mark Mckiernan, *The Voice of One Crying in the Wilderness: Sidney Rigdon, Religious Reformer, 1793–1876* (Lawrence, Kans.: Coronado Press, 1971).

4. A large number of the revelations received during the early years of Mormonism have been compiled and canonized by the Church as *The Doctrine and Covenants of the Church of Jesus Christ of Latter-day Saints,* or more simply, the *Doctrine and Covenants.* Throughout the remainder of this book, the standard LDS convention of referring to this volume as D&C will be followed. First issued in 1835, the D&C has gone through numerous editions since. Unless the wording of the text has been modified significantly from the original, and so identified in these notes, any edition can be consulted with confidence. The passage cited is D&C 100:9.

5. _Latter Day Saints' Messenger and Advocate_ 3 (November 1836): 401–4; hereafter, _Messenger and Advocate_.

6. Campbell's postmillennialism is summarized in Hiram J. Lester, "Alexander Campbell's Millennial Program," _Discipliana_ 48 (Fall 1988): 35–39. A thorough history of how subsequent commentators have analyzed his millennial views is provided in Lester, "Alexander Campbell: A Prophet of an American Millennium" (unpublished paper in author's possession). That a premillennialist like Ridgon and a postmillennialist like Campbell could, for a time, agree on a common commitment to primitivism is best evidenced by the enduring alliance between premillennialist Barton Stone and postmillennialist Campbell, the two most important figures in early nineteenth-century American primitivism. See Richard T. Hughes, "The Apocalyptic Origins of the Churches of Christ and the Triumph of Modernism," _Religion and American Culture: A Journal of Interpretation_ 2 (Summer 1992): 181–214.

7. W. Herbert Hanna, _Thomas Campbell: Seceder and Christian Union Advocate_ (Cincinnati: Standard Publishers Co., 1935), 157–58. Begg's works include _A Connected View of Some of the Scriptural Evidence of the Redeemer's Speedy Personal Return_ (London, 1829) and _Twelve Short and General Reasons for a Literal Premillennial Second Advent_ (London, 1830). Elias Smith wrote _The Whole World Governed by a Jew; or The Government of the Second Adam, as King and Priest_ (Exeter, N.H., 1805) and, beginning in 1808, edited the _Herald of Gospel Liberty_, a periodical dedicated to the quest for the "primitive gospel."

8. Robert Richardson, ed., _Memoirs of Alexander Campbell_, 2 vols. (1868–70; Cincinnati: Standard Publishing Co., 1913), 2:345–46. Campbell also opposed Rigdon's proposal that "all things should be held in common" by contemporary believers just as they had been in the New Testament. See also Alanson Wilcox, _A History of the Disciples of Christ in Ohio_ (Cincinnati: Standard Publishing, 1918), 125.

9. Amos S. Hayden, _Early History of the Disciples in the Western Reserve, Ohio_ (Cincinnati, 1876), 183.

10. _Memoirs of Alexander Campbell_, 1:347. See also Hanna, _Thomas Campbell_, 158.

11. _Messenger and Advocate_ 3 (Nov. 1836): 403.

12. Ibid., 403. The statement about Zion being a "defense" and a "refuge" is found in D&C 115:6.

13. Written as a broadside introduction to the Mormon message, it was quickly reproduced in the Church's official newspaper, _Messenger and Advocate_ 2 (July 1836): 342–46. The following year, as Hyde helped head the first LDS mission to Britain, he reissued it in almost identical words as _A Timely Warning to the People of England_. For several years, it served as

the chief British introduction to the Mormon faith. See Peter Crawley, "A Bibliography of the Church of Jesus Christ of Latter-day Saints in New York, Ohio, and Missouri," *BYU Studies* 12 (Summer 1972): 505; and David J. Whittaker, "Early Mormon Pamphleteering" (Ph.D. diss., Brigham Young University, 1982).

14. *Messenger and Advocate* 2 (July 1836): 342–46. Quotations in the next few paragraphs are taken from this printing of *A Prophetic Warning.*

15. Parley P. Pratt, *A Voice of Warning and Instruction to all People, Containing an Introduction to the Faith and Doctrine of the Church of the Latter-Day Saints, Commonly Called Mormons* (New York: W. Sandford, 1837). Parley Pratt was one of the most prolific pamphleteers in early Mormonism. Since the early Saints had little occasion or inclination to systematize their doctrine, Pratt ended up as one of the most influential "theologians" during the early decades of the church's history. His contributions and impact are ably assessed in Peter Crawley, "Parley P. Pratt: Father of Mormon Pamphleteering," *Dialogue* 15 (Autumn 1982): 13–26; and David J. Whittaker, "Early Mormon Pamphleteering" (Ph.D. diss., Brigham Young University, 1982).

16. *The Evening and the Morning Star* 2 (Dec. 1833): 117. In the early years, this periodical was known simply as the *Star,* a convention which shall be followed hereafter in this book.

17. *Star* 2 (June 1834): 163.

18. *Star* 2 (Jan. 1834): 126. Despite keeping his paper open to other views, Campbell himself was an ardent postmillennialist. This was part of the reason Rigdon broke off formal ties with Campbell's movement in August 1830, just months before the Mormon missionaries arrived in Ohio. Campbell's eschatology is discussed most thoroughly in Hiram J. Lester, "Alexander Campbell's Millennial Program," *Discipliana* 48 (Fall 1988): 35–39; and Lester, "Alexander Campbell: Prophet of an American Millennium, A Historiographic Study" (unpublished paper in author's possession).

The Disciples' encounter with millenarianism at this time is briefly recounted in Hanna, *Thomas Campbell,* 156–59.

19. Ibid., 117.

20. On Dispensationalism, see Sandeen, *The Roots of Fundamentalism;* Weber, *Living in the Shadow;* Norman Kraus, *Dispensationalism in America: Its Rise and Development* (Richmond: John Knox Press, 1958); Arnold D. Ehlert, *A Bibliographic History of Dispensationalism* (Grand Rapids: Baker, 1965); and Clarence Bass, *Backgrounds to Dispensationalism: Its Historical Origins and Ecclesiastical Implications* (Grand Rapids: Eerdmans, 1960).

21. *Star* 2 (Jan. 1834): 126.

22. Ibid., 127.

23. D&C 109:60–67.
24. *Journal of Discourses*, 26 vols. (London: Latter-day Saints' Book Dept., 1855–86), 2:268. Two revelations from the 1830s, though rarely cited in the period under study, later provided scriptural support for the Saints' lineal link to ancient Israel. D&C 64:36 declares that "rebellious" Saints "are not of the blood of Ephraim, wherefore they shall be plucked out." D&C 86:8–10 reads, "Therefore, thus saith the Lord unto you, with whom the priesthood hath continued through the lineage of your fathers. For ye are lawful heirs, according to the flesh, and have been hid from the world with Christ in God. Therefore your life and the priesthood have remained, and must needs remain through you and your lineage until the restoration of all things spoken by the mouths of all the holy prophets since the world began."
25. Victor L. Ludlow, *Isaiah: Prophet, Seer and Poet* (Salt Lake City: Deseret Book, 1982), 171–72. Developing notions of an actual Israelite pedigree through Joseph and Ephraim are briefly discussed in Newell G. Bringhurst, *Saints, Slaves, and Blacks: The Changing Place of Black People Within Mormonism* (Westport, Conn.: Greenwood Press, 1981); and Melodie Moench, "Nineteenth-Century Mormons: The New Israel," *Dialogue: A Journal of Mormon Thought* 12 (Spring 1979): 42–54.

Such attitudes welcomed the influence of British Israelism in America. Relevant studies include Richard Edmund, "British-Israel: A Study of Nineteenth-Century Millennialism" (Ph.D. diss., McGill University, 1980); and Bruce Van Orden, "Anglo-Israelism and the Mormon Church" (unpublished paper delivered at the 1984 meeting of the Mormon History Association).

Not all who trace their roots to Joseph Smith and the early Saints developed a literal identification with Israel. See Robert Ben Madison, "'Heirs According to the Promise': Observations on Ethnicity, Race, and Identity in Two Factions of Nineteenth-Century Mormonism," *The John Whitmer Historical Association Journal* 12 (1992): 66–82.

26. Joseph Smith once declared that "the effect of the Holy Ghost upon a Gentile is to purge out the old blood & make him actually of the seed of Abraham. That man that has none of the blood of Abraham (naturally) must have a new creation by the Holy Ghost." *The Words of Joseph Smith: The Contemporary Accounts of the Nauvoo Discourses of the Prophet Joseph*, ed. Andrew F. Ehat and Lyndon Cook (Provo, Utah: BYU Religious Studies Center, 1980), 4. Some years later, Brigham Young offered his interpretation of the Prophet's remarks: "Joseph said that the Gentile blood was actually cleansed out of their veins, and the blood of Jacob made to circulate in them; and the revolution and change in the system were so great that it caused the beholder to think they were going into fits." *Journal of Discourses* 2:268–69.

27. *Messenger and Advocate* 1 (Jan. 1835): 57.

28. D&C 133:12–13.

29. In over five hundred pages, the Book of Mormon records the spiritual history in the western hemisphere of several groups who migrated from the Middle East. The most prominent was the colony of Lehi. It soon divided into two warring groups—the Nephites and the Lamanites. Though there are notable exceptions throughout the thousand years of history detailed, the Nephites tended to be in covenant with God while the Lamanites disregarded the paths of righteousness.

Like the Bible, the Book of Mormon is divided into books which bear the names of their prophetic authors. Originally, each book was divided only into chapters. In 1879, LDS apostle Orson Pratt divided the text into verses and smaller chapters. Since all subsequent LDS editions have used this format, unless there have been substantive wording changes as well, citations will be made in this manner. Thus, the reference here is Ether 13:4–8.

30. D&C 28:9. The word *Zion* was added to later editions for clarification. The D&C passage quoted actually uses the phrase "on the borders by the Lamanites." This was understood to mean the western border of the United States, particularly in Missouri, for two reasons. First, in the 1830s that was the boundary separating the states from the Indian territory. Second, the Latter-day Saints often referred to the Indians as Lamanites due to their belief that the Indians descended from the peoples discussed in the Book of Mormon.

31. D&C 29:7–8.

32. For the history of Mormonism in Ohio, the most detailed account is Milton V. Backman, *The Heavens Resound: A History of the Latter-day Saints in Ohio, 1830–1838* (Salt Lake City: Deseret Book, 1983).

33. D&C 43:28–30.

34. D&C 57:1–4.

35. D&C 63:24–29. The physical layout of the settlement is discussed in Ronald E. Romig and John H. Siebert, "Jackson County, 1831–1833: A Look at the Development of Zion," in *Restoration Studies III*, ed. Maurice L. Draper (Independence: Herald House, 1986), 286–304.

36. D&C 64:21–24.

37. *Personal Writings of Joseph Smith*, 66–67.

38. This circular was issued as a broadside and reprinted in the *Messenger and Advocate* 3 (Sept. 1837): 561–64.

39. Warren A. Jennings, "The City in the Garden: Social Conflict in Jackson County, Missouri," in *The Restoration Movement: Essays in Mormon History*, ed. F. Mark Mckiernan et al. (Lawrence, Kans.: Coronado Press, 1973), 99–119; Jennings, "Zion Is Fled: The Expulsion of the Mormons from Jackson County, Missouri" (Ph.D. diss., University of Florida, 1962);

Richard L. Bushman, "Mormon Persecutions in Missouri, 1833," *BYU Studies* 3 (Autumn 1960): 11–20; Richard L. Anderson, "Jackson County in Early Mormon Descriptions," *Missouri Historical Review* 65 (Apr. 1971): 270–93; and T. Edgar Lyon, "Independence, Missouri, and the Mormons, 1827–1833," *BYU Studies* 13 (Autumn 1972): 10–19.

40. D&C 116.

41. Leland H. Gentry, "A History of the Latter-day Saints in Northern Missouri from 1836–1839" (Ph.D. diss., Brigham Young University, 1965); Gentry, "Adam-ondi-Ahman: A Brief Historical Survey," *BYU Studies* 13 (Summer 1973): 553–76; Gentry, "The Land Question at Adam-ondi-Ahman," *BYU Studies* 26 (Spring 1986): 45–56; and Max H. Parkin, "A History of the Latter-day Saints in Clay County, Missouri, from 1833–1837" (Ph.D. diss., Brigham Young University, 1976).

42. A reliable, brief overview of these final difficulties can be found in F. Mark Mckiernan, "Mormonism on the Defensive: Far West," *Restoration Movement*, ed. Mckiernan et al., 121–40. Separate topical studies include Peter Crawley, "Two Rare Missouri Documents," *BYU Studies* 14 (Summer 1974): 502–27, which reproduces Sidney Rigdon's 1838 Fourth of July Oration; Reed C. Durham, "The Election Day Battle at Gallatin," *BYU Studies* 13 (Autumn 1972): 36–61; Leland H. Gentry, "The Danite Band of 1838," *BYU Studies* 14 (Summer 1974): 421–50; Alma Blair, "The Haun's Mill Massacre," *BYU Studies* 13 (Autumn 1972): 62–67; and Dean C. Jessee, "'Walls, Grates, Sckreeking Iron Doors': The Prison Experience of Mormon Leaders in Missouri—1838–1839," in *New Views of Mormon History*, ed. Britton and Beecher, 19–42.

Book-length treatments include Gentry, "History of the Latter-day Saints"; and Stephen C. LeSueur, *The 1838 Mormon War in Missouri* (Columbia: University of Missouri Press, 1987). LeSueur's revisionism has been challenged in Richard L. Anderson, "Atchison's Letters and the Causes of Mormon Expulsion from Missouri," *BYU Studies* 26 (Summer 1986): 3–47; and Clark V. Johnson, "The Missouri Redress Petitions: A Reappraisal of Mormon Persecutions in Missouri," *BYU Studies* 26 (Spring 1986): 31–44.

43. D&C 124:49, 51.

44. *Words of Joseph Smith*, 363.

45. James B. Allen, Ronald K. Esplin, and David J. Whittaker, *Men with a Mission: The Quorum of the Twelve Apostles in the British Isles, 1837–1841* (Salt Lake City: Deseret Book, 1992), 87.

46. The quote is from *Words of Joseph Smith*, 415. The editors dispute the 19 July 1840 date given for this address, claiming that "the notion that Zion comprehends all of North and South America" was one of the

"teachings of the Prophet in 1843 and 1844" (419). Dean C. Jessee, however, who first published a transcript of this address, accepts the 1840 date. See Jessee, "Joseph Smith's 19 July 1840 Discourse," *BYU Studies* 19 (Spring 1979): 390–94. The fact that the previously quoted Pratt letter was written in the fall of 1840 supports the earlier dating.

47. This development is succinctly outlined in Bruce R. McConkie, "Come: Let Israel Build Zion," *Ensign* 7 (May 1977): 115–18; and Spencer J. Palmer, *The Expanding Church* (Salt Lake City: Deseret Book, 1978), 33–42. The story of Mormon migration to Utah is told in Gustive O. Larson, *Prelude to the Kingdom: Mormon Desert Conquest* (Francistown, N.H.: Marshall Jones, 1947); Larson, "The Mormon Gathering," in *Utah's History,* ed. Richard D. Poll, (Provo: Brigham Young University Press, 1978); P. A. M. Taylor, *Expectations Westward: The Mormons and the Emigration of their British Converts in the Nineteenth Century* (London: Oliver & Boyd, 1965); Wallace Stegner, *The Gathering of Zion: The Story of the Mormon Trail* (New York: McGraw-Hill, 1964); and William Mulder, *Homeward to Zion: The Mormon Migration from Scandinavia* (Minneapolis: University of Minnesota Press, 1957).

48. Cited in Thomas G. Alexander, *Mormonism in Transition: A History of the Latter-day Saints, 1890–1930* (Urbana: University of Illinois Press, 1986), 288–89.

49. Italics added. The "Articles of Faith" derive from a March 1842 letter that Joseph Smith wrote to John Wentworth, editor of the *Chicago Democrat,* describing the history and faith of the Latter-day Saints. They are reproduced in original form in *Personal Writings of Joseph Smith,* 219–20. Today they constitute part of the canonical LDS volume, *The Pearl of Great Price* (Salt Lake City: The Church of Jesus Christ of Latter-day Saints, 1990). An overview of the history of the Articles can be found in John W. Welch and David J. Whittaker, "'We Believe . . .': Development of the Articles of Faith," *Ensign* 9 (Sept. 1979): 51–55.

50. Pratt, *Voice of Warning,* 82–84. Earlier Pratt had explained that Gog was Ezekiel's term for the Gentile nations (80).

Of related interest is George L. Berlin, "Joseph S. C. F. Frey, the Jews, and Early Nineteenth-Century Millenarianism," *Journal of the Early Republic* 1 (Spring 1981): 27–49.

51. The phrase "come quickly" is found in D&C 33:18; 34:12; 35:27; 39:24; 41:4; 49:28; 51:20; 54:10; 68:35; 87:8; 88:126; 99:5; 112:34. Expressions that the end is "nigh" or "at hand" can be found in D&C 1:12, 35; 29:9, 10; 33:10; 34:7; 35:15, 16, 26; 39:19, 21; 42:7; 43:17; 45:37–39; 49:6; 58:4; 63:53; 104:59; 106:4; 128:24; 133:17.

52. *Messenger and Advocate* 2 (Oct. 1835): 206.

53. *Messenger and Advocate* 1 (Jan. 1835): 58.

54. "Diary of Amos Bottsford Fuller, 1837–1838," typescript, LDS Church Archives, 20.

55. The most common vehicle for such promises was the "patriarchal blessing" given to individual members as a modern recreation of Jacob's prophecies and promises to his twelve sons. Such blessings are analyzed in Irene M. Bates, "Transformation of Charisma in the Mormon Church: A History of the Office of Presiding Patriarch, 1833–1979" (Ph.D. diss., University of California, Los Angeles, 1991).

56. *Star* 2 (June 1834): 162. Similar expressions were made by other premillennialists of the period such as Barton Stone and his Churches of Christ preachers. See Hughes, "Apocalyptic Origins of the Churches of Christ," 181–214.

57. D&C 29:11.

58. The earliest published poems are found in the *Star* and subsequent Church newspapers. The first compilation of hymns is Emma Smith, ed., *A Collection of Sacred Hymns for the Church of the Latter Day Saints* (Kirtland, Oh., 1835). Parley Pratt was one of the most prolific as well as popular hymnwriters in this period. His work can be examined in *The Millennial Hymns of Parley Parker Pratt*, ed. Samuel Russell (Cambridge: Cambridge University Press, 1913). On Mormon hymnody in general, see Michael Hicks, *Mormonism and Music: A History* (Urbana: University of Illinois Press, 1989); Newell B. Weight, "An Historical Study of the Origin and Character of Indigenous Hymn Tunes of the Latter-day Saints" (Ph.D. diss., University of Southern California, 1961); and David S. Wheelwright, "The Role of Hymnody in the Development of the Latter-day Saint Movement" (Ph.D. diss., University of Maryland, 1943).

59. The scriptural reference is Rev. 5:9–12; some examples of their exegesis of this passage include *Star* 2 (Apr. 1834): 146; Pratt, *Voice of Warning*, 85; and *Star* 1 (June 1832): 8.

A more developed understanding of this promise came during the early 1840s when the special temple liturgy known as "the endowment" was first revealed. See Andrew F. Ehat, "Joseph Smith's Introduction of Temple Ordinances and the 1844 Succession Question" (M.A. thesis, Brigham Young University, 1982); and David John Buerger, "The Development of the Mormon Temple Endowment Ceremony," *Dialogue* 20 (Winter 1987): 33–76.

60. *Messenger and Advocate* 3 (Apr. 1837): 482.

61. Pratt, *Voice of Warning*, 147.

62. Ibid., 148–49.

63. 10th Article of Faith, *Pearl of Great Price*, 61.

64. For example, see *Star* 2 (Feb. 1834): 131; *Messenger and Advocate* 1 (Jan. 1835): 58; 3 (Nov. 1836): 403–4; Pratt, *Voice of Warning*, 146–61; and *Elders' Journal* 1 (July 1838): 31–32.

65. Max F. Schultz, *Paradise Preserved: Recreations of Eden in Eighteenth- and Nineteenth-Century England* (Cambridge: Cambridge University Press, 1985), 321.

66. Pratt, *Voice of Warning*, 148.

67. Ibid., 152.

68. Ibid., 159.

69. D&C 133:22–24.

70. *Star* 2 (Feb. 1834): 131.

71. Pratt, *Voice of Warning*, 160.

72. Pratt, *Voice of Warning*, 84.

73. *Star* 1 (July 1832): 16. A characteristic of Phelps's hymn selection and preparation for *Star* was that he occasionally borrowed doctrinally agreeable lines or stanzas from non-Mormon songs and included them in his own compositions, sometimes with slight modification. The lines herein cited are one such example. This quatrain originally formed the final stanza of a popular Protestant hymn in the nineteenth century, "Jerusalem, My Happy Home," but is perhaps better known in its twentieth-century form as the last verse in some arrangements of "Amazing Grace." See William J. Reynolds, *Companion to Baptist Hymnal* (Nashville, Tenn.: Broadman Press, 1976), 165. The first line reads, "When we've been there ten thousand years." Phelps dropped the word *ten* and replaced it with *a*, thus making it clearly millennial in meaning.

74. Thrupp, *Millennial Dreams in Action*, 31.

Chapter 3
Apocalyptic Dualism in Early Mormonism

1. *Elders' Journal* 1 (July 1838): 42. Rigdon is mentioned in *Elders' Journal* 1 (Nov. 1837): 27.

2. *Times and Seasons* 1 (Nov. 1839): 10. *Times and Seasons* was the church's primary American periodical from 1839 to 1846. It was published in Nauvoo, Illinois, until the main body of Saints were forced to leave the city and begin their exodus westward to the Great Basin.

3. Similarly worded declarations are found in three revelations received during the 1830s: D&C 68:9; 84:74; 112:29.

4. Examples in the early literature of how this verse was used include *Messenger and Advocate* 1 (June 1834): 131, 135; 1 (July 1835): 151; 2 (Mar. 1836): 283–84. Of the sixty New Testament passages cited most frequent-

ly in LDS periodical literature between 1832 and 1838, only two (Matthew 24 and Hebrews 11) were quoted more often than Mark 16:16. See Gordon Irving, "The Mormons and the Bible in the 1830s," *BYU Studies* 13 (Summer 1973): 481.

5. *Star* 2 (Sept. 1834): 187; emphasis in original. This statement was later reprinted in the *Times and Seasons* 2 (Nov. 1840): 197.

6. *Times and Seasons* 4 (Feb. 1843): 106.

7. *Words of Joseph Smith*, 156.

8. Ibid., 162.

9. La Roy Sunderland, *Mormonism Exposed and Refuted* (New York: Piercy and Reed, 1838), 34.

10. Parley P. Pratt, *Mormonism Unveiled: Zion's Watchman Unmasked, and its Editor, Mr. L. R. Sunderland, Exposed: Truth Vindicated: the Devil Mad, and Priestcraft in Danger!* (New York: O. Pratt and O. Fordham, 1838), 25.

11. D&C 29:7.

12. *Times and Seasons* 4 (Mar. 1843): 141.

13. D&C 35:12.

14. D&C 38:6.

15. D&C 84:49–53.

16. Parley P. Pratt, *An Answer to Mr. William Hewitt's Tract against the Latter-day Saints* (Manchester, U.K.: W. R. Thomas, 1840), 8.

17. Davidson, *The Logic of Millennial Thought*. Of course, this is not to imply that such thinking is found only among apocalypticists. In her book *Natural Symbols,* Mary Douglas points out that the ideas of "inside and outside, purity within, corruption without" are "common to small bounded communities" generally and can be described as "a form of metaphysical dualism." The doctrine of "two kinds of humanity, one good, the other bad, and the association of the badness of some humans with cosmic powers of evil," she writes, "is basically similar to some of the so-called dualist religions." Mary Douglas, *Natural Symbols: Explorations in Cosmology* (London: Cresset Press, 1970), 118–19. Thus, social dualism has been a common feature of many religious groups besides apocalypticists.

Nor are polarized perceptions of society restricted to the religious. As George F. Kennan wrote, referring to Soviet attitudes towards the outside world, "It is the undeniable privilege of every man to prove himself right in the thesis that the world is his enemy; for if he reiterates it frequently enough and makes it the background of his conduct he is bound eventually to be right." Kennan, "The Sources of Soviet Conduct," *Foreign Affairs* 25 (July 1947): 59.

18. D&C 60:8, 13; 61:30, 32–33; 62:6; 68:1.

19. *Times and Seasons* 2 (Dec. 1840): 250.

20. *Times and Seasons* 6 (June 1845): 939.

21. Another distillation declares that that which "inviteth and enticeth" to sin and evil is from the devil, while that which "inviteth and enticeth" to do good is "inspired of God." Thus, the way to judge is as plain "as daylight is from the dark night" (Moroni 7:12–19).

22. Gager, *Kingdom and Community*, 25.

23. Kenelm Burridge, *New Heaven, New Earth: A Study of Millenarian Activities* (New York: Schocken Books, 1969), 147.

24. E. R. Dodds, *Pagan and Christian in an Age of Anxiety; Some Aspects of Religious Experience from Marcus Aurelius to Constantine* (Cambridge: Cambridge University Press, 1965), 59.

25. Pratt, *An Answer*, 41.

26. D&C 84:114; 61:30–31.

27. *Messenger and Advocate* 1 (Jan.1835): 61. Protesting sects over the centuries, of course, have felt little hesitation in calling down the judgments of God on all who rejected their "greater light." Seventeenth-century Separatists, for instance, considered not only the Church of England to be "the direct target of God's vengeful wrath; but monarchs, magistrates, and entire nations—papists, protestants, and puritans alike—were all included in the doomsday predictions of the separatists." What is more, "they did not expect a simply spiritual judgment to descend from on high, but one that could equally as well include some form of physical devastation." Stephen Brachlow, *The Communion of the Saints: Radical Puritan and Separatist Ecclesiology, 1570–1625* (Oxford: Oxford University Press, 1988), 97, 99.

28. Moorhead, *American Apocalypse*, 7. This propensity among millenarian apocalypticists is illustrated in John M. Werly, "Premillennialism and the Paranoid Style," *American Studies* 18 (Spring 1977): 39–55.

29. The fear of conspiracy in America is ably analyzed by David B. Davis in "Some Themes of Countersubversion: An Analysis of Anti-Masonic, Anti-Catholic, and Anti-Mormon Literature," *Mississippi Valley Historical Review* 47 (Sept. 1960): 205–25.

30. *Messenger and Advocate* 1 (Jan. 1835): 58.

31. James H. Moorhead writes that "opposition could in turn become evidence to the believer that the millennium was indeed approaching and that his zeal should be redoubled." Moorhead, "Social Reform and the Divided Conscience of Antebellum Protestantism," *Church History* 48 (Dec. 1979): 421.

32. Michael Barkun has written that "men cleave to hopes of imminent worldly salvation when the hammerblows of disaster destroy the world they have known." Barkun, *Disaster and the Millennium* (New Haven: Yale University Press, 1974), 1.

33. Russell, ed., *Millennial Hymns of Parley Parker Pratt*, 19. As late as

the early twentieth century, Latter-day Saints still sang these words from a hymn composed by the Mormon apostle Charles Penrose:

> In thy mountain retreat, God will strengthen thy feet;
> On the necks of thy foes thou shalt tread;
> And their silver and gold, as the Prophets have told,
> Shall be brought to adorn they fair head. . . .

> Thy deliverance is nigh, thy oppressors shall die,
> And the Gentiles shall bow 'neath thy rod.
> ("O Ye Mountains High," #198, *Deseret Sunday School Songs* [Salt Lake City: Deseret Sunday School Union, 1909])

The apocalyptic hope, however, is not restricted to those outwardly threatened. Mormons yearned for the destruction of the wicked, regardless of external animosities. William Smith's remarks illustrate the point. "When I consider the condition of mankind," he wrote, "even, what are termed enlightened nations, and through the glass of scriptures see manifest all their blindness, depravity, and hypocrisy, my heart sickens at the sight and I turn away from the contemplation and I am ready to exclaim, O Lord!"

> How long shall such wickedness,
> Be suffered in the land?
> How long before thou make bare
> Thy own Almighty hand?
> (*Times and Seasons* 2 [June 1841]: 445)

34. Joseph Smith, Jr., *History of the Church of Jesus Christ of Latter-day Saints,* ed. B. H. Roberts, 2d ed., 7 vols. (1951; Salt Lake City: Deseret Book Co., 1976), 3:291–92; hereafter, *History of the Church.*

35. *History of the Church,* 4:89. These remarks were made in March 1840, upon the Prophet's return to Nauvoo from Washington, D.C.

36. Joseph Smith to John C. Calhoun, 2 January 1844, in *Times and Seasons* 5 (Jan. 1844): 395. He seems to be recalling an earlier revelation—D&C 101:86–91.

37. *Times and Seasons* 6 (Dec. 1845): 1052. The quotation is from Isaiah 33:1.

38. *Times and Seasons* 6 (July 1845): 952.

39. Davidson, *The Logic of Millennial Thought,* 83.

40. Donald G. Matthews claims that "it is the Apocalypse which is missing from most evaluations of black Christianity." Mathews, *Religion in the Old South* (Chicago: University of Chicago Press, 1977), 231. Also relevant

is Henry Lewis Gates, "The Voice in the Text: Messianism, Millenarianism, and the Discourse of the Black in the Eighteenth Century," in *Millenarianism and Messianism in English Literature and Thought, 1650–1800,* ed. Richard H. Popkin (Leiden: Brill, 1988), 193–210.

41. Albert J. Raboteau, *Slave Religion: The "Invisible Institution" in the Antebellum South* (New York: Oxford University Press, 1978), 291.

42. Solon Foster to Luther Foster, 28 December 1848, Foster Family Correspondence, LDS Church Archives.

43. For examples, see *Star* 1 (Feb. 1833): 67; and 1 (Jan. 1833): 60.

44. D&C 39:16–21.

45. *Times and Seasons* 2 (July 1841): 461.

46. D&C 63:37. Mormons were not alone in so perceiving their mission. Other millenarian primitivists such as the Stoneites (Churches of Christ) held a similar outlook.

47. D&C 84:117. Even in the dedicatory prayer for the Kirtland Temple, Joseph Smith chose to petition the Lord thus: "And whatsoever city thy servants shall enter, and the people of that city receive not the testimony of thy servants . . . let it be upon that city according to that which thou hast spoken . . . terrible things concerning the wicked, in the last days—that thou wilt pour out thy judgments without measure." D&C 109:41, 45.

48. *Messenger and Advocate* 2 (July 1836): 346. The tract was published separately as a broadside entitled *A Prophetic Warning* (Toronto, 1836).

49. Pratt, *Voice of Warning,* 141–42.

50. Reported in *Times and Seasons* 3 (May 1842): 798.

51. *Star* 2 (Jan. 1834): 126.

52. D&C 45:66–69; 115:6; 124:36, 109.

53. *History of the Church,* 1:315–16.

54. *Times and Seasons* 2 (Jan. 1841): 276.

55. *Messenger and Advocate* 3 (Nov. 1836): 404.

56. In the dedicatory prayer for the Kirtland temple, the Lord was petitioned thus: "And whatsoever city thy servants enter, and the people of that city receive their testimony, let thy peace and thy salvation be upon that city; that they may gather out of that city the righteous, that they may come forth to Zion, or to her stakes, the places of thine appointment, with songs of everlasing joy; and until this be accomplished, let not thy judgments fall upon that city." D&C 109:39–40.

57. A good discussion of both substance and style in early Mormon preaching is Barbara J. Higdon, "The Role of Preaching in the Early Latter Day Saint Church, 1830–1846" (Ph.D. diss., University of Missouri, 1961). The quotation is D&C 63:58.

58. D&C 105:24; *Star* 1 (July 1832): 14.

59. D&C 109:43–44.

60. Cited in Arrington and Bitton, *The Mormon Experience,* 193.

61. Today's LDS missionaries are influenced by a different psychology of motivation, and talk of impending destruction or imminent punishments is perceived as being too harsh.

62. Examples of their discussion of the passage from Acts can be found in *Star* 1 (Sept. 1832): 30; 2 (June 1833): 161; and *Times and Seasons* 2 (Apr. 1841): 359. Examples of how the Mormons used the passage from Thessalonians are *Star* 2 (May 1834): 155; *Messenger and Advocate* 1 (Jan. 1835): 56–57; and *Times and Seasons* 1 (Dec. 1839): 26.

63. *Times and Seasons* 2 (Mar. 1841): 351. Such sentiments, of course, had long been a part of sectarian Protestantism. Two centuries earlier, Roger Williams had also looked forward to the day when Christ would come "in flaming fire to burne up millions of ignorant and disobedient." Cited in *The Complete Writings of Roger Williams,* ed. Reuben E. Guild et al. (Providence: Narragansett Club Publications, 1866–74; New York: Russell and Russell, 1963), 1:334.

64. Pratt, *Voice of Warning,* 71.

65. Pratt, *A Letter to the Queen, Touching the Signs of the Times, and the Political Destiny of the World* (Manchester, U.K., 1841), 6. See also Malachi 4:1–3.

66. D&C 63:53–54.

67. *Messenger and Advocate* 3 (Nov. 1836): 403. In a 16 March 1841 sermon (*Words of Joseph Smith,* 65), for the first time on record, Joseph Smith advanced the idea that there would be "wicked" men on the earth during the millennium. When he did, it represented an abrupt about-face from a decade of Mormon consensus to the contrary, and it would be at least another decade before the idea really caught hold even among church leaders. As late as 1857, Orson Hyde was still talking of all the wicked being consumed at the Second Coming (see *Journal of Discourses,* 26 vols. [London: Latter-day Saints' Book Depot, 1855–86], 5:355–56). On the other hand, Brigham Young clearly felt that there would be "wicked" men—unbelievers—on the earth during the millennium (see *Journal of Discourses,* 2:316, 7:142).

68. Received in February 1832, the "Vision" was canonized and is now found in D&C 76. The earliest available copy of the revelation was published in the *Star* in July 1832. See Robert J. Woodford, "The Historical Development of the Doctrine and Covenants" (Ph.D. diss., Brigham Young University, 1974).

69. *History of the Church,* 1:245. Such an idea had also occurred to earlier religionists. "The idea of different degrees of felicity in future life, as differences of reward was widely prevalent" among the early Church fa-

thers. This was also true even of some later Protestant divines. "In opposition to Rome, the influence of personal merit on the future state was denied by these theologians; but some of them, while admitting that blessedness is essentially the same for all, hold to several *degrees* of blessedness." John McClintock and James Strong, eds., *Cyclopedia of Biblical, Theological, and Ecclesiastical Literature,* 10 vols. (New York: Harper and Brothers, 1867–81; Grand Rapids: Baker Book House, 1969), 3:315, 317.

70. Mormons find support for both this vision and the terms employed in 1 Corinthians 15:40–42.

71. See D&C 76:33, 51, 75, 103.

72. What few comments were made are sufficiently superficial that they offer no real interpretation or elucidation of the Vision and certainly no repudiation of traditional Christian soteriology. For an account of some who advanced doctrinally unacceptable positions, see *History of the Church,* 1:366. For an early but brief discussion that was apparently acceptable, see *Star* 1 (June 1832): 6; 1 (July 1832): 22 (this source is reproduced in *History of the Church,* 1:283, and *Star* 1 [February 1833]: 69).

73. Some have felt that the absence of discussion of the Vision of the Three Degrees of Glory was by design, that due to its revolutionary nature it was considered too advanced for those still needing "milk," and that it was therefore intentionally suppressed during the early years. Such thinking is based on the Prophet's recorded counsel to the English missionaries to "remain silent concerning the gathering, the vision, and the book of Doctrine and Covenants, until such time as the work was fully established" (*History of the Church,* 2:492).

The assumption is that similar restrictions must have been in effect in the United States. This inference is problematic, however. In the first place, there is almost no documentary evidence for it. On the contrary, there is evidence to show that such a limitation was *not* in effect. American missionaries constantly talked of "the gathering." It was central to their millenarian message. They were also occasionally encouraged to preach the "late revelations" (*Times and Seasons* 4 [Apr. 1843]: 175, for example). And Orson Pratt, at least, on three different occasions in three different years (22 Sept. 1833, 5 Jan. 1834, and 17 May 1835), preached on the Vision. *The Orson Pratt Journals,* ed. Elden J. Watson (Salt Lake City: Watson, 1975), 26, 30, 62.

Since in the Prophet's statement the Vision was merely listed along with other delicate doctrines, rather than being singled out, can its neglect in America be considered intentional when the other controversial concepts were freely advocated? Furthermore, it should be remembered that even in the Prophet's proscription, provision was made for a later exposure when "the work was fully established." Yet there is no evidence of anything more than passing mention of the Vision in any of the American locations—Kirtland, Far West, or early Nauvoo—where the Church had already been fully established.

74. One exception to this is the following from W. W. Phelps: "All men have a right to their opinions, but to adopt them for rules of faith and worship, is wrong, and may finally leave the souls of them that receive them for spiritual guides, in the telestial kingdom: For these are they who are of Paul, and of Apollos . . . but received not the gospel." *Star* 1 (Feb. 1833): 69. Also interesting along this line, though from a decade later, is Joseph's poeticized version:

> These are they that came out for Apollos and Paul;
> For Cephas and Jesus, in all kinds of hope;
> For Enoch and Moses, and Peter and John;
> For Luther and Calvin, and even the Pope.
> (*Times and Seasons* 4 [Feb. 1843]: 85)

Another exception which illustrates the conceptual confusion apparent when these kingdoms were mentioned is Wilford Woodruff's record of Zebedee Coltrin's prophecy upon his head when he was ordained a "seventy": "Also that I should visit COLUB [Kolob] & Preach to the spirits in Prision & that I should bring all of my friends or relatives forth from the Terrestrial Kingdom (who had died) by the Power of the Gospel." *Wilford Woodruff's Journal, 1833–1898*, 9 vols., ed. Scott G. Kenney (Salt Lake City: Signature Books, 1983–85), 1:119 (3 Jan. 1837).

75. *Times and Seasons* 4 (Feb. 1843): 81–85.

76. Philip Schaff, *The Principle of Protestantism As Related to the Present State of the Church* (Chambersburg, 1845), 114, cited in Winthrop S. Hudson, *Religion in America*, 3d ed. (New York: Charles Scribner's Sons, 1981), 8. Modern historians of religion concur. Sydney E. Ahlstrom, for example, speaks of its "enormous impact on subsequent history" and calls it "by far the most influential doctrinal symbol in American Protestant history." Ahlstrom, *A Religious History of the American People*, 2 vols. (New Haven: Yale University Press, 1972; Garden City, N.Y.: Image Books, 1975), 1:118, 177.

77. Phillip Schaff, ed., *The Creeds of Christendom*, 3 vols. (New York: Harper and Brothers, 1877; Grand Rapids: Baker Book House, 1966), 3:671.

This contrasts with the Roman Catholic ideas of Purgatory and Limbo. Purgatory is defined as "the state, place, or condition in the next world, which will continue until the last judgment, where the souls of those who die in the state of grace, but not yet free from all imperfection, make expiation for unforgiven venial sins or for the temporal punishment due to venial and mortal sins that have already been forgiven and, by so doing, are purified before they enter heaven" (*New Catholic Encyclopedia*, 1967 ed., s.v. "Purgatory"). Limbo is "the state and place either of those souls who did not merit hell and its eternal punishments but could not enter heaven before the Redemption (the fathers' Limbo); or those souls who are eternally excluded from the beatific vision because of original sin alone (the children's Limbo)" (*New Catholic Encyclopedia*, 1967 ed., s.v. "Limbo").

However, eighteenth- and even early nineteenth-century continental Catholicism differed little from Protestantism in its didactic use of descriptions of hell and damnation to motivate the populace to godly living. In France, Father Jacques Bridaine preached numerous sermons on hell which were far more lurid than those of his contemporary, Jonathan Edwards, who is popularly stereotyped in that role. Moreover, Jean-Baptiste Massillon, court preacher to young Louis XV, published an influential sermon entitled "On the Small Number of the Elect," a piece one might expect to have been of Calvinist origin. See Ralph Gibson, "Hellfire and Damnation in Nineteenth-Century France," *Catholic Historical Review* 74 (July 1988): 383–402.

78. Some of the more obvious examples from the Book of Mormon of a polarized afterlife are 1 Nephi 15:29–36; 2 Nephi 9:11–19; and Alma 40:11–26.

79. D&C 29:27–28.

80. D&C 101:65–66.

81. In the current lexicon of Mormon theology, "eternal life" is "the kind, status, type, and quality of life that God himself enjoys." It is reserved only for those in the highest level of the highest glory, the "Celestial Kingdom." On the other hand, to be "cast out with the devil and his angels, to inherit the same kingdom" is a fate reserved only for those once faithful but now fallen foes of God's church known as "sons of perdition." Bruce McConkie, *Mormon Doctrine*, 2d ed. (Salt Lake City: Bookcraft, 1966), 237, 746. Thus, today, these two outcomes describe only the polar ends of afterlife possibilities.

82. *Star* 1 (Mar. 1833): 77.

83. *Times and Seasons* 4 (Feb. 1843): 85.

84. The definitive study is Russell E. Miller, *The Larger Hope: The First Century of the Universalist Church in America, 1770–1870* (Boston: Unitarian Universalist Association, 1979). Good, brief introductions to Universalism are provided in George H. Williams, *American Universalism: A Bicentennial Essay* (Medford, Mass.: Universalist Historical Society, 1971); and Marini, *Radical Sects*.

85. *Messenger and Advocate* 1 (July 1835): 150–52. Lewis O. Saum has

documented the widespread antipathy to Universalism among the "common man" in antebellum America. See his *Popular Mood of Pre–Civil War America* (Westport, Conn.: Greenwood Press, 1980), 44–47.

86. *Messenger and Advocate* 1 (July 1835): 151. In a later reminiscence, Brigham Young suggested that such strong anti-Universalist sentiment even led some Saints to find fault with the Vision itself because it seemed too generous with salvation. *Journal of Discourses*, 26 vols. (London: Latter-day Saints' Book Depot, 1855–56), 16:42. (*Journal of Discourses* is a collection of talks given in Utah by LDS church leaders over a span of thirty years.)

87. Philastus Hurlbut's work was incorporated in Eber D. Howe, *Mormonism Unvailed* (Painesville, Ohio, 1834); Origen Bacheler, *Mormonism Exposed* (New York, 1838); and La Roy Sunderland, *Mormonism Exposed and Refuted* (New York, 1838). There is neither direct mention nor allusion to the Vision in any of these works.

88. John Corrill, *A Brief History of the Church of Christ of Latter Day Saints (Commonly Called Mormons)* (St. Louis, 1839), 47.

89. Caswall admits dependence on Corrill. Henry Caswall, *The Prophet of the Nineteenth Century* (London, 1843), 98–99. Jonathan Baldwin Turner, *Mormonism in All Ages* (New York: Platt and Peters, 1842), 243.

One exception to this general oversight is a recently discovered tract (shared by David Whittaker, Mormon Archivist at the BYU Library) published in England about 1840. It provides the only contemporary reaction to the Vision longer than a sentence or two. The unnamed author, simply designated "a lover of truth," read the Vision as a Universalist manifesto. It seemed to him that the Vision dangerously extended the net of salvation beyond Reformed Protestant assumptions, thus removing the deterrent of threatened damnation. *Remarks on the Doctrines, Practices, &c. of the Latter-Day Saints: Setting forth the Marvellous Things Connected with the New Light from America* (Preston, U.K., n.d.). Since this pamphlet was published by Joseph Livesey, who also published another anti-Mormon tract by the Methodist minister Richard Livesey, it may be that Richard Livesey was the author.

90. William Harris, *Mormonism Portrayed* (Warsaw, Ill.: Sharp and Gamble, 1841), 23. Harris is mentioned in the context of faithful missionary service in *Messenger and Advocate* 3 (Jan. 1837): 446.

91. Pratt, *Voice of Warning*, 217–18. These ideas are placed in context in Colleen McDannell and Bernhard Lang, *Heaven: A History* (New Haven: Yale University Press, 1988).

92. Harris's recollection is confirmed in the words of this early Mormon song:

The heaven of sectarians is not the heaven for me;
So doubtful its location, neither on land nor sea.
But I've a heaven on the earth—
The land and home that gave me birth,—
A heaven of light and knowledge—
O, that's the heaven for me, &c.
(*Times and Seasons* 6 [Feb. 1845]: 799)

93. *Words of Joseph Smith,* 214.

94. Ibid., 368.

95. For this and subsequent quotations from the King Follett address, I have used Stan Larson's amalgamation of the various contemporary accounts. See Stan Larson, "The King Follett Discourse: A Newly Amalgamated Text," *BYU Studies* 18 (Winter 1978): 193–208. The quotation is from p. 205.

A total of seven verses in the Book of Mormon directly equate "torment" with a "lake of fire and brimstone" (2 Nephi 9:16, 19, 26; 28:23; Jacob 6:10; Mosiah 3:27; and Alma 12:17). A symbolic connection, however, seems necessary only in Mosiah 3:27 and Alma 12:17, where the word *as* is used to link the two terms. For example, "Then is the time when their torments shall be *as* a lake of fire and brimstone, whose flame ascendeth up forever and ever" (Alma 12:17; emphasis mine). For individuals accustomed to a literal hermeneutic, the remaining passages would not have seemed unusual. In well-worn cadences, Jacob 6:10 speaks of going "away into that lake of fire and brimstone, whose flames are unquenchable, and whose smoke ascendeth up forever and ever, which lake of fire and brimstone is endless torment"; 2 Nephi 28:23 also warns of a "place" prepared for them, "even a lake of fire and brimstone, which is endless torment." It is easy enough to see how such verses with their spatial allusions would not have forced abandonment of traditional perceptions of a physical hell.

Of related interest is the textual change from the 1830 edition in 2 Nephi 9:16. Originally it read, "And they shall go away into everlasting fire, prepared for them; and their torment is a lake of fire and brimstone" (1830 ed., 80). Later the important word *as* was inserted, and today this verse and the other two mentioned above are invoked to provide scriptural justification for the metaphorical interpretation Joseph Smith began explicitly employing in the last months of his life (for example, McConkie, *Mormon Doctrine,* 280–81). Significantly, I could find no instance in which either Joseph Smith or any other Latter-day Saint used these verses in such a fashion during the period studied. In fact, Smith's use of traditional jargon to describe hell is conspicuous as late as his 1843 poem. Whereas in the original scriptural text of the Vision the word *hell* is found only once, the Prophet uses it six times in his poem. In terms familiar to Christians from any century, he talks of the ungodly who suffer "in hell-fire, and vengeance, the doom of the damn'd." No passage, however, is more striking than this quatrain describing the fate of the sons of perdition:

> They are they who must go to the great lake of fire,
> Which burneth with brimstone, yet never consumes,
> And dwell with the devil, and angels of his,
> While eternity goes and eternity comes.
> (*Times and Seasons* 4 [Feb. 184]: 83)

96. Larson, "King Follett Discourse," 207. The duration of postmortal punishment was an issue raised by the Universalists.

97. The early revelation is D&C 19:5–12. The "chains of hell" are given symbolic meaning in Alma 12:9–11, but, again, the verses were not discussed in the early years.

98. Larson, "King Follett Discourse," 207–8.

99. Smith began discussing the topics of the "unpardonable sin" and the "sons of perdition" in depth about the same time he was also modifying his conception of hell and the afterlife, that is, during the final months of his life (see *Words of Joseph Smith*, 330, 334–35, 342, 347–48, 353–54, 360–61). It is true that in June 1833, Smith mentioned the sons of perdition, but, as has already been noted, this was only to say that not enough was known about them or their destiny to justify discussing it (*History of the Church*, 1:366).

100. This is perhaps best illustrated in the case of John Taylor. Throughout this period, Taylor was closely associated with Smith both as editor of the *Times and Seasons* and, from September 1843, as a member of the Anointed Quorum, a select group composed of those who were the first to experience the Mormon temple ceremony. John Taylor was thus well exposed not only to Smith's public but also to his private teachings. Yet, in a *Times and Seasons* editorial published less than a year after Smith's death, John Taylor declared that "hell" is literally "in the midst of the earth, and when Sodom and Gomorrah were destroyed they sunk down to hell, and the water covered up the unhallowed spot. . . . No wonder we have earthquakes, hot springs and convulsions in the earth," he continued, "if the damned spirits of six thousand years . . . have gone down *into the pit*. . . . No wonder the earth groans and is in pain to be delivered as saith the prophet." *Times and Seasons* 6 (Feb. 1845): 792.

If a man as intelligent and literate as John Taylor either did not understand or ignored the Prophet, one can imagine to what degree the finer doctrinal subtleties that Joseph Smith was introducing in the late Nauvoo period actually settled into the conscious understanding of the ordinary member. Scholars are liable to error if they simply assume that once an idea was revealed or once it was taught by the Prophet the Saints immediately assimilated it into their mental universes.

Chapter 4
The Bible, the Mormons, and Millenarianism

1. Perry Miller, "The Old Testament in Colonial America," in *Historical Viewpoints*, ed. John A. Garraty (New York: Harper and Row, 1970), 1–95. See also Nathan O. Hatch and Mark A. Noll, *The Bible in America: Essays in Cultural History* (New York: Oxford University Press, 1982).

2. Philip L. Barlow, *Mormons and the Bible: The Place of the Latter-day Saints in American Religion* (New York: Oxford University Press, 1991) contains several chapters on Mormon use of the Bible during the pre-Utah period.

3. Cited in Stephen J. Stein, "Transatlantic Extensions: Apocalyptic in Early New England," in *The Apocalypse in English Renaissance Thought and Literature: Patterns, Antecedents, and Repercussions*, ed. C. A. Patrides and Joseph Wittreich (Ithaca: Cornell University Press, 1984), 266–298. Typological thought among the Puritans is explored in John R. Knott, Jr., *The Sword of the Spirit: Puritan Responses to the Bible* (Chicago: University of Chicago Press, 1980); Mason I. Lowance, *The Language of Canaan: Metaphor and Symbol in New England from the Puritans to the Transcendentalists* (Cambridge: Harvard University Press, 1980); Theresa Toulouse, *The Art of Prophesying: New England Sermons and the Shaping of Belief* (Athens: University of Georgia Press, 1987); Bozeman, *To Live Ancient Lives;* and Charles L. Cohen, "Two Biblical Models of Conversion: An Example of Puritan Hermeneutics," *Church History* 58 (June 1989): 182–96.

4. The analysis is based upon three major published collections of Joseph Smith's communications—*Words of Joseph Smith, Personal Writings of Joseph Smith,* and *Teachings of the Prophet Joseph Smith,* ed. Joseph Fielding (Salt Lake City: Deseret News Press, 1938).

5. The ability to identify so readily with biblical episodes and individuals, however, was elsewhere on the wane. See Hans W. Frei, *The Eclipse of Biblical Narrative: A Study in Eighteenth- and Nineteenth-Century Hermeneutics* (New Haven: Yale University Press, 1974).

6. Sacvan Bercovitch, "The Typology of America's Mission," *American Quarterly* 30 (1978): 133–55; Bercovitch, *The American Jeremiad* (Madison: University of Wisconsin Press, 1978); Conrad Cherry, ed., *God's New Israel: Religious Interpretations of American Destiny* (Englewood Cliffs: Prentice-Hall, 1971).

7. *Personal Writings of Joseph Smith,* 285.

176   *Notes to Pages 60–63*

8. Ibid., 375.

9. Ibid., 317.

10. *Wilford Woodruff's Journal,* 1:125.

11. *Personal Writings of Joseph Smith,* 376.

12. Ibid., 376.

13. Ibid., 377. Core, or Cora (Korah), Datham, and Abiram were the leaders of a revolt against Moses and Aaron and were swallowed up in the earth for their rebellion (Numbers 16).

14. *Personal Writings of Joseph Smith,* 472–73.

15. *Words of Joseph Smith,* 111.

16. *Teachings of the Prophet Joseph Smith,* 22.

17. For the religion scholar John F. Wilson, it was bringing such literary figuralism to bear on Mormon millennial thought that compelled him to distance the Saints from postmillennialism. "If figural elements are part of the movement's self understanding," he explained, "the degree of dependence upon human initiative required to secure the kingdom should not be overinterpreted. This is to say, if the Prophet and his associates viewed themselves as, so to speak, acting out revelatory roles in this world written in another and transmitted through scriptures, the degree of the 'initiative' they were required to take would seem to be less striking than it is ordinarily held to be." Wilson, "Some Comparative Perspectives on the Early Mormon Movement and the Church-State Question, 1830–1845," *Journal of Mormon History* 8 (1981): 63–77.

18. In the words of one scholar, "we may say the New Testament method of interpreting the Old was generally that of typology. Types and prophecies of the coming of Christ were sought throughout the Old Testament" and "were readily found." The early Christians "regarded the events described in the Old Testament as prefigurations of events in the life of Jesus and his church." Robert M. Grant and David Tracy, *A Short History of the Interpretation of the Bible,* 2d ed. (Philadelphia: Fortress Press, 1984), 36–37.

Jan Shipps is sensitive to this aspect of LDS thought in her book, *Mormonism: The Story of a New Religious Tradition.*

19. *Teachings of the Prophet Joseph Smith,* 280.

20. *Words of Joseph Smith,* 180–81.

21. Ibid., 68.

22. Orson Hyde, *A Voice from Jerusalem, or a Sketch of the Travels and Ministry of Elder Orson Hyde, Missionary of the Church of Jesus Christ of Latter Day Saints, to Germany, Constantinople, and Jerusalem* (Liverpool, 1842), 18.

23. American Protestants, of course, had long spoken of an American Zion, but they did so in the usual typological terms, never anticipating on their continent the actual presence of a glistening New Jerusalem.

Information found in this and subsequent paragraphs relies on Peter Toon, ed., *Puritans, the Millennium and the Future of Israel* (Cambridge: Clark, 1970); David S. Katz, *Philo-Semitism and the Readmission of the Jews to England, 1603–1655* (Oxford: Clarendon Press, 1982); Katz, *Sabbath and Sectarianism in Seventeenth-Century England* (Leiden: Brill, 1988); Richard H. Popkin, "Jewish Messianism and Christian Millenarianism," in *Culture and Politics from Puritanism to the Enlightenment,* ed. Perez Zagorin (Berkeley: University of California Press, 1980), 79–83; *Millenarianism and Messianism in English Literature and Thought, 1650–1800* (Leiden: Brill, 1988); Popkin, "Millenarianism in England, Holland and America: Jewish-Christian Relations in Amsterdam, London and Newport, Rhode Island," in *Philosophy, History and Social Action,* ed. S. Hook, W. L. O'Neill, and R. O'Toole (Norwell, Mass.: Kluwer Academic Publishers, 1988), 349–71; and Popkin, "The Lost Tribes, the Caraites and the English Millenarians," *Journal of Jewish Studies* 37 (Autumn 1986): 213–27.

24. Mayr Verete in his 1981–82 Clark Lecture, "The Idea of the Restoration of Israel in English Thought," argued that when Calvinist theologians reinterpreted the phrase "all Israel" in verses 25–26 to mean the historical Jews rather than taking it to be a symbolic reference to the church, Christian Zionism was born. See Popkin, ed., *Millenarianism and Messianism,* 10–11.

Helpful context is also provided in E. Elizabeth Johnson, *The Functions of Apocalyptic and Wisdom Traditions in Romans 9–11* (Atlanta: Scholars Press, 1989); and James W. Watts, "The Remnant Theme: A Survey of New Testament Research, 1921–1987," *Perspectives in Religious Studies* 15 (Summer 1988): 109–29.

25. Christopher Hill, "'Till the Conversion of the Jews,'" in *Millenarianism and Messianism,* ed. Popkin, 12–36, demonstrates how widespread in seventeenth-century England was the idea that the conversion and restoration of the Jews was the crucial antecedent to the millennium. The pre-Reformation view is discussed in Robert C. Stacey, "The Conversion of the Jews to Christianity in Thirteenth-Century England," *Speculum* 67 (1992): 263–83.

26. In Reformed Protestant soteriology, conversion was not simply cognitive acceptance of theological propositions; it was a work of divine grace from start to finish. Therefore, contemporary writers spoke of "the calling of the Jews" when referring to their conversion. Early Christian descriptions of the end times are reviewed in Danielou, *The Theology of Jewish Christianity,* 377–404; Lea, "A Survey of the Doctrine of the Return of Christ in the Ante-Nicene Fathers," 163–77; and Daley, *The Hope of the Early Church.*

27. Henry Finch, *The Calling of the Iewes* (London, 1621). See Franz

Kobler, "Sir Henry Finch (1558–1625) and the First English Advocates of the Restoration of the Jews to Palestine," *Transactions of the Jewish Historical Society of England* 16 (1952): 101–20.

28. Increase Mather, *The Mystery of Israel's Salvation, Explained and Applied: or, a Discourse Concerning the General Conversion of the Israelitish Nation* (London, 1669). See Carl Frederick Ehle, Jr., "Prolegomena to Christian Zionism in America: The Views of Increase Mather and William E. Blackstone Concerning the Doctrine of the Restoration of Israel" (Ph.D. diss., New York University, 1977). Mather's son, Cotton, was also an influential colonial American eschatologist. See John S. Erwin, *The Millennialism of Cotton Mather* (Lewiston: Edwin Mellen Press, 1990).

Regina S. Sharif, *Non-Jewish Zionism: Its Roots in Western History* (London: Zed Press, 1983); and Mayr Verete, "The Restoration of the Jews in English Protestant Thought," *Middle Eastern Studies* 8 (1972): 3–50, provide excellent surveys of Christian Zionism.

29. Mel Scult, *Millennial Expectations and Jewish Liberties: A Study of the Efforts to Convert Jews in Britain up to the Mid-Nineteenth Century* (Leiden: Brill, 1978) traces the changing attitudes about the national conversion of the Jews.

30. Millenarians generally espoused both the conversion and territorial restoration of the Jews prior to the Second Coming. Some, however, had more grandiose visions of the restored Jewish state than others. See Whalen, "Millenarianism and Millennialism," 124–25, 160–70.

31. Varying LDS ideas on this and related matters are explored in Steven Epperson, *Mormons and Jews: Early Mormon Theologies of Israel* (Salt Lake City: Signature Books, 1992).

32. Watson, *The Orson Pratt Journals*, 23, 25, 26, 48, 52, 65. Orson Pratt elaborated on his ideas of the Jews gathering in unbelief in *New Jerusalem; or, the Fulfillment of Modern Prophecy* (Liverpool, 1848); and later in addresses in Utah. See *Journal of Discourses*, 18:64, 20:147.

33. *Wilford Woodruff's Journal*, 2:271 (16 Aug. 1843). Woodruff later expressed the view that the Jews would not be converted until Christ returned (4:362–66 [12 Dec. 1855], 4:401 [17 Feb. 1856], 7:457 [26 Feb. 1879]).

34. As W. W. Phelps summarized it, "Judah will be gathered: and when the Lord shows himself to them, with the wounds he received of them, more than eighteen hundred years before, they will know him, and rejoice in the Holy One of Israel." *Star* 1 (Feb. 1833): 67.

35. D&C 45:51–53.

36. *Star* 2 (Mar. 1834): 141.

37. *Star* 1 (Aug. 1832): 21. The excerpt is from *The Reformer* 12 (Dec. 1831): 109.

38. Hyde, *A Voice from Jerusalem,* 14.

39. Ibid., 15.

40. *Times and Seasons* 2 (May 1841): 408.

41. On occasion, the Saints actually referred to the Indians as "Jews." See, for instance, D&C 19:27; 57:4.

Excellent histories of the idea of the Hebraic origins of the Indian are Richard H. Popkin, "The Jewish Indian Theory," in *Menasseh ben Israel and His World,* ed. Joseph Kaplan et al. (Leiden: Brill, 1989); and Walter Hart Blumenthal, "The 'Lost Ten Tribes': Prehistoric Peopling of America: A Bibliographical Survey of the Early Theory of Israelitish Derivation, and the Origin of the American Indians," manuscript, American Jewish Archives at Hebrew Union College, Cincinnati, 1930.

Of related interest are Lee E. Huddleston, *Origins of the American Indians: European Concepts, 1492–1729* (Austin: University of Texas, 1967); Margaret T. Hogden, *Early Anthropology in the Sixteenth and Seventeenth Centuries* (Philadelphia: University of Pennsylvania Press, 1964); Robert Wauchope, *Lost Tribes and Sunken Continents: Myth and Method in the Study of American Indians* (Chicago: University of Chicago Press, 1962); Robert F. Berkhofer, Jr., *The White Man's Indian: Images of the American Indian from Columbus to the Present* (New York: Vintage, 1979); *Hebrew and the Bible in America: The First Two Centuries,* ed. Shalom Goldman (Hanover, N.H.: University Press of New England, 1993). Richard Slotkin, *Regeneration Through Violence: Mythology of the American Frontier, 1600–1860* (Middletown: Wesleyan University Press, 1973) places this notion in the broad background of American literary history.

42. *Proclamation of the Twelve Apostles of the Church of Jesus Christ of Latter-day Saints* (Liverpool: Wilford Woodruff, 1845), 4, 13. It was also published in New York the same year.

43. Latter-day Saints believed that the lost tribes would come first to the American Zion to receive certain blessings before moving on to their millennial inheritance in the Holy Land. "And they who are in the north countries shall come in remembrance before the Lord; and their prophets shall hear his voice, and shall no longer stay themselves; and they shall smite the rocks, and the ice shall flow down at their presence. And an highway shall be cast up in the midst of the great deep . . . and the boundaries of the everlasting hills shall tremble at their presence. And there shall they fall down and be crowned with glory, even in Zion, by the hands of the servants of the Lord, even the children of Ephraim. And they shall be filled with songs of everlasting joy. Behold, this is the blessing of the everlasting God upon the tribes of Israel" (D&C 133:26–34). Parley Pratt finds their eventual settlement in the Holy Land predicted in a variety of biblical passages. See Pratt, *Voice of Warning,* 55–60, 71–73, 171–80.

44. *History of the Church,* 2:52.
45. *Messenger and Advocate* 1 (Nov. 1834): 18.
46. *Personal Writings of Joseph Smith,* 271.
47. Ibid., 274.
48. Ibid., 273. As support for the general theme of the restoration of Israel, the Prophet also cited, but did not comment on, these common millenarian passages: Joel 2:32, Isaiah 26:20–21, Jeremiah 31:12, Psalms 50:5, and Ezekiel 34:11–13.
49. *Personal Writings of Joseph Smith,* 274.
50. From David Katz's study, *Sabbath and Sectarianism,* it is noteworthy how often in transatlantic sectarian Protestantism since the English Civil War that a literalist fascination with the Old Testament and an interest to study the Hebrew language have linked up with a millenarian eschatology. See also Daniel Liechty, *Andreas Fischer and the Sabbatarian Anabaptists: An Early Reformation Episode in East Central Europe* (Scottdale: Herald Press, 1988). Not surprisingly, Joseph Smith and many of his closest associates also studied Hebrew. See Louis C. Zucker, "Joseph Smith as a Student of Hebrew," *Dialogue* 3 (Summer 1968): 41–55.

Richard Popkin has pointed out how "increased Christian knowledge of Jewish source materials and Jewish ideas" at times "intensified Millenarian theorizing and expectations." Popkin, "Millenarianism in England, Holland, and America," 365.

51. D&C 132:1–3, 40, 45. Studies on polygamy are reviewed in Davis Bitton, "Mormon Polygamy: A Review Article," *Journal of Mormon History* 4 (1977): 101–18. Subsequent works include Lawrence Foster, *Religion and Sexuality* (New York: Oxford University Press, 1981); Linda King Newell and Valeen Tippetts Avery, *Mormon Enigma: Emma Hale Smith—Prophet's Wife, 'Elect Lady', Polygamy's Foe, 1804–1879* (Garden City: Doubleday, 1984); Richard S. Van Wagoner, *Mormon Polygamy: A History* (Salt Lake City: Signature Books, 1986); and B. Carmon Hardy, *Solemn Covenant: The Mormon Polygamous Passage* (Urbana: University of Illinois Press, 1992).

52. *Words of Joseph Smith,* 42.

53. Ibid., 43–44. In 1829, before the Church was even organized, the Aaronic priesthood was conferred on Joseph Smith with the promise that it would "never be taken again from the earth, until the sons of Levi do offer again an offering unto the Lord in righteousness" (D&C 13). Several years later, a revelation promised that "the sons of Moses and also the sons of Aaron shall offer an acceptable offering and sacrifice in the house of the Lord, which house shall be built unto the Lord in this generation, upon the consecrated spot [Zion] as I have appointed" (D&C 84:31). Finally, in the revelation instructing the Saints to build a "house of the

Lord" in Nauvoo, they were told that it would be a place for "your memorials for your sacrifices by the sons of Levi" (D&C 124:39).

Ascertaining exactly what was intended or understood by these verses is difficult since there is virtually no period discussion of them extant. They can be read literally to establish continuity with Smith's discourse here being quoted, or they can be taken symbolically. Literal restoration of sacrificial ritual seems implicit in Smith's later remark that the 144,000 mentioned in Revelation represented "the number of priests who should be appointed to administer in the daily sacrifice" (*Words of Joseph Smith*, 170). Support for a metaphorical reading of sacrifices and offerings, however, can be found in D&C 59:8–12; 95:16; 96:6; 97:8, 27; 124:1, 49, 51, 75, 103–4; 126:1; 132:50–51. On one occasion Smith mentioned the future offering of the sons of Levi and declared, "Let us, therefore, as a church and a people, and as Latter-day Saints, offer unto the Lord an offering in righteousness; and let us present in his holy temple, when it is finished, a book containing the records of our dead, which shall be worth of all acceptation" (D&C 128:24).

54. Taylor, *The Mediation and Atonement* (Salt Lake City: Deseret News, 1882), 119–23.

55. Sidney B. Sperry, *Doctrine and Covenants Compendium* (Salt Lake City: Bookcraft, 1960), 394.

56. Personal correspondence cited in *Doctrines of Salvation: Sermons and Writings of Joseph Fielding Smith*, 3 vols., ed. Bruce R. McConkie (Salt Lake City: Bookcraft, 1956), 3:94.

57. McConkie, *Mormon Doctrine*, 666.

58. Widtsoe, *Evidences and Reconciliations* (Salt Lake City: Bookcraft, 1943), 194–96.

59. The Council of Twelve, *Priesthood and Church Government* (Salt Lake City: Deseret Book, 1939), 5n.

60. See Andrew F. Ehat, "Joseph Smith's Introduction of Temple Ordinances and the 1844 Succession Question" (M.A. thesis, Brigham Young University, 1982); and Buerger, "The Development of the Mormon Temple Endowment Ceremony," 33–76.

61. Foremost in this connection is the work of Hugh Nibley. See Nibley, "Christian Envy of the Temple," *Jewish Quarterly Review* 50 (Oct. 1959): 97–123; (Jan 1960): 229–40; *What Is a Temple? The Idea of the Temple in History* (Provo: Brigham Young University Press, 1963); and *The Message of the Joseph Smith Papyri: An Egyptian Endowment* (Salt Lake City: Deseret Book, 1975). His students have produced numerous articles relevant to the subject, some of which are conveniently collected in *The Temple in Antiquity: Ancient Records and Modern Perspectives*, ed. Truman G. Madsen (Provo:

Brigham Young University Press, 1982). Michael Quinn argues that the similarities between the Mormon temple ceremony and the "ancient mysteries" are more profound than parallels with Masonry. See Quinn, *Early Mormonism and the Magic World View* (Salt Lake City: Signature Books, 1987), 184–91.

Polemical tracts that argue for a close relationship between Mormonism and Masonry include Samuel H. Goodwin, *Mormonism and Masonry* (Washington, D.C.: The Masonic Association of the United States, 1924); and Mervin B. Hogan, *Mormonism and Freemasonry: The Illinois Episode* (Salt Lake City: Campus Graphics, 1980). Anthony W. Ivins, *The Relationship of "Mormonism" and Freemasonry* (Salt Lake City: Deseret News Press, 1934); and E. Cecil McGavin, *Mormonism and Masonry* (Salt Lake City: Bookcraft, 1956), on the other hand, downplay the kinship. The story of Masonic attitudes toward Mormon participation in Masonry is reviewed in Michael W. Homer, "Masonry and Mormonism in Utah, 1847–1984," *Journal of Mormon History* 18 (Fall 1992): 57–96.

Valuable as a historical introduction is Kenneth W. Godfrey, "Joseph Smith and the Masons," *Journal of the Illinois State Historical Society* 64 (Spring 1971): 79–90.

62. *Personal Writings of Joseph Smith*, 62.

63. D&C 24:16.

64. D&C 24:15. D&C 60:15 instructs the brethren to do this "not in their presence, lest thou provoke them, but in secret . . . as a testimony against them in the day of judgment." Further mention of the matter is made in D&C 75:20–22; 84:92; and 99:4. The apostolic practice is referred to in Matthew 10:14–15; Luke 10:10–12; and Acts 13:51.

65. *Personal Writings of Joseph Smith*, 182–83.

66. *History of the Church*, 7:264. According to Illinois governor Thomas Ford, after the martyrdom of Joseph and Hyrum Smith, cursings were not only pronounced "upon their enemies," but as well "upon the country, upon government, upon all public officers" for neither redressing their earlier grievances nor preventing the murder of their leaders when supposedly under state custody. Ford, *History of Illinois*, 361, as cited in *History of the Church*, 7:41.

67. Ibid., 7:544. It should be noted that "belief in special providences as divine reward or, more usually, punishment, was not the exclusive property of any religious group, but rather common to all of Christendom." Peter W. Williams, *Popular Religion in America: Symbolic Change and the Modernization Process in Historical Perspective* (Urbana: University of Illinois Press, 1980), 123. In his study of the folklore of the Methodist itinerant preachers contemporary to the Mormons, Donald Byrne remarked that "the God of these preachers was an avenging clan god, determined to

protect his own and to lay low their detractors." Many groups other than just the Mormons inserted their own name in the axiom "God protects the Methodist." Byrne, *No Foot of Land: Folklore of American Methodist Itinerants* (Metuchen, N.J.: Scarecrow Press and the American Theological Library Association, 1975), 99.

68. D&C 98:40.

69. *Messenger and Advocate* 1 (June 1835): 138. The author is merely listed as "P." That Smith was responsible for seeing that it was published, see *History of the Church*, 2:228.

70. D&C 98:23–46.

71. Alma 43:46–47.

72. D&C 103:24–26.

73. *Personal Writings of Joseph Smith*, 183.

74. *Words of Joseph Smith*, 217.

75. Ibid., 217–18.

76. Ibid., 218.

77. Ibid., 219.

78. Ibid., 258.

79. Ibid., 129.

80. D&C 101:81–92. As has already been pointed out in chapter 3, the Saints were regularly reminded that there was a crucial difference between invoking the principle of divine vengeance and becoming personally vindictive. "Pray ye, therefore," directed the Lord immediately after the stern declarations just quoted, "that their ears may be opened unto your cries, that I may be merciful unto them, that these things may not come upon them." D&C 101:92.

81. *Personal Writings of Joseph Smith*, 95.

82. Ibid., 319.

83. Ibid., 392.

Chapter 5
The Book of Mormon and the Millenarian Mind

1. See Gary Wills, *Inventing America: Jefferson's Declaration of Independence* (New York: Doubleday, 1978).

2. The extent of this attitude toward scripture is discussed in George M. Marsden, "Everyone One's Own Interpreter?: The Bible, Science, and Authority in Mid-Nineteenth-Century America," in *The Bible in America: Essays in Cultural History*, ed. Nathan O. Hatch and Mark A. Noll (New York: Oxford University Press, 1982), 79–100.

3. References analyzed in the tables do not include Book of Mormon passages cited only because they were being defended from ridicule

raised against them in anti-Mormon tracts. The concern here is with how the book was used when the Saints set their own agenda.

4. *Personal Writings of Joseph Smith*, 273.

5. *Star* 1 (Jan. 1833): 57. The editor at this time, and almost certainly the author of this unsigned article, was W. W. Phelps.

6. Pratt, *Voice of Warning*, 191. This portion of the text was deleted by Pratt in his second edition (1839), and was not restored in subsequent editions.

7. 3 Nephi 21:12–13; cf. Micah 5:8–9. See also 3 Nephi 16:15 and 20:16–17.

8. Pratt, *Mormonism Unveiled*, 13.

9. Ibid., 15.

10. Charles B. Thompson, *Evidences in Proof of the Book of Mormon* (Batavia, N.Y., 1841), 229–30.

11. One of the earliest examples of this is Howe, *Mormonism Unvailed*, 145–46, 197. Many later anti-Mormon books borrowed extensively from Howe. That the fear did not cease after the Saints left Missouri is apparent from its perpetuation in subsequent works. See, for example, James H. Hunt, *Mormonism* (St. Louis: Ustick and Davies, 1844), 280–83.

The phrase "paranoid style" originated with Richard Hofstadter in his lead essay in *Paranoid Style in American Politics* (New York: Wiley, 1965).

12. John King to John Chambers, 14 July 1843, as cited in Ronald W. Walker, "Seeking the 'Remnant': The Native American During the Joseph Smith Period," *Journal of Mormon History* 19 (Spring 1993): 1–33.

13. *Millennial Star* 2 (July 1841): 43. In an effort to appease agitated Missourians, leading Mormons not only acknowledged that talk of a Mormon-Indian alliance was inflammatory, but declared that the Mormons themselves were just as worried about Indian trouble as other Missourians and that the Saints would be among the first to take up arms against Indian aggression. See *Messenger and Advocate* 2 (Aug. 1836): 357.

14. The 1981 edition of the Book of Mormon follows the 1840 edition, rendering the latter phrase "a *pure* and delightsome people"; italics mine.

15. *Messenger and Advocate* 2 (Oct. 1835): 193.

16. *Star* 1 (Dec. 1832): 54.

17. *Star* 1 (Sept. 1832): 32.

18. Pratt, *Voice of Warning*, 191.

19. *Times and Seasons* 6 (Mar. 1845): 829–30.

20. Ibid., 830.

21. Information in this and subsequent paragraphs is drawn from Sharif, *Non-Jewish Zionism;* Verete, "The Restoration of the Jews in English Protestant Thought"; *With Eyes Toward Zion: Scholars Colloquium on America–Holy Land Studies,* ed. Moshe Davis (New York: Arno Press, 1977);

The Holy Land in American Protestant Life, ed. Robert T. Handy (New York: Arno Press, 1981); and Ruth Mouly and Roland Robertson, "Zionism in American Premillenarian Fundamentalism," *American Journal of Theology and Philosophy* 4 (Sept. 1983): 97–109.

22. As Jewish Zionism flourished in subsequent years, Mormon interest continued unabated. See Truman G. Madsen, "The Mormon Attitude Toward Zionism," *Haifa University Lecture Series,* ed. Yaakov Goldstein (Haifa: Haifa University Press, 1980), lecture 5; Eldin Ricks, "Zionism and the Mormon Church," *Herzl Year Book* 5 (1963): 147–74.

23. *The Prophet,* 14 Dec. 1844: n.p. Noah's talk was subsequently published as M. M. Noah, *Discourse on the Restoration of the Jews* (New York, 1845). For background information, see Jonathan D. Sarna, *Jacksonian Jew: The Two Worlds of Mordecai Noah* (New York: Homes & Meir, 1981).

24. *Millennial Star* 1 (May 1840): 18–19.

25. *Wilford Woodruff's Journal,* 8:52 (21 Sep. 1881).

26. *Gospel Reflector* 1 (1841): 129.

27. *Messenger and Advocate* 2 (Oct. 1835): 194.

28. Little is certain about the origin of *References to the Book of Mormon,* but bibliographers conclude that the four-page item of unknown authorship was probably printed in Kirtland in 1835. Chad J. Flake, ed., *A Mormon Bibliography, 1830–1930* (Salt Lake City: University of Utah Press, 1978), 545; Peter Crawley, "A Bibliography of the Church of Jesus Christ of Latter-day Saints in New York, Ohio, and Missouri," *BYU Studies* 12 (Summer 1972): 505.

29. As part of the first European edition of the Book of Mormon, Brigham Young and Willard Richards included a six-page "index" which they had prepared. Hugh G. Stocks, "The Book of Mormon, 1830–1879: A Publishing History" (M.A. thesis, University of California, Los Angeles, 1979), 69–72. Stocks points out that "all subsequent LDS editions before 1920 include it virtually unchanged, but they correctly label it as a table of contents and place it in the front of the book" (69).

Because the reference guides are only a few pages in length and because they are organized as tables of contents, traditional notes listing page numbers would be of little help. Individuals wishing to consult the original sources should use these documents as they do any other table of contents by looking down through the sequential listings for the Book of Mormon book being referenced.

30. John W. Dodds, *The Age of Paradox: A Biography of England 1841–1851* (New York: Rinehart, 1952), cited in Leonard J. Arrington, *Brigham Young, American Moses* (New York: Knopf, 1985), 85.

31. Robert P. Crawford, *An Index, or Reference to the Second and Third Editions of the Book of Mormon, Alphabetically Arranged* (Philadelphia, 1842).

In standard index fasion, this document is arranged alphabetically and should be consulted accordingly.

32. Geoffrey Rowell, *Hell and the Victorians: A Study of the Nineteenth-Century Theological Controversies Concerning Eternal Punishment and the Future Life* (Oxford: Clarendon Press, 1974); Jeffrey Burton Russell, *Mephistopheles: The Devil in the Modern World* (Ithaca: Cornell University Press, 1986); and James Turner, *Without God, Without Creed: The Origins of Unbelief in America* (Baltimore: Johns Hopkins University Press, 1985).

33. On Universalism specifically, see Miller, *The Larger Hope*. For the broader, liberal assault on "the good old Calvinistical Way" in eighteenth-century New England, see Norman Fiering, *Jonathan Edward's Moral Thought and its British Context* (Chapel Hill: University of North Carolina Press, 1982); and Robert H. Wilson, III, *The Benevolent Deity: Ebenezer Gay and the Rise of Rational Religion in New England, 1696–1787* (Philadelphia: University of Pennsylvania Press, 1984). An even broader background is painted in Henry F. May, *The Enlightenment in America* (New York: Oxford University Press, 1976).

34. Cited in Miller, *The Larger Hope*, 45–56.

35. Thompson, *Evidences in Proof of the Book of Mormon*, 191, 231–32.

36. *Personal Writings of Joseph Smith*, 270–72.

37. *Star* 2 (Jan. 1834): 126.

38. *Star* 1 (Mar. 1833): 74.

39. Donald F. Durnbaugh, *The Believers' Church: The History and Character of Radical Protestantism* (New York: Macmillan, 1968); Richard T. Hughes, ed., *The American Quest for the Primitive Church* (Urbana: University of Illinois Press, 1988); Hughes and C. Leonard Allen, *Illusions of Innocence: Protestant Primitivism in America, 1630–1875* (Chicago: University of Chicago Press, 1988); Hughes, "Christian Primitivism as Perfectionism: From Anabaptists to Pentecostals," in *Reaching Beyond: Chapters in the History of Perfectionism*, ed. Stanley M. Burgess (Peabody, Mass.: Hendrickson, 1986), 213–55; and Hatch, *The Democratization of American Christianity*.

40. Hatch, *The Democratization of American Christianity*; and Marsden, "Everyone One's Own Interpreter."

41. D&C 10:45.

42. *Times and Seasons* 2 (16 Aug. 1841): 507.

43. *Messenger and Advocate* 2 (Jan. 1836): 251.

44. *Millennial Star* 1 (Aug. 1840): 75.

45. Smith, ed., *A Collection of Sacred Hymns*, 95–96.

46. *Millennial Star* 2 (Aug. 1841): 63–64.

47. *Nauvoo Neighbor* 2 (28 Aug. 1844): 2; reprinted in *Times and Seasons* 5 (2 Sept. 1844): 635. Joseph Smith was murdered in the Carthage, Illinois, jail on 27 June 1844.

48. *Elders' Journal* 1 (July 1838): 39–42; also *History of the Church* 3:49–54. The interpretation also appears in Noah Packard, *Political and Religious Detector: In Which Millerism Is Exposed* (Medina, Oh., 1843), 26–27.

49. *Star* 1 (Mar. 1833): 79. The passage cited is 3 Nephi 20:23.

50. *Times and Seasons* 2 (Apr. 1841): 359–60. The passage cited is 1 Nephi 22:20–22, 24.

51. *History of the Church*, 4:106. Hyde published the account of his mission as *A Voice from Jerusalem, or a Sketch of the Travels and Ministry of Elder Orson Hyde, Missionary of the Church of Jesus Christ of Latter Day Saints, to Germany, Constantinople, and Jerusalem* (Liverpool, 1842). In the late 1970s, the LDS church dedicated a garden spot on the Mount of Olives to Hyde and included a bronze plaque containing his prayer in Hebrew, Arabic, and English.

Epperson, *Mormons and Jews*, provides a reading of Hyde's mission that downplays any conversionist intent either immediate or ultimate. Context for the mission is provided in Naomi Shepherd, *The Zealous Intruders: The Western Rediscovery of Palestine* (San Francisco: Harper & Row, 1987); and Lester I. Vogel, *To See a Promised Land: Americans and the Holy Land in the Nineteenth Century* (University Park: Pennsylvania State University Press, 1992).

52. Isaiah 51:18–19 as quoted by Hyde, *Times and Seasons* 1 (Aug. 1840): 156.

53. *Times and Seasons* 1 (Aug. 1840): 156–57.

54. *Millennial Star* 6 (Dec. 1845): 191–92. Similar interpretations can be found in *Times and Seasons* 6 (15 Nov. 1845): 1037; *Millennial Star* 7 (15 Jan. 1846): 26; and *Millennial Star* 7 (1 Feb. 1846): 35.

Chapter 6
Moderate Millenarians

1. Oliver, *Prophets and Millennialists*, 14–18.

2. David F. Aberle, "A Note on Relative Deprivation Theory as Applied to Millenarian and Other Cult Movements," in *Millennial Dreams in Action*, ed. Thrupp, 209.

3. *Personal Writings of Joseph Smith*, 271–72.

4. Pratt, *Voice of Warning*, 100.

5. D&C 24:13–14 even made an exception to its injunction against seeking to perform miracles for the signs mentioned in the Marcan commission. This was justified on the grounds that those seeking the truth were entitled to see the scriptural promise of signs following faith "be fulfilled; for ye shall do according to that which is written." Apparently, some got carried away with this liberty and church leaders later had to

direct that "officers hold out no invitations as has been frequently the case to a display of the various gifts in your church meetings." Spiritual gifts were not to be "exercised before the public, unless the individual cannot help it." As a general rule the Saints were to "be content to exercise the gifts among themselves." *Millennial Star* 3 (Dec. 1842): 144.

6. *Personal Writings of Joseph Smith,* 219.

7. Cited in *Millennial Star* 10 (Oct. 1848): 302–3.

8. *Messenger and Advocate* 1 (Apr. 1835): 97.

9. *Star* 1 (Oct. 1832): 38. "Antimissionism," which included opposition to all reform societies, not just missionary societies, was a thoroughly primitivist position. Such sentiments flourished throughout the Ohio river valley among Baptists, Christians, Campbellites, and even some Methodists as demonstrated in Bertram Wyatt-Brown, "The Antimission Movement in the Jacksonian South: A Study in Regional Folk Culture," *Journal of Southern History* 36 (Nov. 1970): 501–29. Franklin E. Rector saw antimissionism as a significant part of why Campbell and his Reformers could no longer find a home in Regular Baptist associations. See Rector, "Behind the Breakdown of Baptist-Disciple Conversations on Unity," *Foundations* 4 (1961): 120–37; and Bill J. Humble, "The Missionary Society Controversy in the Restoration Movement" (Ph.D. diss., State University of Iowa, 1964). See also Hatch, *The Democratization of American Christianity,* 174–78; and Byron C. Lambert, *The Rise of Anti-Mission Baptists: Sources and Leaders, 1800–1840* (New York: Arno, 1980).

10. *Star* 2 (June 1834): 163.

11. *Personal Writings of Joseph Smith,* 220. Especially as the Saints were able to experience a more stable community life, they were influenced by many of the same developments discussed in A. Gregory Schneider, *The Way of the Cross Leads Home: The Domestication of American Methodism* (Bloomington: Indiana University Press, 1993).

12. D&C 89.

13. *Messenger and Advocate* 1 (July 1835): 154.

14. *Elders' Journal* 1 (May 1837): 511.

15. "Kirtland Council Minute Book," typescript, LDS Church Archives, 256–57.

16. *Times and Seasons* 5 (1 Mar. 1844): 460.

17. Once the Mormons arrived in Utah and could more effectively control the environment for leisure activities, they were more accommodating to certain forms of entertainment and recreation. See Davis Bitton, "Early Mormon Lifestyles; or the Saints as Human Beings," in *The Restoration Movement: Essays in Mormon History,* ed. F. Mark Mckiernan (Lawrence, Kans.: Coronado Press, 1973), 273–305; and R. Laurence Moore, "Learning to Play: The Mormon Way and the Way of Other Americans," *Journal of Mormon History* 16 (1990): 89–106.

18. *Messenger and Advocate* 2 (Nov. 1834): 223.
19. D&C 88:118.
20. *Times and Seasons* 5 (1 Nov. 1844): 697.
21. D&C 42:40.
22. *Journal of Discourses*, 14:18.
23. *Messenger and Advocate* 3 (Dec. 1836): 421.
24. Ibid., 422.
25. *References* was published in the 1830s. Young and Richards did not hear about plural marriage until after their return from England, and Crawford would not have known about it in Philadelphia in 1842.
26. "Marriage," D&C (Kirtland, 1835) 101:4. This section was deleted in the 1876 edition and replaced by what is now D&C 132.
27. Foster, *Religion and Sexuality*, 239. This argument is developed in Hardy, *Solemn Covenant.*
28. *Messenger and Advocate* 2 (Apr. 1836): 289–91. That such views were not uncommon among Northern clergy is demonstrated in Larry E. Tise, *Proslavery: A History of the Defense of Slavery in America, 1701–1840* (Athens: University of Georgia Press, 1988).
29. The best overall histories of Mormon attitudes toward blacks and slavery are Newell G. Bringhurst, *Saints, Slaves and Blacks: The Changing Place of Black People within Mormonism* (Westport, Conn.: Greenwood Press, 1981); and Lester E. Bush, Jr., and Armand L. Mauss, eds., *Neither White nor Black: Mormon Scholars Confront the Race Issue in a Universal Church* (Midvale, Utah: Signature Books, 1984). See also Chester Lee Hawkins, "Selective Bibliography on African-Americans and Mormons, 1830–1990," *Dialogue* 25 (Winter 1992): 113–31.
30. Richard H. Brown links proslavery, antiabolitionist Northerners with the Democracy in "The Missouri Crisis, Slavery, and the Politics of Jacksonianism," *South Atlantic Quarterly* 65 (Winter 1966): 55–72. Not only were the Democrats solidly anti-abolitionist, but Vernon L. Volpe demonstrates that in the 1840 election even many of the Whigs were forced to adopt a similar position. See Volpe, "The Anti-Abolitionist Campaign of 1840," *Civil War History* 32 (Dec. 1986): 325–39.
31. See Edmund S. Morgan, "Slavery and Freedom: An American Paradox," *Journal of American History* 59 (June 1972): 5–29.
32. D&C 101:79.
33. 2 Nephi 30:6; 5:21; 3 Nephi 2:15. 2 Nephi 30:7; Words of Mormon 1:8; 4 Nephi 1:10; Mormon 5:17; Moroni 9:12 have since been used to suggest a metaphorical reading.
34. *Messenger and Advocate* 1 (Mar. 1835): 82.
35. Mark P. Leone, *Roots of Modern Mormonism* (Cambridge: Harvard University Press, 1979), 27; Hansen, *Mormonism and the American Experience*, 205.
36. Marvin S. Hill, C. Keith Rooker, and Larry T. Wimmer, "The Kirt-

land Economy Revisited: A Market Critique of Sectarian Economics," *BYU Studies* 17 (1977): 391–472.

37. *Words of Joseph Smith*, 250. See also *History of the Church*, 1:381, 3:301, 5:281. Apostle Heber C. Kimball expressed similar views as recorded in 7:466.

38. Robert B. Flanders, *Nauvoo: Kingdom on the Mississippi* (Urbana: University of Illinois Press, 1965).

39. Arrington, Fox, and May, *Building the City of God*, 79–294.

40. Darrett B. Rutman, "Assessing the Little Communities of Early America," *William and Mary Quarterly*, 3d ser., 43 (1986): 163–78.

41. Nathan O. Hatch, "Elias Smith and the Rise of Religious Journalism in the Early Republic," in *Printing and Society in Early America*, ed. William L. Joyce et al. (Worcester: American Antiquarian Society, 1983), 274.

42. *History of the Church*, 5:401.

43. Ibid., 6:238.

44. Ibid., 3:9. *Personal Writings of Joseph Smith*, 354, omits the word "political."

45. Cited in Hatch, *The Democratization of American Christianity*, 29.

Helpful context is provided in Richard H. Shyrock, *Medicine and Society in America, 1660–1850* (New York: New York University Press, 1960); and Catherine L. Albanese, "Physic and Metaphysic in Nineteenth-Century America: Medical Sectarians and Religious Healing," *Church History* 55 (Dec. 1986): 489–502. Thomson himself is discussed in John Duffy, *The Healers: A History of American Medicine* (Urbana: University of Illinois Press, 1979); and William G. Rothstein, *American Physicians in the Nineteenth Century: From Sects to Science* (Baltimore: Johns Hopkins University Press, 1972).

Mormon attitudes toward medicine are explored in Lester E. Bush, "The Mormon Tradition," in *Caring and Curing: Health and Medicine in the Western Religious Traditions*, ed. Ronald L. Numbers and Darrel W. Amundsen (New York: Macmillan, 1986), 397–420; and Robert T. Divett, *Medicine and the Mormons: An Introduction to the History of Latter-day Saint Health Care* (Bountiful, Utah: Horizon, 1981). On the LDS experience with botanic medicine in particular, see N. Lee Smith, "Herbal Remedies: God's Medicine?" *Dialogue* 12 (Autumn 1979): 37–60; and Smith, "Why Are Mormons So Susceptible to Medical and Nutritional Quackery?" *Journal of the Collegium Aesculapium* 1 (Dec. 1983): 29–43.

46. *Wilford Woodruff's Journal*, 2:108 (26 June 1841).

47. Hatch, *The Democratization of American Christianity;* Sydney E. Ahlstrom, *A Religious History of the American People*, 2 vols. (1972; Garden City, N.Y.: Image Books, 1975). For a history of popular anti-Calvinism in the post-Revolution years, see Marini, *Radical Sects*. For a broader analysis and

attention to the elite reaction, see Daniel Walker Howe, "The Decline of Calvinism: An Approach to its Study," *Comparative Studies in Society and History* 13 (1972): 306–27.

48. *Millennial Star* 1 (Jan. 1841): 217–25.

49. D. Michael Quinn, *Early Mormonism and the Magic World View* (Salt Lake City: Signature, 1987) is the most comprehensive study. Also suggestive are Bushman, *Joseph Smith and the Beginnings of Mormonism;* the articles in *BYU Studies* 24 (Fall 1984); and Alan Taylor, "The Early Republic's Supernatural Economy: Treasure Seeking in the American Northeast, 1780–1830," *American Quarterly* 38 (Spring 1986): 6–34.

50. Keith Thomas, *Religion and the Decline of Magic* (New York: Scribner's, 1971); Bryan R. Wilson, *Magic and the Millennium* (New York: Harper & Row, 1973). For a different view, see Valerie I. J. Flint, *The Rise of Magic in Early Medieval Europe* (Princeton: Princeton University Press, 1991).

51. Relevant texts include Helaman 12:18; 13:17–23, 30–37; Mormon 1:18–19; 2:10.

52. Marvin S. Hill notes, "Some historians, including Fawn Brodie, have tended to view a belief in magic in much the same way that Obediah Dogberry did, as chicanery and fraud—proof that Smith's religious claims were not genuine. A more temperate view has recently emerged among scholars of religion, and it is now clear that magic is but one means people employ in efforts to make contact with the divine. Belief in magic was not at odds with the Smith family's religious attitudes and can be seen instead as evidence of them." Hill, *Quest for Refuge: The Mormon Flight from American Pluralism* (Salt Lake City: Signature Books, 1989), 4.

53. James G. Frazer, *The Golden Bough* (1890; New York: St. Martin's Press, 1980). Helpful for disentangling these distinctions is Dorothy Hammond, "Magic: A Problem in Semantics," *American Anthropologist* 72 (1970): 1349–56. See also the anthropologist Hildred Geertz's critique (and response by Keith Thomas) of the methodological validity of Thomas's *Religion and the Decline of Magic* wherein the old functionalist dichotomies are perpetuated: Hildred Geertz, "An Anthropology of Religion and Magic, I," and Keith Thomas, "An Anthropology of Religion and Magic, II," *Journal of Interdisciplinary History* 6 (Summer 1975): 71–89, 91–109.

54. Gustav Jahod, "A Classical Fallacy: Magical 'Thinking' vs. 'Thought,'" in *Psychology and Anthropology* (New York: Academic Press, 1982), 181. See also Tom Settle, "The Rationality of Science versus the Rationality of Magic," *Philosophy of the Social Sciences* 1 (1971): 176–91.

55. Howard Kerr and Charles L. Crow, eds., *The Occult in America: New Historical Perspectives* (Urbana: University of Illinois Press, 1983); Herbert Leventhal, *In the Shadow of the Enlightenment: Occultism and Renaissance Sci-*

ence in Eighteenth-Century America (New York: New York University Press, 1976); David D. Hall, *Worlds of Wonder, Days of Judgment: Popular Religious Belief in Early New England* (New York: Knopf, 1989); Richard Godbeer, *The Devil's Dominion: Magic and Religion in Early New England* (New York: Cambridge University Press, 1992); John L. Brooke, *The Heart of the Commonwealth: Society and Political Culture in Worcester County, Massachusetts, 1713–1861* (Amherst: University of Massachusetts Press, 1990); Jon Butler, "Magic, Astrology and the Early American Religious Heritage, 1600–1760," *American Historical Review* 84 (Apr. 1979): 317–46; and Butler, *Awash in a Sea of Faith: Christianizing the American People* (Cambridge: Harvard University Press, 1990). Mormon attitudes are explored in Erich Robert Paul, *Science, Religion, and Mormon Cosmology* (Urbana: University of Illinois Press, 1992).

56. For critiques of the "revolutionary" interpretation of the Council of Fifty, see D. Michael Quinn, "The Council of Fifty and its Members, 1844–1945," *BYU Studies* 20 (Winter 1980): 163–97; and Andrew F. Ehat, "'It Seems Like Heaven Began on Earth': Joseph Smith and the Constitution of the Kingdom of God," *BYU Studies* 20 (Spring 1980): 253–79.

57. *Proclamation of the Twelve Apostles of the Church of Jesus Christ of Latter-day Saints* (New York, 1845), 6–7.

58. *History of the Church,* 5:499.

59. *Words of Joseph Smith,* 367.

60. *Times and Seasons* 5 (Mar. 1844): 470–71.

61. Mormon admiration for the Constitution of the United States is thoroughly explored in *"By the Hands of Wise Men": Essays on the U.S. Constitution,* ed. Ray C. Williams (Provo: Brigham Young University Press, 1979).

62. Robert L. Kelley, *The Cultural Pattern in American Politics: The First Century* (New York: Knopf, 1979), 166.

63. Smith, "The Book of Mormon in a Biblical Culture," 18.

Chapter 7
Apocalyptic Adversaries: Mormonism Meets Millerism

1. *History of the Church,* 5:271–72.

2. Information about William Miller and the Millerite movement presented in subsequent paragraphs is drawn principally from the following works: Gaustad, ed., *The Rise of Adventism;* P. Gerard Damsteegt, *Foundations of the Seventh-Day Adventist Message and Mission* (Grand Rapids: Eerdmans, 1977); David L. Rowe, *Thunder and Trumpets: Millerites and Dissenting Religion in Upstate New York, 1800–1850* (Chico, Calif.: Scholars Press, 1985); Everett N. Dick, "The Millerite Movement, 1830–1845," in *Advent-*

ism in America: A History, ed. Gary Land (Grand Rapids: Eerdmans, 1986), 1–35; Ronald L. Numbers and Jonathan M. Butler, eds., *The Disappointed: Millerism and Millenarianism in the Nineteenth Century* (Bloomington: Indiana University Press, 1987); and Ruth Alden Doan, *The Miller Heresy, Millennialism, and American Culture* (Philadelphia: Temple University Press, 1987).

3. Cited in Rowe, *Thunder and Trumpets,* 6.

4. William Miller, *Evidence from Scripture and History of the Second Coming of Christ about the Year 1843; Exhibited in a Course of Lectures* (Troy, N.Y.: Kemble & Hooper, 1836); hereafter, *Lectures.*

5. Rowe, *Thunder and Trumpets,* x.

6. William Miller, *Views of the Prophecies and Prophetic Chronology* (Boston: Moses A. Dow, 1841), 33–35.

7. *The Midnight Cry* 4 (15 June 1843): 107.

8. Miller, *Lectures,* 198

9. Miller, *Views of the Prophecies,* 77–98, 225–31.

10. Rowe, *Thunder and Trumpets,* 120.

11. David T. Arthur, "Millerism," in *The Rise of Adventism,* ed. Gaustad, 165–71.

12. Cited in Rowe, *Thunder and Trumpets,* 135.

13. Leon Festinger, Henry Riecken, and Stanley Schlacheter, *When Prophecy Fails: A Social and Psychological Study of a Modern Group that Predicted the Destruction of the World* (New York: Harper & Row, 1956).

14. *The Midnight Cry* 6 (1 Aug. 1844).

15. Cited in Rowe, *Thunder and Trumpets,* 135.

16. *The Midnight Cry* 6 (12 Oct. 1844).

17. Recent studies such as those listed in note 2 dispel myths about ascension robes and hill-top awaitings. The early adventist Mary A. Seymour remarked, "As to the charge of having robes ready for the ascension, we do not deny . . . they are linen, the righteousness of the Saints. . . . In these robes we shall be caught up to meet our coming King." *Voice of Truth and Glad Tidings* 5 (29 Jan. 1845): 2.

18. Rowe, *Thunder and Trumpets,* 139.

19. David Brion Davis, "Some Themes of Counter-Subversion: An Analysis of Anti-Masonic, Anti-Catholic, and Anti-Mormon Literature," *The Mississippi Valley Historical Review* 47 (Sept. 1960): 205–24.

20. See, for example, *Signs of the Times* 3 (6 Apr. 1842): 8; 3 (13 Apr. 1842): 13; 3 (25 May 1842): 61; 3 (8 June 1842): 79–80; 3 (15 June 1842): 88; 3 (22 June 1842): 96; and 3 (27 July 1842): 131, 135.

21. Joshua V. Himes, *Mormon Delusions and Monstrosities* (Boston, 1842). Campbell's section appeared a decade earlier as *Delusions: An Analysis of the Book of Mormon* (Boston: Benjamin H. Greene, 1832). Himes

used the 1842 reprint of Sunderland's *Mormonism Exposed,* which was originally published in 1838.

22. This supports the observation of Stephen Stein and Catherine Albanese that in the latest studies of Millerism "the 'marginal' Millerites are shown to be participants in the cultural center of religious life in the mid-nineteenth century," that in important ways they were "representative of the religious outlook of nineteenth-century America." Cited in Numbers and Butler, *The Disappointed,* xi. This is also clearly in evidence in Doan, *The Miller Heresy, Millennialism, and American Culture.* R. Laurence Moore, *Religious Outsiders and the Making of Americans* (New York: Oxford University Press, 1986) provides a revisionist look at the whole notion of an American religious "mainstream."

23. Cited in Bruce L. Shelley, *Church History in Plain Language* (Waco, Tex.: Word Books, 1982), 80.

24. Even though it clearly bears the marks of being an in-house work written to edify fellow Seventh-day Adventists, volumes 3 and 4 of Le Roy Edwin Froom's *Prophetic Faith of Our Fathers: The Historical Development of Prophetic Interpretation* (Washington, D.C.: Review and Herald, 1954) still provide the most detailed account of millennial doctrines from the period. Comprehensive and helpful is the 110-page "Bibliographical Essay" at the end of Gaustad, *The Rise of Adventism.*

25. Examples of Mormon ridicule of the Millerites can be found in *Times and Seasons* 3 (Oct. 1842): 940; 4 (Feb. 1843): 105, 109; 4 (Mar. 1843): 114–16; 4 (Apr. 1843): 169–71; 4 (Sept. 1843): 307–8; and 5 (Jan. 1844): 391.

26. Hardy's pamphlet was *Hypocrisy Exposed, or J. V. Himes Weighed in the Balance of Truth, Honesty, and Common Sense, and Found Wanting; Being a Reply to a Pamphlet Put Forth by Him, Entitled, Mormon Delusions and Monstrosities* (Boston, 1842).

27. Packard, *Political and Religious Detector,* 27.

28. *Times and Seasons* 4 (Mar. 1843): 113.

29. *The Midnight Cry* 4 (13 Apr. 1843): 11.

30. *Words of Joseph Smith,* 179–80. Richard L. Anderson dates this prayer to sometime before February 1835 when, at the charter meeting of the Quorum of the Twelve Apostles, Joseph Smith remarked that "fifty-six years should wind up the scene" (*History of the Church,* 2:182). Fifty-six years added to 1835 makes 1891. Anderson feels that 1891 is close enough to Smith's eighty-fifth birthday (23 Dec. 1890) that they both originated from the same source. Anderson, "Joseph Smith and the Millenarian Time Table," *BYU Studies* 3 (Spring/Summer 1961): 55–66. Whatever the relationship, the 1835 comment had little immediate impact since expressions from the prophet and his followers about an imminent end continued unabated into the 1840s. It took Millerism to

provide the context that made Smith's prayer meaningful, regardless of when it occurred.

31. *Words of Joseph Smith,* 168–69. This was later canonized as D&C 130:15–17.

32. *Times and Seasons* 5 (Mar. 1844): 454.

33. Ibid., 427.

34. *Words of Joseph Smith,* 336. See also pp. 327–36.

35. Ibid., 332.

36. *Times and Seasons* 5 (Feb. 1844): 427.

37. *History of the Church,* 5:272.

38. *Times and Seasons* 1 (Mar. 1840): 69. Higbee and Pratt's statement also seems to be a refutation of the whole tradition of attempting to ascertain the year of Christ's return.

39. *Times and Seasons* 3 (July 1842): 835. Opposition to Millerism on similar grounds can be found in William I. Appleby, *A Few Important Questions for the Reverend Clergy to Answer, Being a Scale to Weigh Priestcraft and Sectarianism* (Philadelphia, 1843).

40. *Words of Joseph Smith,* 180. In another address, Smith declared that "Zion and Jerusalem must both be built up before the coming of Christ ~~This will near a half of a century~~ How long it will take to do this[?] 10 years Yes more than 40 years will pass before this work will be accomplished and when these cities are built then shall the coming of the Son of man be" (417).

41. Moses Martin, *A Treatise on the Fulness of the Everlasting Gospel* (New York, 1842), 43.

42. *Wilford Woodruff's Journal,* 2:270–71 (6 Aug. 1843).

43. Ibid.

44. Martin, *Treatise,* 43–44.

45. Miller, *Lectures,* 4. See entire introduction.

46. Oliver, *Prophets and Millennialists.*

47. *Wilford Woodruff's Journal,* 2:107–8 (25 June 1841).

48. *Words of Joseph Smith,* 161.

49. Ibid., 185.

50. Ibid., 185.

51. Ibid., 187. Smith reasoned, "The popular religionists of the day say that the beasts spoken of in [Revelation] represent Kingdoms. Very well, on the same principle we can say that the twenty four Elders spoken of represent beasts, for they are all spoken of at the same time, and represented as all uniting in the same acts of praise and devotion." He added, "there is no revelation any where to show that the beasts meant any thing but beasts" and "we may spiritualize and express opinions to all eternity but that is no authority." *Words of Joseph Smith,* 186, 189.

52. Ibid., 186–87. A decade earlier Joseph Smith had written that the

seven-headed, ten-horned beast mentioned in Revelation 13 was a "sign, in the likeness of the kingdoms of the earth." Encountering Millerism, however, prompted a different response: "Some say it means the kingdoms of the world. . . . Suppose we admit that it means the kingdoms of the world, what propriety would there be in saying, [verse 4] who is able to make war with myself. If these spiritualizing interpretations are true, the book contradicts itself in almost every verse, but they are not true." *Words of Joseph Smith,* 187.

In the early 1830s, Joseph Smith provided a number of revisions to the biblical text which he intended to publish as a "translation" of the Bible. Since he worked with the King James Version rather than the original languages, it was not a translation in the usual sense. Emendations were felt to come through inspiration. To this day his revisions are known among Latter-day Saints as the "inspired version" or the Joseph Smith Translation (JST). See Robert J. Matthews, *"A Plainer Translation": Joseph Smith's Translation of the Bible* (Provo: Brigham Young University Press, 1975); and Barlow, *Mormons and the Bible,* 46–61. An edition of the Bible incorporating Smith's revisions is published by the Reorganized Church of Jesus Christ of Latter Day Saints entitled *Inspired Version: The Holy Scriptures Containing the Old and New Testaments, An Inspired Revision of the Authorized Version* (Independence, Mo.: Herald Publishing House, 1944). The quotation about the "sign" is from *Inspired Version,* Revelation 13:1.

53. Miller, *Lectures,* 5.

54. Miller, *Lectures,* 36–53. A synopsis of fifteen different scriptural ways for arriving at 1843 is presented in *The Midnight Cry* 4 (15 June 1843): 107–9.

55. *Times and Seasons* 4 (Feb. 1843): 104. See entire article, pp. 103–5.

56. Ibid., 103, 105.

57. Ibid., 105.

58. Ibid., 105. Taylor's comments may illuminate a previously obscure passage in D&C 130, recorded in the midst of the Millerite discussion. Verse 4 mentions "God's time, angel's time, prophet's time, and man's time." Man's time was obvious, God's time was assumed to be 1000 earth years to one divine day, and angel's time was commented on in the next verse. But why the additional category of "prophet's time"? If it was being cited in the same sense John Taylor used it, then a "prophet's time" referred to the particular equation which had to be applied to that prophet's words to get his prophetic numbers correctly computed.

59. William I. Appleby, *A Dissertation on Nebuchadnezzar's Dream* (Philadelphia, 1844), 21.

60. Franklin D. Richards, "Scriptural Items" and "Words of the Prophets," n.p., n.d. (1841 written on cover), manuscript located in the LDS Church Archives.

61. D&C 5:14. Also see D&C 33:5, 109:73.

62. *Words of Joseph Smith,* 180.

63. Appleby, *Dissertation on Nebuchadnezzar's Dream,* 24.

64. *Words of Joseph Smith,* 180.

65. *The Midnight Cry* 4 (15 June 1843): 108.

66. *Words of Joseph Smith,* 180. 1890 was the year Smith would have turned eighty-five and before which, he concluded, the Second Coming would not occur.

67. Joseph Smith did not routinely discuss such topics. Quite to the contrary, he counseled that "if the young elders would let such things alone it would be far better." *Words of Joseph Smith,* 171.

68. That "community of discourse" is ably evoked in Oliver, *Prophets and Millennialists,* and Harrison, *The Second Coming.*

69. A year after the Prophet's death and as far away as Alabama it was necessary to discuss "the inconsistency of young elders trying to explain John's seven headed and ten horned monster, and such like things that occur in the scriptures." *Times and Seasons* 5 (July 1844): 573.

70. "Despite the fact that church leaders declined to make *official* pronouncements even approximating the time, there was enough preaching from the pulpit on its imminence, enough watching the 'signs of the times,' and enough private speculation in both high and low places that it was an uncommon Mormon who did not have some feeling that he could witness the winding up scenes in his own lifetime." James B. Allen, *Trials of Discipleship: The Story of William Clayton, a Mormon* (Urbana: University of Illinois Press, 1987), 303. See also Reinwand, "An Interpretive Study of Mormon Millennialism."

Chapter 8
The Millenarian Appeal of Mormonism in England

1. Dean L. May, "A Demographic Portrait of the Mormons, 1830–1980," in *After 150 Years: The Latter-day Saints in Sesquicentennial Perspective,* ed. Thomas G. Alexander and Jessie L. Embry (Provo, Utah: Charles Redd Center for Western Studies, 1983), 39–69. May estimates British membership at 9,882 and the worldwide total at 30,000 as the exodus to Utah commenced (4). As late as 1870, the U.S. Census showed that a third of the population of Salt Lake County were born in Britain. See Ronald W. Walker, "Cradling Mormonism: The Rise of the Gospel in Early Victorian England," *BYU Studies* 27 (Winter 1987): 34n.

2. The broader story of all aspects of early British Mormonism has been told in *Mormons in Early Victorian Britain,* ed. Richard L. Jensen and Malcolm R. Thorp (Salt Lake City: University of Utah Press, 1989); V. Ben Bloxham et al., eds., *Truth Will Prevail: The Rise of the Church of Jesus Christ*

of Latter-day Saints in the British Isles, 1837–1987 (Cambridge: Cambridge University Press, 1987); *BYU Studies* 27 (Winter 1987): entire number; and *BYU Studies* 27 (Spring 1987): entire number. Allen et al., *Men with a Mission* offers a detailed history of the years discussed in this study, as well as a reproduction of many important primary sources.

3. Excellent surveys of religion in England from which the following paragraphs are derived include David L. Edwards, *Christian England*, 3 vols. (Grand Rapids: Eerdmans, 1980–84); Ernest Gordon Rupp, *Religion in England, 1688–1791* (Oxford: Clarendon Press, 1986); Ernest E. Best, *Religion and Society in Transition: The Church and Social Change in England, 1560–1850* (New York: Mellen, 1982); John R. H. Moorman, *A History of the Church of England* (London: A. C. Black, 1953); Alan D. Gilbert, *Religion and Society in Industrial England, 1740–1914* (London and New York: Longman, 1976); W. R. Ward, *Religion and Society in England 1790–1850* (London: Batsford, 1972); and Owen Chadwick, *The Victorian Church*, 2 vols. (New York: Oxford University Press, 1966).

4. Bill Speck, *Reluctant Revolutionaries: Englishmen and the Revolution of 1688* (Oxford: Oxford University Press, 1988). *History Today* 38 (July 1988) is dedicated in its entirety to the Glorious Revolution in commemoration of its tercentenary anniversary.

5. Malcolm Thorp, "The Religious Backgrounds of Mormon Converts in Britain, 1837–1852," *Journal of Mormon History* 4 (1977): 51–65. Edward R. Norman, *Church and Society in England, 1770–1970* (Oxford: Oxford University Press, 1976) challenges the accuracy of the "clerical corruption" stereotype, but, as Thorp notes, nineteenth-century Anglican reforms were "too little and too late to ease the popular image of an indifferent clerical establishment." He also comments that Mormon "reminiscences seldom reveal deep commitment to [the Church of England]" and concludes that Anglicanism, for LDS converts at least, had been "more a family tradition than a source of spiritual satisfaction." Thorp, "The Field is White Already to Harvest," in Allen et al., *Men with a Mission*, 329, 335.

6. The most comprehensive history of British Dissent is Michael R. Watts, *The Dissenters: From the Reformation to the French Revolution* (New York: Oxford University Press, 1978). The story is carried into the 1800s with Paul Sangster, *A History of the Free Churches* (London: Routledge, 1983); David M. Thompson, ed., *Nonconformity in the Nineteenth Century* (London: Routledge and Kegan Paul, 1972); and Horton Davies, *The English Free Churches*, 2d ed. (London: Oxford University Press, 1963).

A study of particular value for its treatment of Preston and other early Mormon Lancashire beachheads is Paul T. Phillips, *The Sectarian Spirit: Sectarianism, Society and Politics in Victorian Cotton Towns* (Toronto: University of Toronto Press, 1982).

7. Thorp, "Religious Backgrounds," 60. For statistics on denominational affiliation in Britain, see R. Currie, A. Gilbert, and L. Horsley, *Churches and Churchgoers: Patterns of Church Growth in the British Isles Since 1700* (Oxford: Oxford University Press, 1977).

8. Deryck W. Lovegrove, *Established Church, Sectarian People: Itinerancy and the Transformation of English Dissent, 1780–1830* (Cambridge: Cambridge University Press, 1988); and Richard Carwardine, *Transatlantic Revivalism: Popular Evangelicalism in Britain and America, 1790–1865* (Westport, Conn.: Greenwood Press, 1978), 59–84.

9. The attendance figure and times mentioned are from Joseph Fielding Diary, 31 March 1838, typescript, 18, Special Collections, BYU Library. The other quotations are from Heber C. Kimball, *Journal of Heber C. Kimball, an Elder of the Church of Jesus Christ of Latter-day Saints* (Nauvoo, 1840), 32–33.

10. This is based on Thorp's analysis of 280 conversion accounts providing sufficient information to identify prior religious involvements. See Thorp, "Religious Backgrounds," 60, for a statistical table. A slightly different arrangement of this data is found in Thorp, "The Field is White Already to Harvest," 333. The Anglican-to-Methodist ratio is documented in Currie et al., *Churches and Churchgoers*.

It also appears that most Mormon converts in Canada in the 1830s had previously been Methodists of one kind or another. See Larry C. Porter, "Beginnings of the Restoration: Canada, An 'Effectual Door' to the British Isles," in *Truth Will Prevail*, ed. Bloxham et al., 3–43; Richard E. Bennett, "'Plucking not Planting': Mormonism in Eastern Canada, 1830–1850," in *The Mormon Presence in Canada*, ed. Brigham Y. Card et al. (Logan: Utah State University Press, 1990), 19–34; and Bennett, "A Study of the Church of Jesus Christ of Latter-day Saints in Upper Canada, 1830–1850" (M.A. thesis, Brigham Young University, 1975).

11. Studies of English Methodism are myriad. Perhaps the most comprehensive and up-to-date is the three-volume *History of the Methodist Church in Great Britain*, ed. R. E. Davies, A. R. George, and E. G. Rupp (London: Epworth Press, 1965–83). Recent monographs also useful for what follows include David N. Hempton, *Methodism and Politics in British Society, 1750–1850* (Stanford: Stanford University Press, 1984); John M. Turner, *Conflict and Reconciliation: Studies in Methodism and Ecumenism in England, 1740–1982* (London: Epworth Press, 1985); and Anthony Armstrong, *The Church of England, the Methodists, and Society, 1700–1850* (Totowa, N.J.: Rowman and Littlefield, 1973). On Wesley himself, see Henry D. Rack, *Reasonable Enthusiast: John Wesley and the Rise of Methodism* (London: Epworth Press, 1990).

12. Cited in Garrett, *Spirit Possession and Popular Religion*, 104.

13. Hempton, *Methodism and Politics*, 216, 230, makes the point that

Methodism must not be treated "as a monolith" since there were "many Methodisms in many places at many times." In volume 2 of Davies et al., *History of the Methodist Church,* separate chapters treat "The Wesleyan Methodists" and "Other Methodist Traditions," pp. 213–329. One study quite attuned to such variation is Deborah M. Valenze, *Prophetic Sons and Daughters: Female Preaching and Popular Religion in Industrial England* (Princeton: Princeton University Press, 1985). Also useful for its specific focus on areas frequented by Mormon missionaries is D. A. Gowland, *Methodist Secessions: The Origins of Free Methodism in Three Lancashire Towns: Manchester, Rochdale, and Liverpool* (Manchester: University of Manchester Press, 1979).

14. The standard work on Primitive Methodism is Julia S. Werner, *The Primitive Methodist Connexion: Its Background and Early History* (Madison: University of Wisconsin Press, 1984). Also valuable is *From Mow Cop to Peake, 1807–1932: Essays to Commemorate the 175th Anniversary of the Beginnings of Primitive Methodism, May 1982* (Yorkshire: Wesley Historical Society, Yorkshire Branch, 1982), and R. W. Ambler, *Ranters, Revivalists and Reformers: Primitive Methodism and Rural Society, South Lincolnshire 1817–1875* (Hull: Hull University Press, 1989). In terms of the institutionalization that may have prompted the United Brethren schism, Turner remarks that "Wesleyanism was not the only Methodism that can be shown in development. Primitive Methodism illustrates much more sharply the transition from sect to denomination so beloved of modern sociologists." *Conflict and Reconciliation,* 82.

On the United Brethren, see Job Smith, "The United Brethren," *Improvement Era* 13 (July 1910): 818–23; and Smith's diary, pp. 1–5, in LDS Church Archives. The story of the conversion of many of this group is also told in Allen et al., *Men with a Mission,* 147–55, 331–32; and V. Ben Bloxham, "The Apostolic Foundations, 1840–1841," in *Truth Will Prevail,* ed. Bloxham et al., 132–44.

15. See Valenze, *Prophetic Sons and Daughters;* Ambler, *Ranters, Revivalists, and Reformers;* and Phillips, *The Sectarian Spirit.*

16. *Millennial Star* 2 (June 1841): 23.

17. Robert Currie, *Methodism Divided* (London: Faber, 1968), and John C. Bowmer, *Pastor and People* (London, 1975) make clear that the Methodism of the pulpit was not always the Methodism of the pew. Valenze, *Prophetic Sons and Daughters,* and Gowland, *Methodist Secessions,* also illustrate that generalizations are dangerous, and that an alternative to formal schism was the private gathering of the pious while retaining nominal affiliation with the parent body. Finally, a spate of regional studies in Methodism, too, qualifies the stereotypes. As just one example, David Luker demonstrated how "Cornish Wesleyan Methodism was clearly

something very different from orthodox Wesleyanism." See Luker, "Revivalism Theory and Practice: The Case of Cornish Methodism," *Journal of Ecclesiastical History* 37 (1986): 603–19.

18. Harrison, *The Second Coming*, 132.

19. Cited in Harrison, *The Second Coming*, 153.

20. Cited in Valenze, *Prophetic Sons and Daughters*, 87.

21. Harrison, *The Second Coming;* Oliver, *Prophets and Millennialists;* and Hopkins, *A Woman to Deliver Her People.*

22. Ibid. and Ronald R. Nelson, "Apocalyptic Speculation and the French Revolution," *Evangelical Quarterly* 53 (Oct.–Dec. 1981): 194–206.

23. Willard Richards Journal, Vol. 12, p. 4, typescript, LDS Church Archives.

24. Sandeen, *Roots of Fundamentalism*, 57–58.

25. Little is known today about Robert Aitken, though some information can be found in Malcolm Thorp, "Early Mormon Confrontations with Sectarianism, 1837–1840," in *Mormons in Early Victorian Britain*, 49–69; Gowland, *Methodist Secessions;* and *British Dictionary of National Biography*, 1:206.

26. Cit. in Orson F. Whitney, *Life of Heber C. Kimball* (Salt Lake City: Stevens and Wallis, 1945), 149–50.

27. Robert Aitken, *The Second Coming of Christ: A Sermon* (London: G. & C. Fowler, 1839), 7–8.

28. Ibid., 11.

29. *Wilford Woodruff's Journal*, 1:498 (23 Aug. 1840); 1:512 (10 Sep. 1840).

30. Kimball, *Journal*, 48.

31. Fielding Diary, 51–58, 98, 111; John Taylor to Leonora Taylor, 30 Jan. 1840, in *Men with a Mission*, 360–71.

32. Alfred Cordon, "An Abridgement of His Journal," typescript, BYU Library; *Millennial Star* 2 (Dec. 1841): 126; 3 (June 1842): 30.

33. G. R. Balleine, *Past Finding Out: The Tragic Story of Joanna Southcott and Her Successors* (London: S.P.C.K., 1956) has a chapter on this group. Oliver, *Prophets and Millennialists*, and Harrison, *The Second Coming*, deal with Wroe as well.

34. Hopkins, *A Woman to Deliver Her People* is the standard treatment.

35. Cit. in Harrison, *The Second Coming*, 147–48.

36. *Millennial Star* 2 (Aug. 1841): 54. The tract referred to is Pratt, *A Letter to the Queen.*

37. Still the most important study of the Irvingites is P. E. Shaw, *The Catholic Apostolic Church* (New York: King's Crown Press, 1946). Irving's nephew, G. Carlyle, produced *The Collected Writings of Edward Irving*, 5 vols. (London, 1866). More recent studies intent on emphasizing the experi-

ential primitivism of Irving are Rowland A. Davenport, *Albury Apostles: The Story of the Body Known as the Catholic Apostolic Church (Sometimes Called the "Irvingites")*, 2d ed. (London: Neiligo, 1974); Arnold Dallimore, *Forerunner of the Charismatic Movement: The Life of Edward Irving* (Chicago: Moody Press, 1983); Charles Gordon Strachan, *The Pentecostal Theology of Edward Irving* (London: Darton, Longman and Todd, 1973); and Strachan, "Theological and Cultural Origins of the Nineteenth-Century Pentecostal Movement," in *Essays on Apostolic Themes*, ed. Paul Elbert (Peabody, Mass.: Hendrickson Publishers, 1985), 144–57.

38. *Times and Seasons* 3 (Apr. 1842): 746. A modern comparison between the two movements is Robert L. Lively, Jr., "The Catholic Apostolic Church and the Church of Jesus Christ of Latter-day Saints: A Comparative Study of Two Minority Millenarian Groups in Nineteenth-Century England" (Ph.D. diss., University of Oxford, 1977).

39. Oliver, *Prophets and Millennialists*, 99–149.

40. Cit. in Shaw, *Catholic Apostolic Church*, 34.

41. Ibid., 32. See also Strachan, "Theological and Cultural Origins," 144–57; and Davenport, *Albury Apostles*.

42. *History of the Church*, 2:230–34. Hewitt apparently became Preceptor of the Painesville Academy. His connections to Irvingism and his visit to the Mormons, however, caused him problems with the Congregational minister in Painesville. See *Painesville Telegraph*, 26 Feb. and 4 Mar. 1836.

43. *Personal Writings of Joseph Smith*, 164.

44. Porter, "Beginnings of the Restoration," 3–43; Bennett, "'Plucking not Planting,'" 19–34; and Bennett, "A Study of the Church of Jesus Christ of Latter-day Saints in Upper Canada."

The leading historian of Mormonism in Scotland discusses the setting described in Strachan, "Theological and Cultural Origins," and suggests that the Irvingites "may have helped prepare the groundwork for the Mormon success." Frederick S. Buchanan, "The Ebb and Flow of Mormonism in Scotland, 1840–1900," *BYU Studies* 27 (Spring 1987): 29. Of related interest is Buchanan, *"A Good Time Coming": Mormon Letters to Scotland* (Salt Lake City: University of Utah Press, 1988).

45. Fielding Diary, 1.

46. Ibid., 2.

47. The case for Irvingite influence is argued in G. St. John Stott, "John Taylor's Religious Preparation," *Dialogue* 19 (Spring 1986): 123–28.

48. *Messenger and Advocate* 2 (May 1836): 318. It is probable that Pratt was referring to works like Canadian Irvingite Adam Hood Burwell's *Voice of Warning and Instruction Concerning the Signs of the Times, and the Coming of the Son of Man, to Judge the Nations, and Restore All Things* (Kingston, Can.,

1835), perhaps the inspiration for Pratt's own similarly titled book produced the next year.

49. Shaw, *The Catholic Apostolic Church*, 112–16; Porter, "Beginnings of the Restoration," 22–25; B. H. Roberts, *The Life of John Taylor: Third President of the Church of Jesus Christ of Latter-day Saints* (Salt Lake City, 1892), 32–33; Stott, "John Taylor's Religious Preparation," 124–26; and Richard Bennett, "From Colony to Homeland: Upper Canada and the Introduction of Mormonism to Great Britain" (unpublished paper in author's possession).

According to Joseph Fielding, the dangerous doctrines they had imbibed, all Irvingite basics, included such millenarian teachings as "the first and second resurrection, the destruction of the wicked in the last days by the judgments of God, the coming of Christ to reign on the earth in the millennium and the apostasy of the Gentile churches." Joseph Fielding to Parley Pratt, 20 June 1841, in *Millennial Star* 2 (Aug. 1841): 50–52. Taylor added that the group believed "that there ought to be Apostles and Prophets, Pastors, Teachers and Evangelists, that men had not the gift of the Holy Ghost" and that they believed "in all the gifts and blessings as experienced in the former days." Qtd. in Stott, "John Taylor's Religious Preparation," 124.

50. Parley P. Pratt, *The Autobiography of Parley Parker Pratt* (1874; Salt Lake City: Deseret Book, 1985), 139–40.

51. Ibid. Overall, however, Fielding reported that as a result of the visit of Caird and companions to Toronto "to establish Mr. Irving's principles . . . many of our old friends joined them." Fielding, *Millennial Star* 2 (August 1841): 52. This included the group's host, William Patrick. Shaw, *The Catholic Apostolic Church*, 112–16.

52. *Messenger and Advocate* 2 (May 1836): 318.

53. Cited in Ronald W. Walker, ed., "The Willard Richards and Brigham Young 5 September 1840 Letter From England to Nauvoo," *Brigham Young University Studies* 18 (1978): 472.

54. Oliver, *Prophets and Millennialists*, 218.

55. *History of the Church*, 4:222–23.

56. *Millennial Star* 3 (Apr. 1843): 197.

57. Whitney, *Life of Heber C. Kimball*, 146.

58. The hymn is cited in Turner, *Conflict and Reconciliation*, 47.

Epilogue
Mormonism, Millenarianism, and Modernity

1. John F. Wilson, "Modernity," in *Encyclopedia of Religion*, ed. Mircea Eliade (New York: Macmillan, 1988), 17–22.

2. Alexander, *Mormonism in Transition;* Mark P. Leone, *Roots of Modern Mormonism;* Gordon and Gary Shepherd, *A Kingdom Transformed: Themes in the Development of Mormonism* (Salt Lake City: University of Utah Press, 1984); Richard O. Cowan, *The Church in the Twentieth Century* (Salt Lake City: Bookcraft, 1985); Allen and Leonard, *The Story of the Latter-day Saints;* Arrington and Bitton, *The Mormon Experience;* Hansen, *Mormonism and the American Experience;* Shipps, *Mormonism;* and Armand L. Mauss, "Assimilation and Ambivalence: The Mormon Reaction to Americanization," *Dialogue* 22 (Spring 1989): 30–67. From another angle, Mario S. DePillis, "The Persistence of Mormon Community into the 1990s," *Sunstone* 15 (Sep. 1991): 28–49 looks at how Mormons have managed to maintain their communitarian quality amidst modernity.

3. Williams, *Popular Religion in America,* 12.

4. Mircea Eliade, *Cosmos and History: The Myth of the Eternal Return* (New York: Harper & Row, 1954); Eliade, *The Sacred and the Profane* (New York: Harper & Row, 1957); and Eliade, *Myth and Reality* (New York: Harper & Row, 1963). Especially relevant is Robert A. Segal, "Eliade's Theory of Millenarianism," *Religious Studies* 14 (1978): 159.

5. John C. Dwyer, *Church History: Twenty Centuries of Catholic Christianity* (New York: Paulist Press, 1985), 352.

6. Peter L. Berger, *A Rumor of Angels* (Garden City: Doubleday, 1969), 39–40.

7. Charles E. Garrison, *Two Different Worlds: Christian Absolutes and the Relativism of Social Science* (Newark: University of Delaware Press, 1988).

8. That other groups also retain supernaturalism in their eschatology is demonstrated in Paul Boyer, *When Time Shall Be No More: Prophecy Belief in Modern American Culture* (Cambridge: Harvard University Press, 1992).

9. Shepherd and Shepherd, *A Kingdom Transformed,* 196.

Index

GRANT UNDERWOOD is associate professor of religion at Brigham Young University, Hawaii. He has served a term on the executive council of the Mormon History Association as well as on the board of editors for the *Journal of Mormon History*. He has been a summer fellow with the National Endowment for the Humanities, a Starkoff Fellow at the American Jewish Archives, and has been active in the American Academy of Religion. He has published a number of articles on Mormon history in journals including *Church History, Pacific Historical Review,* and the *Journal of Mormon History*. His greatest satisfaction and sense of accomplishment comes from joining his wife, Sheree, in loving and rearing seven wonderful children, including two sets of twin girls.